STORM
WARNING

BILLY GRAHAM
STORM WARNING

WORD PUBLISHING
Dallas·London·Vancouver·Melbourne

STORM WARNING

Library of Congress Cataloging-in-Publication Data

Graham, Billy, 1918–
    Storm warning / Billy Graham.
        p. cm.
    Rev. ed. of: Approaching hoofbeats. c1983.
    Includes bibliographical references.
    ISBN 0–8499–0983–X (Hardcover)
    ISBN 0–8499–3681–0 (Mass Paper)
    1. Four Horsemen of the Apocalypse.   2. Eschatology.
    I. Graham, Billy, 1918– Approaching hoofbeats. II. Title.
    BS2825.2.G734 1992
    236—dc20   92–34807
                                                                       CIP

56789 OPM 7654321

Printed in the United States of America

Contents

Foreword

The Bible is a book for today. The more complex and uncertain the world becomes, the more we need God's truth for moral guidance. The ancient creeds of the Christian church, some of which date back nearly seventeen hundred years, held that the Bible is "the infallible rule of faith and practice," and it is as practical today for bringing harmony and peace on earth as it ever was. To disregard the place of Scripture in our lives, or to allow the principles of God's purpose for men and women on this planet to fall into disuse, would be tragic. We need the Word of God today as never before in history.

It is no accident that the most popular, most valuable book in Russia, Romania, Hungary, Czechoslovakia, Bulgaria, Albania, and Germany today is the Bible. People deprived of its wisdom and vision grow weary. God spoke through the prophet Hosea, "My people are destroyed for lack of knowledge." Wherever the Word of God is hidden or ignored, there will be certain destruction.

As we witness the events now unfolding in Eastern Europe, the European Community, the Russian Federation, and the Middle East, there is ample cause for optimism. From many points of view the world seems to be entering a time of peace and calm. But no one should run up the all-clear flags just yet. There is still cause for alarm; there are storms on the horizon. We are plagued by rising debt, growing crime, new expressions of racial and ethnic hatred, disintegrating moral values, sexually transmitted diseases and the AIDS epidemic, the collapse of the traditional family unit, escalating drug and alcohol abuse, and increasingly hostile attacks against the Christian church. Is this all coincidence or is it perhaps a symptom of something else?

We live today in the most complex and sophisticated period in recorded history. Science, technology, and ideas have literally reshaped the dimensions of our world, and a mere handful of modern nations now holds the power to determine the fate and future of the planet.

But what would happen if such might and power fell into the hands of unscrupulous, unprincipled leaders? Already we are caught up in a whirlwind of economic uncertainty with new alignments of power and commerce on the horizon. The United Nations and other international organizations seem almost powerless to ensure lasting peace.

At this very moment Asia, Europe, and the Americas are forging strong regional economic alliances. What new threats might suddenly appear if competition, protectionism, or extreme nationalism were to push the world once again into armed camps? As we witness the outbursts of violence in Germany, Yugoslavia, Russia, France, Britain, and the United States, can anyone doubt what must follow? The death of European Communism and the defeat of Saddam Hussein gave the world a much-needed rest, but we cannot afford to be lulled to sleep quite so easily. We have reason to believe that all the surprises are not quite over, and the hurricane may truly be yet to come.

This is a book about warnings—about the apocalypse— the ultimate end game. Included is an account of the startling and detailed writings of John the apostle found in the Book of Revelation. Transmitted by the last surviving disciple of Jesus Christ, it is an account of the events that will most certainly take place at the end of this present age.

Part of this material was included, in slightly different form, in an earlier book, *Approaching Hoofbeats*, in 1983. In this new work I have added a discussion of Matthew 24:3-37, in which Jesus described for His disciples the signs of the end times. Both of these narratives are presented here in the context of my own ministry on six continents spanning nearly fifty years.

Since the Greater Los Angeles Crusade of 1949, when our ministry first came into the national spotlight, I have had the privilege of preaching to more than 100 million people in eighty-four countries. During this time, I have preached from the historic pulpits of Moscow, Cracow, Prague, Budapest, Wittenburg, Berlin, Dresden, Paris, London, Brussels, Amsterdam, and many other places where news is now being made.

Since 1954, I have made eight separate trips to Germany, both east and west of the Wall, and I was honored to speak at the Brandenburg Gate while the Wall was still coming down. I have stood in the places where history was made. I have seen with my own eyes the part that men and women of faith have played in these earth-shaking events, and I have heard with my own ears their cries for freedom.

Any history of the political events of our time is incomplete and invalid if it does not include a discussion of the Bible, the impact of Christianity, and the role of faith in changing the hearts and minds of people all over the world. I have met these men and women—the ones who are changing the world around us—in places like the Gethsemane Church in Berlin, where the New Forum came together; in Timisoara, Romania, where the dissension began; in Moscow, Kiev, Budapest, Warsaw, and Leipzig.

This is where the real revolutions are happening. For what is taking place in the world today is not just a protest but a revolution in the human heart—a change designed by God Himself for just such a time as this. And that is what this book is about.

The task of writing, researching, and referencing a work of this scope is never easy. It takes the contributions of many diligent people and many long hours. I am grateful to all the people who are a part of this work through their participation in our ministry efforts over the years. In addition, I would like to express my thanks to Dr. Jim Black for his major work in researching and coordinating the development of the manuscript; to Kip Jordon, Joey Paul, and the Word staff; and to my associates—Dr. John Akers; Fred and Millie Dienert; my secretary, Stephanie Wills; and especially to my wife, Ruth—all of whom were involved in the editing process. Above all, I want to thank you, the reader, for sharing in the experience. You hold the future in your hands. I pray that God will give you the wisdom to use it wisely.

Billy Graham
Montreat, North Carolina
July 1992

Part 1

Storm Clouds on the Horizon

1

The Winds of Change

*A*ll my experiences of disasters around the world, both manmade and natural, did not prepare me for what I saw in South Florida in September 1992. Hurricane Andrew had carved a path of devastation more than thirty miles wide, and it was a picture of absolute chaos for as far as the eye could see. Not a single house or building had been spared.

I had been asked by Florida Governor Lawton Chiles to come down to meet with the people in the hardest-hit areas of the state, especially Homestead and the other communities where Andrew had done such severe damage. On Saturday, September 5, we had the privilege of holding a religious service for those people who so desperately needed encouragement. Just a few days before these same people had been routinely going about their lives unconcerned with the swirls of small dark clouds that satellites had detected somewhere off the west coast of Africa.

At first it was just a typical tropical depression. But it began to grow in size and momentum and slowly moved westward across the sea. Weather forecasters worldwide noted the season's first hurricane but quickly added that it was too far from anything to cause concern.

That assessment changed radically over the next three days as the storm approached Caribbean waters. Each day the weather advisories were more pronounced: small craft warnings, gale warnings, tropical storm warnings,

and—when the winds surged past forty-eight knots—
hurricane warnings.

Andrew's first landfall was at 11 P.M. on Sunday, August 23, in the Bahamas. Four people were killed on the island of Eleuthera, and property damage was the most extensive in the island's history. Four hours later, the palm trees in South Florida began to dance in the wind with the first gusts from Andrew.

My daughter, GiGi, and her husband Stephan called us that evening from their home near Fort Lauderdale. "We're sitting here, waiting for Andrew," she said. "We aren't exactly sure where it's going to hit, but it should be here within the next four hours." They were taking what precautions they could, but they were going to stick it out at home. GiGi's words gave the storm a new sense of drama and urgency for Ruth and me.

Further south, near Florida City, Herman Lucerne was also preparing to ride the storm out. A former mayor of Florida City, Herman was a renowned outdoorsman and fishing guide. At the age of seventy-eight, he was known to many people as "Mr. Everglades," because that great swampland was his stomping ground. He had lived there all his life. When he heard the storm warnings, he took the usual precautions, just as he had done for countless other hurricanes. He had seen so many in the past, he was convinced he would weather another.

Andrew hit South Florida around 4 A.M.

During those long, deadly hours, Hurricane Andrew unleashed a fury of devastating proportions. For the first time, a storm passed directly over the National Hurricane Warning Service in Coral Gables, and it ripped the radar array from the top of the six-story structure. The center's anemometer was destroyed shortly after it recorded 164-mile-per-hour winds with wind gusts off the scale. The winds that blasted the tip of Florida left thirty-three people dead, destroyed more than sixty-three thousand homes, left 1.3 million people without water or electricity, and did more than $30 billion in damage. But it didn't stop there.

Nineteen hours later, the hurricane had crossed the Gulf of Mexico and struck the coast of Louisiana, where it killed again, leaving fifty thousand people homeless and hundreds of thousands without water or electricity.

The newspapers said that this was the greatest natural disaster ever to strike the United States.

As soon as Ruth and I could get through, we were on the phone with GiGi and Stephan. They said that 100-mile-an-hour winds had blasted their neighborhood, knocking down trees and light poles in the area. They survived unhurt, but they assured me that they would never try to ride out another hurricane. They had learned their lesson and were grateful to have a second chance.

Tragically in Florida City, Herman Lucerne would never get another chance. He didn't survive Andrew. He relied on his experience, but this time his usual precautions were not enough.

Twenty-three years earlier, in Pass Christian, Mississippi, a group of people were preparing to have a "hurricane party" in the face of a storm named Camille. Were they ignorant of the dangers? Could they have been overconfident? Did they let their egos and pride influence their decision? We'll never know.

What we do know is that the wind was howling outside the posh Richelieu Apartments when Police Chief Jerry Peralta pulled up sometime after dark. Facing the beach less than 250 feet from the surf, the apartments were directly in the line of danger. A man with a drink in his hand came out on the second-floor balcony and waved. Peralta yelled up, "You all need to clear out of here as quickly as you can. The storm's getting worse." But as others joined the man on the balcony, they just laughed at Peralta's order to leave. "This is my land," one of them yelled back. "If you want me off, you'll have to arrest me."

Peralta didn't arrest anyone, but he wasn't able to persuade them to leave either. He wrote down the names of the next of kin of the twenty or so people who gathered there to party through the storm. They laughed as he took their names. They had been warned, but they had no intention of leaving.

It was 10:15 P.M. when the front wall of the storm came ashore. Scientists clocked Camille's wind speed at more than 205 miles per hour, the strongest on record. Raindrops hit with the force of bullets, and waves off the Gulf Coast crested between twenty-two and twenty-eight feet high.

News reports later showed that the worst damage came at the little settlement of motels, go-go bars, and gambling houses known as Pass Christian, Mississippi, where some twenty people were killed at a hurricane party in the Richelieu Apartments. Nothing was left of that three-story structure but the foundation; the only survivor was a five-year-old boy found clinging to a mattress the following day.

In the Face of Reality

My daughter GiGi, her husband Stephan, Herman Lucerne, and the people in the Richelieu Apartments—they were all defying the odds. They had heard the warnings, and they decided to stay. Today there are storm warnings of a different sort urging us to pay attention to the crises in our world, and I have to wonder if we are not staring blindly into the face of an oncoming storm of apocalyptic proportions.

Jesus said, "For nation will rise against nation, and kingdom against kingdom. And there will be famines, pestilences, and earthquakes in various places. All these are the beginning of sorrows" (Matthew 24:7–8 NKJV). There are storm warnings on every hand and dark clouds brooding on the horizon. There is recession in the United States, and around the world millions are plagued by unprecedented suffering and despair. Truly, we live in a time of troubles. But what does it all mean? Are we really in danger?

In his 1992 State of the Union Address, President George Bush spoke of the undeniable awareness that something profound and unusual is happening in the world; "big changes" he called them. Mr. Bush applauded the death of Communism and America's apparent victory in the Cold War. He said, "In the past twelve months, the world has known changes of almost biblical proportions."

Then, midway through that January address, the president warned of the dangers still ahead with the striking words, "The world is still a dangerous place. Only the dead have seen the end of conflict. And though yesterday's challenges are behind us, tomorrow's are being born."

Yes, there are many hopeful signs and exciting challenges in the changes taking place in the world. As I have watched them develop, the events in Eastern Europe have been exciting, but there are also great dangers. You see them described in detail on the nightly news. They fill the headlines. But while it may be easy to judge the danger of a hurricane, how do you determine the dangers of a society in chaos? Where do you even begin to try?

That is the purpose of this book: to review the state of the world in these troubled times and to examine the circumstances confronting us today in the light of the only reliable standard—the Bible. My purpose is not to arouse groundless fears or to make unfounded charges; rather, I hope to raise some important questions. Can we find any hope in the current world situation? Will there be lasting peace? Is there a better way? How should we live in the face of the world's new challenges and crises?

Tension in Our Streets

I can confirm the feelings of tension in our streets. I travel constantly, and wherever I go today I see the symptoms of America's disappointment and despair. The whole world was shocked by the violence and looting in Los Angeles sparked by the unpopular verdict in the Rodney King case. Just a year earlier we watched media coverage of the hostile confrontations between pro-abortion and pro-life activists in Indianapolis and elsewhere. Before that came the news of rioting in San Francisco. All across America, in one city after another, angry crowds are lashing out in protest on one issue after another.

In April 1992, an Associated Press reporter spoke with Americans from California to Florida, and he discovered a deep sense of anxiety and uncertainty, including feelings of despair. A man in Louisiana spoke of a "nameless, shapeless dread." A World War II veteran from Wisconsin sensed the "forewarning of revolution." A lawyer from Washington State spoke of his growing concern over government mismanagement and abuses of power. A nun in Florida spoke of the "floating anxiety" among the people she meets.

The economic spiral of the eighties has been followed by the seemingly bottomless recession of the nineties. The sheer momentum of such changes has robbed many Americans of their joy and optimism. Lost jobs, broken lives, ruined careers, bankruptcies, shattered marriages, physical and emotional abuse, and a thousand other tragedies have invaded America's homes. What remains in such cases is the somber, joyless, unromantic reality of a nation in deep, deep trouble. And it is only too clear that the emotional roller-coaster ride of the past two decades has been tragically complicated by the moral and spiritual bankruptcy of our society.

The Changing World

But America is not the only trouble spot today. The entire world is in turmoil. While the population of the planet continues to explode at a rate of nearly 100 million births per year, millions more are dying from epidemics, war, famine, starvation, drugs, crime, and violence. We are living in a time of enormous conflict and cultural transformation. The political and social revolutions of our time stagger the imagination.

On the world political scene, the events of the past three years seem to bear the unmistakable stamp of destiny. We have been stunned by shockwaves of change in nation after nation, all around the globe. Many of them have brought hope and freedom to hundreds of millions of people. However, in spite of the outbreak of democracy in Eastern Europe, the collapse of the Berlin Wall, the hundred-hour war in the Persian Gulf, the failed Soviet coup, and the reported death of Communism, we are now seeing the inevitable problems arising from the laborious and problematical unification of Europe.

No sooner had the world witnessed the tragic deaths of young pro-democracy students at Tiananmen Square than we witnessed the equally emotional news of democratic victories in Romania, Poland, Czechoslovakia, Bulgaria, and other former Communist states. In many places, the promoters of change offer a grand vision of world unity. They say that the world has come to the threshold of unparalleled peace and global oneness. In his highly publicized address in Fulton, Missouri, Mikhail Gorbachev called for a strong central government of democratic nations: a new world order to replace the old idioms and stratagems based on nuclear conflict. But while the world applauded his remarks, and perhaps even his sentiments, there was justifiable caution in most quarters.

The bloodbath in Yugoslavia is just one example of the hostile tensions unleashed by these changes. But such turmoil is not entirely unexpected. While the globalists and international affairs specialists continue their chant for "peace, peace," we are reminded that the Bible says that there can be no lasting peace until Christ returns. So the world remains restless and uncertain. While we are expectant and hopeful—and while the world continues to applaud men like Gorbachev when they speak of peace— our fears are not so easily resolved.

We have seen the results of unrestrained greed, corruption, and manipulation on Wall Street, financial mismanagement in the halls of government, fraud and perversion at the highest levels of both church and state. While keeping an eye on the showdown that many observers feel may be brewing even now between the financial superpowers of Europe, Asia, and North America, many people sense the possibility of an even greater unraveling in the world. As we hope for peace, for new opportunities and prosperity, we are constantly confronted by the realities of new problems in this age of crisis.

Search for a New Morality

The riots in South Central Los Angeles captured the eyes and ears of the entire world for a week in the spring of 1992. Angered by a jury's verdict, crazed rioters took the law into their own hands and committed countless treacherous acts more horrible and repellent than the act they were supposedly protesting. Forty-four lives were lost, two thousand people were injured, and property damage was estimated at more than a billion dollars. Commenting on the aftermath of those riots, the editors of *Newsweek* later wrote: "The unrest in L.A. underscored the importance of finding new ways to think about ethnicity, crime and poverty. And . . . the need for new kinds of moral leadership also become painfully clear."

Tabloids and newsmagazines worldwide published page after page of startling photographs that clearly showed the faces of looters and rioters and the remains of fire-gutted buildings. But those scenes of violence on America's streets are only one illustration of the terror at large in the world today.

We have also been disturbed by photographs of war, famine, and pestilence in East Africa, including the grim image on the front pages of our newspapers and on our television screens of mothers and their hopelessly emaciated children in war-ravaged Somalia. The specter of death is seemingly never vanquished on the continent of Africa. But time after time such images point out the fragile line between life and death in the modern world. Somalia's tragedy reads like a carbon copy of a dozen similar wars of recent years. Since November 1991, open warfare has pitted a half-dozen or more factions against one another in that poverty-stricken nation. The head of state fled for his life, leaving behind total anarchy and chaos. In the news photos from Mogadishu, the capital, I could not help but see shades of Biafra, Soweto, Uganda, Liberia, Ethiopia, the Belgian Congo, and countless other bloody African wars of the past forty years.

A May 7, 1992, article by Todd Shields, reporting for the *Washington Post* from Mogadishu, described how that country had been reduced to a shambles by war, poverty, and drought. There was no electrical or mechanical power in the cities. No food, no medical supplies, few things of value that had not been ransacked and ruined. Bands of marauding gunmen kill, loot, and rob at will, even stealing the baby food airlifted to feed starving children in the nation's refugee camps.

Eventually, the fatal shooting of a relief worker caused even the Red Cross to abandon its efforts to bring in food and medical supplies. No one knows what the future may hold there. This is the dismal and shocking reality, but it is only too typical of the horrors we see in the world around us. Some observers suggest that America—like the rest of the world—may be reaching the point of giving up on social concern. We no longer believe we can help the poor and destitute; our emotions have been purged. *Newsweek* described the feeling as a worldwide case of "compassion fatigue."

Should we be surprised that the world has come to such a state? When we see fraud, corruption, and abuse at every level of our society and in every sector of public life, can anyone be expected to continue in the mistaken belief that humanity is somehow perfectible without the intervention of God? Can we expect unending compassion and concern when no amount of mercy can stop the pain?

A Call for Character

In a lecture at the Jonathan Edwards College of Yale University in November 1990, U.S. Secretary of Health and Human Services Dr. Louis W. Sullivan called for a "renewed sense of personal responsibility" in this country. He said that "a high percentage of the disease and disability afflicting the American people is a consequence of unwise choices of behavior and lifestyle." The result, he said, is blighted, stunted, and less fulfilling lives for our citizens and outrageously high medical costs.

Dr. Sullivan portrayed the toll of tobacco and alcohol use both in terms of loss of life and in the dollars-and-cents cost to taxpayers. But he also spoke of the toll of America's unwise choices on morality and our national sense of values. He said:

> I am troubled by diminishing confidence in our willingness and ability as a society and individuals to make sound judgments about healthy human behavior and lifestyles. Linked to this declining faith in ethical and value judgment is an erosion of those institutions that have generated, shaped, and sustained our ethical and cultural standards—family, neighborhood, church, school, and voluntary associations. As a consequence of this institutional decline, we have fewer sources of instruction in healthy, constructive behavior.

The conditions the secretary of health described are the very conditions that have contributed to anger, violence, and hostility in our streets. "All about me, I see the toll of our ethical dilemma, the tragic price of our cultural indifference," Sullivan added. "So many of these problems have their roots in the alienation, isolation, and lack of direction that follow from the collapse of societal standards, and the institutions that generate them."

Sullivan described his Yale address as a plea for a revitalized "culture of character." In fact, the secretary was pleading for a return to such old-fashioned virtues as "self-discipline, integrity, taking responsibility for one's acts, respect for others, perseverance, moderation, and a commitment to serve others and the broader community."

Foundational Values

Truly, the world is in need of moral leadership. But not, as *Newsweek* proposed, some new kind; rather, as Louis

Sullivan proposes, we need the kind of foundational values and personal character the world once understood and respected. We need moral leadership that teaches the difference between right and wrong and teaches us to forgive one another even as we are forgiven by our Father in heaven. We need moral leadership that teaches love for our brothers and sisters of every race and tribe; a morality in which material abundance is never the aim or goal of a society, but merely the result of its industry.

The world needs moral leadership that respects the rights of men and women equally as children of one Father, but in the balance and harmony which the Father designed for us and which He told us is most natural and beneficial to our potential for leading happy and productive lives. In His final days on earth, Jesus said, "If anyone loves me, he will obey my teaching. My Father will love him, and we will come to him and make our home with him" (John 14:23). That is the kind of moral leadership the world needs.

We need a morality that guarantees respect for mothers who mother, for fathers who father, and for all those who live and work together to fulfill God's commandments to pursue our individual destinies as His privileged children. We need families that stay together and pray together. We do not need a new moral order; the world desperately needs the tried and tested moral order that God handed down at Sinai, which He proved through the prophets and patriarchs of old and which He expressed most perfectly in the life, death, and living presence of His own Son, Jesus Christ.

Many people will remember the story reported in *Time* magazine about Joseph Markowski, an AIDS-infected drifter who had been selling his blood at a Los Angeles plasma center. He was a down-and-outer who said that he needed the money. He was charged with attempted murder because he did not care whom he killed with his tainted blood. That is the morality of a self-centered and careless world. Unless we turn to the morality of Jesus Christ, who shed His blood to save lives, the morality of Joseph Markowski is the best the world can expect.

The Emotional Vortex

In my book *World Aflame* (1965), I spoke of the 1960s and 1970s as a time of anger and outrage, as a warfare of conflicting ideologies. While the circumstances of our own time may have changed superficially, I am convinced that the greater social dimensions have not really changed at all. In fact, we are still paying the price for the reckless-ness of the free-thinking sixties. More than ever before, our culture is caught in a web of irresponsibility and self-centeredness. Our society is still trapped in the same con-ditions of desperation and fear that have been propelling us downward relentlessly into an emotional inferno.

As we near the end of this millennium and this momen-tous century, the world seems to be spinning faster and faster. Technology and time itself are racing past us at diz-zying speeds. Who can keep up? Where will it end? We have to wonder if there are any answers for the crises of our time. But we must also ask if there is still hope for us—or is it as bad as we often fear?

The bookstores are full of promises. Books by sages and prophets of every stripe offer instant wealth and wis-dom. For some, the answer is fitness; surely a perfect body will bring happiness. For others the answer is to be found in psychological and emotional well-being, or in making contact with the inner, "spiritual" self. Others try to persuade us that our rights have been violated in some way and that the way to happiness is to take matters into our own hands.

Unfortunately, while the names may be new, at their heart the remedies are old. While some of these prescriptions may suppress the symptoms of the world's pain for a while, none of them can cure the illness. The sickness is deep within the soul of our society, and that has always been God's exclusive territory.

I have asked people from various parts of the world what they think of our chances for the future. Most of them have a pessimistic view. Editorials in the international press are even gloomier than those in American papers. Constantly the words "Armageddon" and "Apocalypse" are used to describe events on the world scene. A decade ago, George Orwell's gloomy book, *1984*, was the image everyone used. Today Orwell's fiction seems pale in comparison to the reality: What we fear today is the Apocalypse itself.

That is the reason I have come back to the story of the four horsemen and the biblical account of the end times in this book, to confront these specters and to examine them in the light of the only reliable eternal truth: God's revealed truth, the Bible. In order to confront the troubles facing our age, I want to examine what the Bible has to say about these times and our hopes for the future.

The Rising Storm

I believe the image of an approaching storm captures the sense of fear and uncertainty I am encountering in my travels. In the midst of every kind of political struggle there is already a storm of resentment in the hearts of many people whom I meet. There is a tempest of rage brewing in our young people. Too often they have been cheated and exploited, not only by the commercialism of this consumer age, but by the educators and sociologists who have stripped them of values, family relationships, and the sense of a greater purpose in life. I see too many young men and women whose virtue has been abused and whose faith in partnership and commitment has been shattered. I truly fear for their future.

I have included much of the material from my book, *Approaching Hoofbeats*, dealing with the four horsemen of the apocalypse, in order to reexamine the biblical teachings on the end of the age. The four horses and their riders described in the sixth chapter of Revelation—the last book of the Bible—remain powerful and evocative images of what may lie just ahead. I also examine in more detail the words of Christ in Matthew 24, in which He spoke of the signs of the end of the age. For in this first book of the New Testament, Christ tells us precisely how the last days of planet Earth will unfold.

In the vivid images of the apostle John's Revelation, we can see the dangers of our age depicted as God perceives them. The first horse has to do with counterfeit religion, with secular, anti-God, and anti-Christian belief systems. In my discussion I have attempted to explore the manifestations of this reality in our world today. I also examine the condition of the modern soul and some of the fraudulent claims to truth offered by the sages of our day.

The second horse deals with war and peace. In addressing both these issues, I have chosen to do so in terms of current world conditions as well as the biblical parallels. The third horse has to do with famine and pestilence, and the fourth represents the trauma of death and the sufferings of hell. These are not meant to be meaningless or vague images, but divine revelation of the realities of the age before Christ's return. Together, the images of the four horsemen represent all the varieties of fear and crisis we are encountering in our time. Today's headlines ring with the warnings of approaching storms, and the

17

language of John's prophetic writings has never seemed so contemporary.

The figurative language of the Apocalypse is indeed complex and profound and at times difficult to understand fully. However, as I cover these chapters I will be as specific and literal as possible, and I have provided commentary from authorities wherever I thought they might help clarify certain terms and concepts. My purpose has not been to dwell specifically on theological issues concerning the Second Coming of Christ, or to offer some personal exposition of events such as the Rapture of the Church, the Tribulation, or the Millennium; however, I do look in depth at the witness of Scripture to the events of our time and to the evidence Jesus Christ expected His followers to know and understand.

In both these passages—in the images of the Apocalypse and in the teachings of Jesus in Matthew 24 concerning the coming end of the age—my purpose is to interpret the text in the most practical and logical way possible. Even though there are portions of the text that employ challenging language, these passages are dramatically relevant to our age and to the problems of a changing world.

Let no one make the dreadful mistake of interpreting such passages as mere fiction or hyperbole. In the face of so much hopelessness in every corner of the globe, we need to recognize the Word of God for what it is: *the* Word of God. So my ultimate goal is to explore these passages in the light of God's message of hope and security and to point to the ultimate source of peace, which is faith in Jesus Christ. There is a way out of despair. There is an answer to the world's crisis. There is a way to have peace with God. That is why this storm warning must be sounded now.

Weathering Life's Storms

I have come to appreciate the complexity of life's storms in a new way over the past three years as I have had to come to grips with a storm of illness in my own life. Even as the world was undergoing enormous political changes in the fall of 1989 and 1990, I began to experience changes of my own.

My first concern was a slight tremor in my hands, which I attributed to my tiring schedule. Before long, however, I experienced some difficulty in walking long distances or in doing simple things, like stepping up to a platform to deliver a sermon. So I went in for some tests at the Mayo Clinic, and my doctors informed me that I was suffering from an early and mild form of Parkinson's disease. Needless to say, that wasn't the kind of news I wanted to hear. But even though the diagnosis came as a surprise, I decided I wasn't going to overreact. I wanted to take things slowly, follow the treatment the doctors prescribed, and see if I couldn't overcome this condition.

Over the past twenty years or so I have had to deal with all sorts of illnesses, some serious, many relatively minor. This has been a new experience for me, but I am glad to report that I am doing fine. I have been told to slow down a little, and my doctors are satisfied with my progress.

By its very nature, the Christian faith involves a certain amount of blood, sweat, and tears. Jesus calls us to be disciples—regardless of the circumstances. When we come to Him, He takes away one set of problems—the burdens of sin, guilt, isolation, hopelessness, and separation from God—and He says to us, "Take my yoke upon you and learn from me" (Matthew 11:29). It is not a yoke that is too heavy for us to bear, for Christ Himself bears it with us. He says, "My yoke is easy and my burden is light" (Matthew

11:30). Nevertheless, He calls us to follow Him, regardless of the cost, and He never promises that our path will always be smooth.

No life is without its own set of problems. When I decided to give my life to Jesus Christ as a young man, it was not because I believed He would take away all my pain. No, I trusted Him because He promised me eternal life, and I believed He would always be with me and give me the strength to cope with the difficulties of this life. I may not have understood all of it at the time, but I believed that in the long run Jesus would help me live a victorious life. And He has done that and more.

Corrie ten Boom used to say, "The worst can happen but the *best* remains." That is a wonderful message, because we all have to endure storms in our lives. When any preacher or teacher of the Word oversells either the material or the spiritual benefits of the Christian life, I believe he is contributing to the work of the horseman who deceives. There is nothing on earth to compare with new life in Jesus Christ, but it will not always be easy, and as I have said, I am learning more of that truth each day.

The Test of Endurance

When I think of physical struggles, I remember a brave young man who came to one of our crusades in a wheelchair. He was suffering the last cruel stages of terminal cancer, and he was angry and bitter about it. He had read too many books promising health to the believer. Too many well-meaning Christians had promised him a miraculous healing from his disease. When he wasn't healed instantly, he grew more and more uncertain.

His loving parents carried him from one faith healer to another, and each one prayed for dramatic healing, but to no avail. The boy had prayed and fasted, and he sincerely believed, but still no miracle cure had taken place. Instead, he was dying. Our crusade was to be the last meeting that young man would ever attend.

Our Youth Night speaker the night he came was Joni Eareckson Tada. Most people know that Joni had been crippled several years earlier in a diving accident. She, too, had prayed for healing. And she, too, remained confined to a wheelchair as a quadriplegic. When she wheeled herself to the microphone that night, she did not oversell the Good News. She confessed her own early anger at remaining crippled after praying and believing in a miracle. Then she told how God met her in her pain and gave her life a new meaning and a new direction in spite of her suffering and disappointment.

Joni dared to tell it like it is. Her honesty set that dying young man free. Letting go of his bitterness and anger, he suddenly stopped seeing himself as a failure, as one who did not have enough faith. Instead, he came to see Christ in and through his pain. Not long after that meeting the young man died, but his parents were able to rejoice that he had not died angry and bitter. He simply gave his life back to his loving Father by giving himself completely to Jesus Christ. Then he went to be with the risen Lord where he would find freedom forever from his suffering.

The Power of God

That does not mean that God never heals in miraculous ways—for I am certain that there are times when He does. But there are also many times when He does not. We cannot understand why some people appear to glide effortlessly through life while others always seem to be in the throes of pain and sorrow. We cannot explain why some withered bodies are healed while others suffer and die. We cannot know why some prayers are answered miraculously while others seem to go unanswered. We cannot pretend that life in Christ will always guarantee victory and material success in this life.

When we tell only the stories of victory, we tell only a part of the truth. When we recount only the answered prayers, we oversimplify. When we imply that the Christian faith involves no yoke and no burden, we tell less than the whole truth. And half-truths, easy answers, and convenient lies are the weapons of deceit.

But in the midst of the suffering, trials, and temptations, Jesus Christ provides His peace and joy. Today that is my own hope: I have not been stopped from doing the things I love to do. I cannot imagine a time when I will not be preaching the Word of God; there is nothing on earth that I would rather be doing. Nevertheless, I realize that I cannot keep up the same pace for another fifty years. I cannot do all the things I used to do.

But for as long as I am able, I will continue to preach, and I will travel as much as I can. I expect to spend more and more time with the various Billy Graham ministries, such as the Cove, our training center near Asheville. And I will continue to give the gospel message through "The Hour of Decision" radio broadcasts and our worldwide television specials as long as God gives me strength.

In a time of stress and uncertainty in his life, the apostle Paul wrote to the church at Philippi: "I have learned in whatever state I am, to be content: I know how to be abased, and I know how to abound. Everywhere and in all things I have learned both to be full and to be hungry, both to abound and to suffer need." And then he added these stirring words: "I can do all things through Christ who strengthens me" (Philippians 4:11–13 NKJV).

That is really what it is all about. So long as we have the assurance that Jesus Christ is in control, no trial is too great, no storm is too overwhelming, no crisis is too much. We can do all things through Christ who gives us strength.

To Proclaim God's Truth

As this book has been researched, written, and revised, we have become even more aware of the dangerous storms sweeping through modern society. I have been confronted more directly than ever by the sinister implications of the dangerous social and political theories that have passed for truth in recent years. As you read this work, perhaps you will see, as I do now, the futility of the wisdom of this world and the emptiness of the secular ideologies that are leading us, day by day, to the very brink of Armageddon.

Despite my concern, I have also become fully convinced of the Christian's responsibility to proclaim the truth of God's Word. We have a mandate to speak out against "the sin that so easily entangles" (Hebrews 12:1): for though we are not of the world, we are still in it, and we are expected to do whatever we can to preserve it.

In this book I have tried to share my concern and to indicate some of the ways Christians can take a stand for righteousness in the world. I have tried to show how each man and woman who truly understands the message of grace and forgiveness can help to prepare others for the future world the Scripture promises.

The people of South Florida thought that they had ample time to prepare for Hurricane Andrew. The population that awaited the storm did as it had been doing for almost a century—windows were covered, loose items were stored, pantries were stocked, and so on. They saw the storm coming, and it looked like the other storms that they had already weathered. But this was a storm that was like no other storm they had ever seen—and not everyone survived it.

There are new storms on the horizon. Storms that seem to signal the end of this age and the coming of the future world Jesus promised. Not everyone will survive those either. It is my hope that this book will be read as a warning to help people adequately prepare, but I am confident that those who put their faith in Jesus Christ *will* survive whatever happens.

In the aftermath of Hurricane Andrew's devastation, as my grandson, Stephan-Nelson, was working night and day helping the survivors to get water and food, he noticed a sign on the roof of one house which read: "Okay, God. You've got our attention. Now what?"

I see storms of apocalyptic proportions on the horizon. God is beginning to get our attention. Now what?

That is what this book is about.

2

Signs of the Times

We sometimes wonder where God is during the storms of life, in all the troubles of the world. Where is God? Why doesn't He stop the evil? The Bible assures us that God will abolish evil when Christ returns. Someday Christ will come with the shout of acclamation, and there will be a dramatic reunion of all those who have trusted in Him.

No wonder Scripture tells us that at that time "every knee should bow, in heaven and on earth and under the earth, and every tongue confess that Jesus Christ is Lord" (Philippians 2:10-11). If you do not receive Christ as Savior and bow to Him now as Lord of your life, the day is coming when you will bow before Him as Judge.

Jesus did not tell us when He is coming back. He said we were not to speculate. "No one knows about that day or hour, not even the angels in heaven, nor the Son, but only the Father" (Matthew 24:36). The sixth chapter of Revelation, as we shall see in chapter 4, gives a strikingly detailed portrait of the end times, but no one knows when these things will be except the Father in Heaven. Not even the angels know. But Jesus also said that there would be certain signs that we could watch for. They are called the "signs of the times," and they are given in detail in chapters 24 and 25 of the Gospel of Matthew—the first book of the New Testament.

Both passages from Matthew and Revelation, taken together, give us a graphic storm warning of events yet to come and provide clearly identifiable signs of the end times. Jesus' own narrative reveals specific details of the fall of Jerusalem and the persecution that would follow. Then in the chapters that follow, Matthew records His triumphal entry into Jerusalem when the crowds hailed Him with palm branches and hosannahs as Messiah. Matthew relates the heartbreaking events of the trials before the Sanhedrin and Pilate, the beatings, the crucifixion, and the thrilling account of Christ's rising from the grave. He provides intimate details of the forty days Jesus spent with the disciples in His glorified body, teaching and challenging them before returning to the throne of Heaven.

But one portion of this story deserves to be examined in greater detail. For when Jesus came up to Jerusalem for that final Passover, He wept over the ancient city. He cried, "O Jerusalem, Jerusalem! the one who kills the prophets and stones those who are sent to her! How often I wanted to gather your children together, as a hen gathers her chicks under her wings, but you were not willing!" (Matthew 23:37 NKJV).

Jesus tried to prepare the disciples for the humiliation He was about to endure—the floggings, the cursings, the mockery, and the shameful death on a cross among thieves—but they did not understand. When He told them He must die and rise again in three days, they were mystified. Surely He was speaking in parables; no man could die and rise again by his own command—unless he were God.

As they passed through the city walls, the people with Him marveled at the size and grandeur of the temple buildings. But Jesus told them that soon these walls, this temple, and all the grand palaces and structures in Jerusalem would be flattened, and "not one stone here will be left on another" (Matthew 24:2).

They were astonished that Jesus would even suggest such a thing. These were just simple fishermen, tax collectors, and tradesmen from the remote northern region of Galilee, but they could see that Jerusalem was a beautiful, grand city. It was the city hailed by the prophets. How could such towering buildings ever be flattened? What army, what force, could do such a thing? So a group of disciples came to Jesus privately and asked Him, "Tell us, when will these things be? And what will be the sign of Your coming, and of the end of the age?"

The Beginning of Sorrows

So Jesus sat down with them and began to teach these things. His answer, recorded in Matthew 24:3-37, offers a dramatic portrait of the last days of planet Earth. Here Jesus revealed the fate of Jerusalem, which was carried out to the letter when it was sacked and burned by the legions of Emperor Titus in A.D. 70. Jesus spoke of the coming of a godless, secular society, and He spoke of the dangers of the heresies conceived by false teachers who would try to pervert the simple message of truth Christ came to deliver. He said to them: "Take heed that no one deceives you. For many will come in My name, saying, 'I am the Christ,' and will deceive many" (Matthew 24:4-5 NKJV).

The rest of the passage, which speaks to the troubles of our own times, reads as follows: "And you will hear of wars and rumors of wars. See that you are not troubled; for all these things must come to pass, but the end is not yet. For nation will rise against nation, and kingdom against kingdom. And there will be famines, pestilences, and earthquakes in various places. All these are the beginning of sorrows."

There has never been a time in history when so many storms have come together in one place and time as they have in the past decade. There have been famines, plagues, and earthquakes for thousands of years, but seldom so many all at once and seldom so concentrated in time and space. The continent of Africa is being devastated by turmoil, famine, and every kind of disease. South America is in political and social chaos. Europe is going through a time of enormous change and uncertainty; no one knows what will happen in Eastern Europe as it undergoes the greatest political upheaval in modern times.

In America we see deepening poverty, racial division, homelessness, crime, physical and sexual abuse, and the disintegration of the traditional family. And these storms are further complicated by plagues of many kinds, including AIDS, tuberculosis, and sexually transmitted diseases. Alcoholism, drug addiction, pornography, and other dangerous behaviors are eating away at society. All of these are combined with earthquakes, physical storms, and natural disasters of many kinds all across the land. But Jesus said these are merely a warning of things yet to come. This is merely the beginning of sorrows.

Jesus warned that the price of believing in Him would be high. Mockery, laughter, persecution, even death would be common, but many would refuse to pay such prices. "Then they will deliver you up to tribulation and kill you," He said, "and you will be hated by all nations for My name's sake. And then many will be offended, will betray one another, and will hate one another. Then many false prophets will rise up and deceive many. And because lawlessness will abound, the love of many will grow cold. But he who endures to the end shall be saved."

I believe this is a realistic portrait of our times. Our confidence has been shocked by scandals in the church, in government, in education, and at every level of authority. We have seen graphic images of police officers beating citizens; we have seen top officials of government and business convicted of cheating, lying, and fraud.

We have seen moral and religious leaders, men who claim to be followers of Jesus, fall into disgrace in the eyes of God and man. And worst of all, we have seen the gospel of Jesus Christ twisted and distorted by false teachers to accommodate the destructive morals and secular behavior of these times. These warnings from the Book of Matthew are not parables or myths; they are the very headlines of our day. They are the evidence of Christ's prophecy fulfilled before our eyes.

But the true church would grow through persecution, Jesus said. It would spring forth from darkness and neglect even as the churches of Romania, Bulgaria, and East Germany have sprung full-blown from the soil of despair. "And this gospel of the kingdom will be preached in all the world as a witness to all the nations," He told them, "and then the end will come."

Unfortunately, the desecrations will not end, for a defamer, a desolator, will defile the altar of God and slander Christ and His people. Jesus said, "Therefore when you see the 'abomination of desolation,' spoken of by Daniel the prophet, standing in the holy place (whoever reads, let him understand), then let those with in Judea flee to the mountains. Let him who is on the housetop not go down to take anything out of his house. And let him who is in the field not go back to get his clothes. But woe to those who are pregnant and to those with nursing babies in those days!"

Just what the nature of that abomination will be is not certain, but it will be a desecration and sacrilege of enormous consequence which will bring about the wrath of God. Then Jesus says,

> And pray that your flight may not be in winter or on the Sabbath. For then there will be great tribulation,

29

such as has not been since the beginning of the world until this time, no, nor ever shall be. And unless those days were shortened, no flesh would be saved; but for the elect's sake those days will be shortened. Then if anyone says to you, "Look, here is the Christ!" or "There!" do not believe it. For false christs and false prophets will rise and show great signs and wonders to deceive, if possible, even the elect. See, I have told you beforehand. Therefore if they say to you, "Look, He is in the desert!" do not go out; or "Look, He is in the inner rooms!" do not believe it. For as the lightning comes from the east and flashes to the west, so also will the coming of the Son of Man be. For wherever the carcass is, there the eagles will be gathered together.

The Final Hours

When the work of the church is nearing fulfillment on earth, Christ told His followers, there would be physical and visible signs that the final days of planet Earth had come. "Immediately after the tribulation of those days," Jesus said, "the sun will be darkened, and the moon will not give its light; the stars will fall from heaven, and the powers of the heavens will be shaken."

The good news for Christians who have remained faithful through trials and persecution will be bad news indeed for everyone who has denied Christ, slandered His people, and followed after false gods.

Jesus told them, "Then the sign of the Son of Man will appear in heaven, and then all the tribes of the earth will mourn, and they will see the Son of Man coming on the clouds of heaven with power and great glory. And He will send His angels with a great sound of a trumpet, and they will gather together His elect from the four winds, from one end of heaven to the other."

Jesus told His followers all of this in concrete and vivid detail. He was not speaking figuratively; this was the unvarnished truth. To be sure that they understood that what He had been telling them was real, not myth or metaphor, He offered the following parable:

> Now learn this parable from the fig tree: When its branch has already become tender and puts forth leaves, you know that summer is near. So you also, when you see all these things, know that it is near— at the doors! Assuredly, I say to you, this generation will by no means pass away till all these things take place. Heaven and earth will pass away, but My words will by no means pass away. But of that day and hour no one knows, not even the angels of heaven, but My Father only. But as the days of Noah were, so also will the coming of the Son of Man be.
>
> Matthew 24:32-37 NKJV

By using a story that was clearly a parable, Jesus illustrated that what He had told them about the end of the age was to be considered as a statement of fact. It was not a metaphor, not a myth. In those stunning images we have a glimpse of what the final storm will look like in Christ's own words. This generation—the age of men and women born into the world system designed by the Greeks and Romans—would survive to see the return of the Messiah. But even as no one had believed Noah's revelation that the flood would come and destroy the world, so in our own time the non-Christian world refuses to believe in the literal return of Jesus Christ. But His return *will* come at a time known only to God.

Imagine how shocking and unsettling these teachings must have been to the disciples of Jesus. Surely they did not fully understand the implications of what He had told them. I suspect that John, the beloved disciple and author of the Apocalypse, came to understand them during his exile on the isle of Patmos, but six decades earlier in A.D. 33 such an understanding would have been utterly inconceivable. Even today many people have difficulty seeing and believing these words.

A Time to Live

For me, the importance of this stirring passage is not that it gives such vivid detail of the end times, but that it assures us of the eternal security of those who put their trust in Jesus Christ. Suffering and death are nothing to look forward to, but death is not really the issue here; Jesus was talking about the ultimate promise of eternal life with God. That is the truth discovered by the young man who came to our crusade Youth Night in his wheelchair. He could not avoid suffering and death in this life, but He had the thrilling certainty of life with Christ ever after.

All of life resounds with the reality of death. Death is all around us, and it is inevitable in every lifetime. The distinguished British author, C. S. Lewis, once wrote that war does not increase death. As tragic as armed conflict truly is, Lewis pointed out that war does not increase the amount of death in the world, because with or without war, death is universal in every generation. Everybody dies.

The Bible says, "it is appointed unto men once to die" (Hebrews 9:27 KJV). All of nature is in the process of dying, yet most people are living their lives as if they will never die. All over the world men and women are living for today with barely a thought of the possibility of eternity.

Nature teaches that everything which has a beginning has an ending. The day begins with a sunrise, but the sun also sets, the shadows gather, and that calendar day is crossed out, never to come again. We will never be able to repeat today. It is gone forever. The seasons come and go, the decades pass, time moves on, and we grow steadily older. One day each of us will die. That is the promise of the natural world.

Nations rise, they flourish for a time, and then they decline. Eventually every empire comes to an end; not even the greatest can last forever. Time and tide and the ravages of sin take their toll on the most noble achievements of man. This is the decree of history and the way of life on this planet.

The Bible also teaches that the world system as we know it shall come to a close. We read in 1 John 2:17: "And the world is passing away, and the lust of it." Jesus said in Matthew 24:35, "Heaven and earth will pass away . . ." And in 2 Peter 3:10 we read: "But the day of the Lord will come as a thief in the night, in which the heavens will pass away with a great noise, and the elements will melt with fervent heat; both the earth and the works that are in it will be burned up."

The words of Jesus Christ are good news for a world in crisis. For He gave us a gospel of hope, good news that offers a workable plan for your life, the good news that God loves you, that He is a God of mercy and that He will forgive you if you confess and forsake your sins and have faith in Him.

Faith in Times of Crisis

The marvelous security of the Christian faith is that it is specifically designed for overcoming the storms of this life and giving us the certainty of the life to come in Heaven. The message of Christ proclaims that the world's days are numbered. Every cemetery testifies that this is true. Our days on this planet are numbered. The Scriptures tell us that life is only a vapor that appears for a moment and then vanishes. Our life is like the grass that withers and the flowers that fade. But for those whose hope is in Christ, we know that we shall overcome. The prophet Isaiah, in one of those marvelous passages that foreshadows the coming of Christ, wrote,

> But those who wait on the LORD
> Shall renew their strength;
> They shall mount up with wings like eagles,
> They shall run and not be weary,
> They shall walk and not faint.
>
> Isaiah 40:31 NKJV

That is the hope of every believer.

But there is another sense in which the world system will end; that is, the world itself will end. Someday soon there will be an end of history. That doesn't mean an end to life but the end of a world that has been dominated by greed, evil, and injustice. The fact that the Bible speaks so often and in such graphic detail about the end of the world indicates that God desires that we find security in Him.

The Revelation of John and Christ's teachings in the Book of Matthew tell us that the present world system will pass away and come to a dramatic end. These passages also tell us that Jesus Christ will come again and that He will set up His kingdom of righteousness and social justice where hatred, greed, jealousy, war, and death will no longer exist. Jesus Himself promised the end of the present evil world system and the establishment of a new order, which is called the kingdom of God.

Jesus used images that were dramatic and compelling, but He did not engage in fantasy. He told His followers, "I am the way and the truth, and the life. No one comes to the Father except through Me" (John 14:6), and He was truth and veracity personified. Jesus indicated that when certain things come to pass, we can be assured that the end is near. He said, "You can read the signs of the weather in the sky, but because of spiritual blindness you cannot read the signs of the times." He indicated that only those who have spiritual illumination and discernment from the Holy Spirit can hope to understand the trends and meanings of history.

The Bible plainly indicates that certain conditions will prevail just before the end. For example, the prophet Daniel said, "even to the time of the end . . . knowledge shall be increased" (Daniel 12:4 KJV). Today there is more knowledge about everything than at any other time in history. I read recently that 90 percent of all the scientists and engineers who have ever lived are alive today. Our high schools, colleges, and universities are turning out nearly 4 million graduates every year.

But although our young people are gaining knowledge, they are not always acquiring wisdom to use that knowledge. In every area of life people are floundering, suffering from neuroses and psychological problems on a scale that we have never known before. Our heads are filled with knowledge, but we are confused, bewildered, frustrated, and without moral moorings.

Power and Glory Forever

Another condition that the Bible says will be present at the end of the world system is power without peace. Many little wars are taking place all over the world, and certainly a major war could break out at any time. Despite the talk of nuclear disarmament and the apparent end of the Soviet Union, the world is still very much under the threat of nuclear war and nuclear accident.

Throughout 1992 the United Nations has been battling with Iraq's Saddam Hussein to isolate and destroy his nuclear capabilities, and it is clear that his intentions remain as militant and belligerent as ever. With the proliferation of nuclear arms on every side of the globe, it is not hard to imagine that somebody could push the wrong button or miscalculate. In a matter of seconds the world could be plunged into a third world war that nobody wants. Jesus said, "And you will hear of wars and rumors of wars. . . . For nation will rise against nation, and kingdom against kingdom" (Matthew 24:6–7 NKJV).

But as the United Nations attempts to mediate hostilities in dozens of nations around the globe, the world is still an armed camp. Billions of dollars, rubles, marks, and pounds are spent for weapons that quickly become obsolete or are replaced with newer ones which cost even more. The United States alone spent hundreds of billions of dollars in 1991 on armaments. In short, the atmosphere of the world is still threatening. While the world cries, "Peace, peace," there is no peace.

I often hear people ask, "Why is there so little peace in the world when we have such unprecedented knowledge and unlimited potential?" We are trying to build a peaceful world, but there is no peace within people's hearts. The Los Angeles riots were, as every reporter noted, evidence of a deep-seated anger and bitterness welling up in America's soul. The Bible assures us that we cannot build a new world on the old, unregenerate hearts of people. The new world will only come about when Jesus Christ, King of kings and Lord of lords, reigns supreme.

Most of us are familiar with these memorable words from Handel's famous oratorio, *The Messiah*, taken from the writings of the prophet Isaiah:

For unto us a Child is born,
Unto us a Son is given;
And the government will be upon His shoulder.
And His name will be called
Wonderful, Counselor, Mighty God,
Everlasting Father, Prince of Peace.
Of the increase of His government and peace
There will be no end,
Upon the throne of David and over His kingdom,
To order it and establish it with judgment and
    justice
From that time forward, even forever.
The zeal of the LORD of hosts will perform this.

Isaiah 9:6–7 NKJV

These words are the best promise of security in a world of tension and turmoil. The King of kings is the hope of every man, woman, and child of every tribe and nation that knows the name of Christ. His kingdom is forever.

The signs of insecurity and the shouts of revolution heard around the world are perhaps the death rattle of an era in civilization—perhaps they signal the end of civilization as we have known it. In either event, it is now God's turn to act, and Scripture promises that He will act dramatically. He will send His Son, Jesus Christ, back to this earth. He is the Lord of history. The storms of change in the former Soviet Union are no surprise to Him; nothing we have seen in the headlines is taking God by surprise. Events are moving rapidly toward some sort of climax, but it will be according to God's timing, when His Son returns to be the rightful ruler of the world.

Before that time comes, however, God wants to rule in our hearts. He sent His Son into the world to be the ruler of our hearts. The Bible says that sin shall not have dominion over us if Jesus Christ is in our hearts as Lord and Master. The danger lies in the fact that there are two rulers who want to control us: our self and Jesus Christ. Either self will reign in our lives, or Jesus Christ will reign. "No one can serve two masters," Jesus said (Matthew 6:24). The Bible challenges us, "choose for yourselves this day whom you will serve" (Joshua 24:15 NKJV).

Solomon wrote in the Proverbs, "There is a way that seems right to a man, but in the end it leads to death" (Proverbs 14:12). If you want to have peace with God and find security for these times of trouble, you must answer one very important question: *Who is the ruler of your life?* Are you trying to be the master of your own fate? Are you trying to be the captain of your own soul? Do you believe you can navigate life's storms without the Master at the helm? Or is the kingdom of God within you?

Jesus Christ can come into your heart right now if you will turn from your sins and receive Him as Savior. He loves you. He knows you by name, and He wants to forgive you. You can enter the new kingdom, the new world that will be born under His leadership when He comes again. There is no doubt that the world to come will be a theocracy, but it will be a joyous, exciting, incredibly beautiful place with Jesus Christ in complete and loving control.

Now, before looking further into the revelations of Scripture and especially the writings of John, I would like to retrace briefly the events of the past decade as I have seen them develop all across the European continent. I would like us to start at the Berlin Wall, since that symbolic dividing line between Christian and anti-Christian beliefs was such a perfect picture of the moral and philosophical dilemma of our day.

3

A Changing Landscape

Nothing characterizes the storms of controversy and change taking place in the world today so much as the collapse of Communism in Eastern Europe and the reformation of the once-great Soviet Union. The suddenness of these changes has baffled scholars, Soviet observers, diplomats, and even the CIA. In a matter of days, our history books, maps, dictionaries, and textbooks were invalidated. After August 1989, the world would no longer be the same. We entered the decade of the 1990s with a new challenge and a new direction.

The suddenness of the changes in Eastern Europe and the Baltic States tends to obscure the gradual trend toward change that had been developing for some time. I encountered aspects of it—including the deep hunger for change—during my many trips to Eastern Europe and the Soviet Union over the past decades. While no one could have predicted precisely how the changes in Russia, East Germany, Romania, and the other Communist countries would come about or when they would occur, I sensed along with many other observers a yearning for change in the hearts of the people.

When I held my first crusade in Berlin in 1954, the tensions in Europe were high. During those emotional years following the end of World War II, the Cold War was born, but the term "Cold War" hardly expressed the deep uncertainty and fear felt by most Europeans at that time.

When I met the people of Berlin, I could feel their anxiety. Consequently, I was not really surprised when the Berlin Wall was erected in 1961; the hostility between the democrats in the West and the Communists in the East was just too intense. Considering the nature and consequences of their ruthless doctrines, it was inevitable that the Soviets and East Germans would eventually have to lock democracy out.

Before the wall went up, disagreement and discord between the United States and the Soviet Union—and military adventures such as the American-sponsored Bay of Pigs invasion in Cuba in April 1961—seemed to bring the world to the threshold of war. While Soviet Premier Nikita Khrushchev and President John Kennedy stood toe-to-toe, each daring the other to blink, thousands of East Germans were fleeing into West Berlin. The mass exodus was an embarrassment and provoked the Communists to lock their doors. In August of that year, Khrushchev ordered the Germans to put up the wall.

The Berlin Wall was more than just concrete and barbed wire; it was above all a grim metaphor of mankind's capacity for hatred, stretching twenty-nine miles through the heart of the German capital and another seventy-five miles around the city, and finally stretching along the entire frontier. Guard stations with lookout towers and machine-gun posts all along its length monitored the no man's land between east and west, making West Berlin more like a prison camp than a civilized European city. For nearly three decades, hundreds of men, women, and children were gunned down by Communist guards as they tried to cross that hostile killing field to freedom.

When the wall finally came down in 1989, it was again precipitated by the flight of more than 120,000 East Germans into Hungary and then across the border into Austria.

Once more, the flight from Communism was an enormous embarrassment to the East German government. Tens of thousands of skilled workers fled, confirming the disappointment and unhappiness of life under the Communist regime. Ultimately, the humiliation was too much for the East German government to handle, and their repressive attempts were unsuccessful in the face of a sudden groundswell of resistance.

Erich Honecker was soon driven into exile in the Soviet Union. He had invited Mikhail Gorbachev to Berlin in October 1989 to join in the celebration of the fortieth anniversary of the founding of Communist East Germany. But the people in the streets of Berlin, Dresden, and Leipzig were demanding reforms and threatened to march against Gorbachev. The government spread rumors of Tiananmen-Square-type repression if the people did not remain calm. In reality, the government no longer had the muscle to support such threats. The Soviets refused to help them, and ultimately Honecker, the last hard-liner, was overthrown.

After a period of utter confusion, Egon Krenz headed the provisional East German government, and on November 9, 1989, his administration announced that the Berlin Wall would no longer serve as a barrier between East and West. That announcement was the beginning of the incredible cycle of events that ultimately led to the reunification of the two Germanies on October 3, 1990.

Divided Hopes and Expectations

I vividly remember our rally in 1960 in Berlin, just one year before the wall went up. More than a hundred thousand people came for our week-long crusade. That was at the beginning of the Kennedy era in America, and even amid the general desperation of the German people, there was a sense of cautious optimism and expectation. We saw a desire for openness and a concerted effort to communicate between the different organizations and churches in Germany at that time, but even so, the more extravagant hopes and ambitions of the people were often stifled. I could see then that the political divisions in Germany and Eastern Europe were growing deeper and more troubled.

Ever since 1945, dialogue between people, nations, and the churches of East and West was severely restricted. During our crusades, we found communications difficult, and widespread cooperation was sometimes difficult to obtain. But that didn't stop us. From 1954 to 1990, I was privileged to hold eight crusades and rallies in Germany, and each time we sensed the fear and worry in the people, combined with their hunger for truth and meaning in their lives.

During those thirty-six years, I addressed more than a million people in ten East and West German cities, including three crusades in Berlin. In addition, from 1977 to 1990 we held meetings in every Eastern Bloc country except Bulgaria and Albania.

One of our most pleasant surprises was the 1957 crusade in Berlin when more than a hundred thousand people came to hear the gospel—many from the Eastern Zone. They didn't know much about me or my ministry at that time. They had read stories in the newspapers about the success of the London Crusade, and they came perhaps out of curiosity. But I remember that when I gave the invitation for people to receive Christ, it looked as if the whole audience was coming forward. I had to tell them to go back to their seats. There were too many for our counselors to handle on the field of the stadium. So I said that if they wanted to receive Christ and have their life changed they should write us a letter. Within days we received more than sixteen thousand letters, and that was just the beginning. It was a vivid indication of deep spiritual hunger. From there we went all across Europe; it was a spiritual phenomenon.

Living Between Fear and Hope

When I came back to Berlin in January 1990 to meet privately with the leaders of the East and West German republics, I went there to ask about the possibility of holding an all-Germany crusade in 1992. We were greeted enthusiastically by representatives of the German Evangelical Alliances from East and West. Two Protestant bishops—Dr. Martin Kruse from West Berlin and Dr. Gottfried Forck from East Berlin—came to offer support and prayer. And Dr. Georg Sterzinsky, the Roman Catholic bishop of Berlin, contacted us by letter to offer his encouragement.

Almost in unison, these leaders told me that the German people were desperate for the good news. They said that on both sides of the ideological wall which still separated the two Germanies, men and women were living "between fear and hope," and they pleaded for us to come to Germany, not in 1992, but right then in 1990.

So we did. We hastily changed our itineraries, and on March 10, 1990, we set up our microphones at the Platz der Republik, the great open area in front of the Reichstag, the former parliament building, and right next to the historic Brandenburg Gate. On this historic site where Nazis once paraded by torchlight, marshaling ethnic bitterness and hatred, we came to bring the good news of the gospel.

On the very spot where the evil ambitions of the Third Reich were born, we came to proclaim the gospel of Jesus Christ. The Nazis had promised the German people a thousand-year regime of military might and power and awful judgment; I spoke to them of the good news of forgiveness and the love of God. It was a different story for a different time. It was a message for a people struggling between the failures of history and ideology and their hopes for peace and security.

The entire world watched via satellite when the Berlin Wall came down. I suspect a large part of the shock expressed by the world was not because the hideous wall had at last fallen, but that the emotional and political barriers to peace were being taken away, stone by stone.

When I consider the changes that have occurred in just the past few years, I marvel at the hand of God in world affairs. The Bible says,

> The kings of the earth take their stand
> and the rulers gather together
> against the LORD
> and against his Anointed One.
> "Let us break their chains" they say,
> "and throw off their fetters."
>
> The One enthroned in heaven laughs;
> the Lord scoffs at them.
> Then he rebukes them in his anger
> and terrifies them in his wrath,
> saying,
> "I have installed my King
> on Zion, my holy hill."
>
> Psalm 2:2–6

It also decrees, "Look at the nations and watch—and be utterly amazed. For I am going to do something in your days that you would not believe even if you were told" (Habakkuk 1:5). Such mighty happenings give us a hint of the power that God will unleash at the close of the age. The events which have transpired on the continent of Europe since the summer of 1989 actually help us to understand just how awesome God's plans for the world really are.

The Image of Peace

The place where I stood to address the German people on that afternoon in March 1990 was only yards away from a shattered section of the Berlin Wall where workers with saws and torches were ripping out the bars that supported the barriers. By a show of hands, I learned that more than half of the fifteen thousand to seventeen thousand people who came out to brave the wind and rain were from East Germany. They listened attentively and hopefully, and I wanted to give them a message of peace, a message as big as their dreams.

I told these expectant men and women that the world was watching them by satellite and that Christians everywhere were praying for them. I said it was "with tears of rejoicing and happiness as we watched you coming through the wall." Because of these events, there was a new "hope that peace was on its way to our world." "God has answered our prayers," I assured them, and the changes taking place in the world prove that He cares for us.

Despite the miserable cold and torrents of rain, those hungry people listened intently as I asked questions I knew they were already asking themselves, questions people going through times of turmoil inevitably ask themselves. "How can you find meaning and happiness in your life?" The crowd grew quiet as I spoke of their hopes and fears. "How can you become free of guilt?" There was so much history here in this ancient city, so many memories. Then I asked the question we all must eventually ask, "What will happen after death?"

Among the people gathered around the podium that day were about 120 journalists. I'm sure that was one of the largest press contingents I have ever addressed from the pulpit.

In the press conference the day before, the men and women of the press corps had many questions of their own: "Does Billy Graham regard the dismantling of the Iron Curtain as an answer to prayer?" I told them yes, it was. Christians in the East and the West had been praying for decades for this day. I told them that the prospect of liberation, reunification, and the freedom to worship God made this "the happiest hour for Germany."

We can never thank God enough for what has happened here, I said, but there is another dangerous storm looming on Germany's horizon: the loss of moral and spiritual values. Pornography, prostitution, drugs, violence, and other signs of moral decay are already in evidence throughout West Germany, and now they threaten the east as never before. I recalled speaking to a group of wide-eyed East Germans at the wall a day or two earlier who told me that they were both hopeful and frightened. They were hopeful that peace and freedom would improve their way of life, but they were frightened by the scenes of greed and materialism they saw in the West. They said they would rather remain behind the wall, in poverty and bondage to Communism, than discover that "freedom" was nothing more than moral decadence, corruption, sin, violence, and greed, all qualities that characterize so much of the West today. I thought those were incredibly wise and stirring sentiments from people who had already suffered so much.

The Longings of the Soul

Over the years I have preached more often in Germany than in any other non-English-speaking country. I mentioned that fact to this group, and I told them how much I cared for them; I told the young people of Germany that my prayer for them was that they would not be cheated by hedonism and materialism. Such things cannot satisfy the longings of their souls—only God can do that.

On the night before the big public meeting, we held a rally for a thousand church workers in the famous Gethsemane Church in the eastern sector. This is the place where Christians and democrats met nightly during the years prior to the breakthrough. Brave men and women of every class and vocation came here to encourage each other, to seek God's blessings, and to protect the dissidents who dared speak out against the repressive Communist regime.

I read to them from the books of Isaiah and Ephesians and told them that I believed that God had given them an opportunity to spark revival in Germany. "This divided city longs for a church which is a living answer to the message of Christ," I said. "Let us look at its people with mercy and love. Let us learn to pray together, no matter what political background we come from."

Many of the greatest men of faith had lived and taught on this soil. Great saints of the Roman Church were born here; Luther launched the Protestant Reformation at Wittenburg. With all my heart, I said to them, "I believe that a strong revival can spring from Germany, if Germany does not miss the chance."

I asked each person to make a new commitment to Jesus Christ that night, and hundreds of hands went up. There was, indeed, a sense of renewal and revival in that church, just as there was the following afternoon when Jürgen Wohlrabe, president of the West Berlin Parliament, addressed our gathering. Wohlrabe said, "Your words touch hearts because you convey the message which was given to us two thousand years ago and which we have forgotten or ignored. You point out to your audiences that today the words of the gospel are as valid as ever."

Referring to recent political events, the statesman said, "Our personal and social life is not determined by material values. We should find orientation and direction for our lives in the Christian faith and in our personal responsibility."

Throughout that week we saw the hand of God at work in Berlin. A taxi driver who carried people to the various events told us he wasn't interested in our message, but as he heard my remarks from the loudspeakers and as he saw the genuine love and brotherhood in the faces of our workers and helpers, he realized we had something he needed. He said he wanted more. A young Hungarian told us his life had been changed a year earlier when I spoke at the People's Stadium in Budapest. Another man told of how he had been arrested at the border while coming to our crusade in 1960. Two soldiers of the East German People's Army made a special trip to "fellowship with other Christians."

There were many such stories. One man came because his late grandfather had told him so much about the American preacher, Billy Graham, he had to hear for himself. One woman reached out to me as I was arriving for the service and handed me her card indicating that she was accepting Jesus Christ in her life for the first time. She had completed the card with the only marker she had, her lipstick.

I have gained a deep sense of compassion and affection for the people of Eastern Europe over the years. I have shared in their hopes, their joys, and their sorrows. I was touched by them, and I have had the great privilege of preaching in their churches.

One of those special occasions was in Cracow, Poland, in 1978, when Karol Cardinal Wojtyla was the chief prelate in that city. Just as we were leaving Poland, on September

16, Wojtyla was elected to the highest office of the Roman Catholic Church, and he was installed as Pope John Paul II in a solemn enthronement service on September 22, 1978.

The Message of Peace

Of the many opportunities I have had to preach in the East, the chance to speak from the pulpit of the Moscow Baptist Church in May 1982 still stands out as one of my personal highlights. In those days, more than a decade ago, no one dared even dream of the kinds of changes we have seen over the past three years. During the spring of that year, there were hotly debated political battles over nuclear proliferation and other volatile issues. So when I went to Moscow to preach and to deliver an address at a religious conference on the subject of peace, many Westerners apparently thought I had lost my mind, and they said so.

The leaders at the conference represented most of the major religions of the world, and they were considering a wide variety of issues. The possibility of a nuclear holocaust had been weighing heavily on my heart, and since war has always been primarily a moral and spiritual issue, I felt I needed to speak about it and offer a Christian perspective. Unfortunately, a few Christians were the most vocal in their criticism of me. The world press was generally divided. Some scolded me or called me naive, and I was misquoted on occasion. But others—especially many of the press who traveled with me or actually covered the events in Moscow—were more sympathetic.

Nevertheless, today I believe those remarks were instrumental in opening the eyes of many Eastern Europeans to the good news of Jesus Christ and the message of peace He offered. On my trips to the Soviet Union, Hungary, Czechoslovakia, Poland, and Germany over the past ten years, many people have come to tell me that my Moscow address made a profound impact on their lives. Because of the way, the time, and the place in which those remarks were presented, I would like to repeat a portion of the address here, and then to elaborate on the work taking place there now.

The Russian Address

I said in part to the conferees assembled in Moscow:

"The whole human race sits under a nuclear sword of Damocles, not knowing when someone will push the button or give the order that will destroy much of the planet. The possibility of nuclear war, therefore, is not merely a political issue. . . .

"The nuclear arms race is primarily a moral and spiritual issue that must concern us all. I am convinced that political answers alone will not suffice, but that it is now time for us to urge the world to turn to spiritual solutions as well.

A Troubled Planet

"Pope John Paul II has stated, 'Our future on this planet, exposed as it is to nuclear annihilation, depends on one single factor: humanity must make a moral about-face.' But the question that confronts us is, how can this happen? Technologically, man has far exceeded his moral ability to control the results of his technology. Man himself must be changed. The Bible teaches that this is possible through spiritual renewal. Jesus Christ taught that man can and must have a spiritual rebirth.

"I am convinced one of the most vivid and tragic signs of man's rebellion against God's order in our present generation is the possibility of a nuclear war. I include here the whole scope of modern weapons capable of destroying life—conventional, biochemical, and nuclear weapons. I know that the issue of legitimate national defense is complex. I am not a pacifist, nor am I for unilateral disarmament. Police and military forces are unfortunately necessary as long as man's nature remains the way it is. But the unchecked production of weapons of mass destruction by the nations of the world is a mindless fever which threatens to consume much of our world and destroy the sacred gift of life.

"From a Christian perspective, therefore, the possibility of a nuclear war originates in the greed and covetousness of the human heart. The tendency toward sin is passed on from generation to generation. Therefore, Jesus predicted that there would be wars and rumors of wars till the end of the age. The psalmist said, 'In sin did my mother conceive me' [Psalm 51:5 KJV]. Thus, there is a tragic and terrible flaw in human nature that must be recognized and dealt with.

Peace Among Men

"The word 'peace' is used in the Bible in three main ways. First, there is spiritual peace. This is peace between man and God. Second, there is psychological peace, or peace within ourselves. Third, there is relational peace, or peace among men.

"Sin, the Bible says, has destroyed or seriously affected all three of these dimensions of peace. When man was created he was at peace with God, with himself, and with his fellow humans. But when he rebelled against God, his fellowship with God was broken. He was no longer at peace with himself. And he was no longer at peace with others.

"Can these dimensions of peace ever be restored? The Bible says yes. It tells us man alone cannot do what is necessary to heal the brokenness in his relationships—but God can, and has.

"The Bible teaches that Jesus Christ was God's unique Son, sent into the world to take away our sins by His death on the cross, therefore making it possible for us to be at peace—at peace with God, at peace within ourselves, and at peace with each other. That is why Jesus Christ is central to the Christian faith. By His resurrection from the dead, Christ showed once and for all that God is for life, not death. The Orthodox tradition and its Divine Liturgy especially make central this jubilant and glorious event. The Bible states, 'For the wages of sin is death, but the gift of God is eternal life in Christ Jesus our Lord' [Romans 6:23]. The ultimate sign of man's alienation is death; the ultimate sign of God's reconciling love is life.

"Throughout all Christendom you will notice there is one symbol common to all believers—the cross. We believe it was on the cross that the possibility of lasting peace in all of its dimensions has been made. The Bible says about Christ that 'God was pleased to have all his fullness dwell in him, and through him to reconcile to himself all things . . . by making peace through his blood, shed on the cross' [Colossians 1:19-20]. The Bible again says, 'For he himself is our peace, who has made the two one and has destroyed the barrier, the dividing wall of hostility. . . . He came and preached peace to you who were far away and peace to those who were near' [Ephesians 2:14, 17].

"The Christian looks forward to the time when peace will reign over all creation. Christians all over the world pray the prayer Jesus taught His disciples: 'Thy kingdom come. Thy will be done in earth, as it is in heaven' [Matthew 6:10 KJV]. Only then will the spiritual problem of the human race be fully solved.

"Both the Bible and the Christian creeds teach that there will be a universal judgment. Christ will come again, in the words of the ancient Apostles' Creed, 'to judge the quick and the dead.' But then the kingdom of God will be established, and God will intervene to make all things new. That is our great hope for the future.

"But in the meantime God is already at work. The kingdom of God is not only a future hope but a present reality. Wherever men and women turn to God in repentance and faith and then seek to do His will on earth as it is done in heaven, there the kingdom of God is seen. And it is in obedience to Jesus Christ, who is called in the Bible the Prince of Peace, that Christians are to cooperate with all who honestly work for peace in our world."

Thy Kingdom Come

If I were preparing this address over again I would probably expand this point to say that those who are members of God's kingdom live in an alien world as pilgrims and strangers. The kingdom is "already" present in the lives of the believers who glorify Him by word and deed in the church and in society. But the world is "not yet" the kingdom, for, as we have already seen, the world is under the rule and reign of the prince of this world—Satan. Nevertheless, King Jesus has conquered Satan, and all those who have acknowledged Christ as King and who have, by so doing, been reconciled to God are possessed by the King. Is Christ the king of your life?

Jesus dwells within them by His Holy Spirit. The crucified King has received all authority and His indwelling Spirit is greater than Satan and his demon powers: "The one who is in you is greater than the one who is in the world" (1 John 4:4). Believers alone have been "rescued . . . from the dominion of darkness and brought . . . into the kingdom of the Son he loves" (Colossians 1:13).

It is then true that believers bear fruit in every good work upon the earth but believers cannot change the world into the kingdom. Only the return of the King to rule upon the earth can result in His will being done upon earth as it is in heaven. With this inward hope and this indwelling power of the kingdom to come, is it any wonder that Christians strive to extend the kingdom in the hearts of people and work toward a peace that enables the spread of the gospel (1 Timothy 2:4)?

God reigns supreme over the world, leading it providentially toward the day of the kingdom to come (Acts 1:6-7). This is the day of grace for the world, when Jesus returns to establish His kingdom of glory. Humanity now lives between the times of Christ's ascension to the Father and His return "on the clouds of the sky, with power and great glory" (Matthew 24:30).

Then why should Christians serve the cause of peace? First, because they have been instructed to love the lost of this world. Second, because they love that creation of God which has been cursed and corrupted by sin. Third, because they love those created in the image of God, Who wills that all should come to repentance (2 Peter 3:9).

The signs of the kingdom are not always political, although they always have political implications. Jesus' signs were given to lead people to faith, not to political reform (John 20:30-31). Jesus' life by the Spirit within believers draws sinners to the cross and reconciliation. The fruits of righteousness and peace then permeate society.

The Source of Reformation

In the fall of 1982, I returned to Europe to hold other crusades and to meet with various political and religious leaders. I preached from Martin Luther's pulpit in the City Church of Wittenburg on October 17—where Luther posted his Ninety-five Theses in 1517 and sparked the Protestant Reformation. In my sermon, I cited Luther's writings and teachings, and I sensed a bond of friendship with the East Germans—especially those in Wittenburg. Many came to accept Christ at that service. Later I went on to Dresden where I had been asked to preach in the great Church of the Cross, which had been gutted by the bombings of World War II and restored in subsequent years. The night I spoke, the church was filled with more than seven thousand people. I was startled at how many young faces there were in the crowd. Someone estimated that 85 percent of the audience were under thirty years of age. At the invitation, twenty-five hundred raised their hands to indicate their desire to receive Christ.

Today we know that young people like these and their elders were the spark that ignited the flames of change in that part of Europe. They were the evangelical activists who met at Gethsemane Church, who formed prayer vigils, who worked silently and openly whenever possible to foster the hopes of freedom in the East. They were God's people seeking His righteousness. Paul wrote to the Corinthian church, "where the Spirit of the Lord is, there is liberty" (2 Corinthians 3:17). Clearly these people were destined to achieve their freedom. As we shall see in the following chapters, they were even spoken of by the apostle John in the Book of Revelation. For they represent the people of God among the Gentiles—the children of God who would "suffer many things" and proclaim the name of Christ to the ends of the earth.

As we begin in the following chapter to lift the veil on the revelations of things to come, I would like to examine briefly the context and framework of John's writing, his confinement in the Roman labor camp at Patmos, and the way in which he received his vital messages from the Spirit of God. In this second section I have focused largely on the early chapters of John's work; in subsequent chapters I will examine the specific images of the book along with applications to the mounting storm clouds and controversies of our own time.

Part 2

The Lightning over Patmos

4

Inside the Apocalypse

In the history of the church, the Book of Revelation has been neglected, misunderstood, and misinterpreted by more people than any other book. In his own treatise on the book, biblical scholar William Barclay wrote, "The Revelation is notoriously the most difficult and bewildering book in the New Testament; but doubtless, too, we shall find it infinitely worthwhile to wrestle with it until it gives us its blessing and opens its riches to us."

For centuries, the mysterious images of John's book were considered by many too enigmatic and surreal to be understood. But it is surprising how political events of the past few years—from the Persian Gulf War to the collapse of the Soviet Union—have shed a new and penetrating light on these seemingly cryptic messages, so that today they seem much less fantastic and bewildering than they once did.

Many of the passages I used to think were symbolic I now see as obvious evidence of the approaching storm. Until recently, the revelations of John have not often been taught or preached in some of our churches because they seemed too esoteric and obscure for most people. Nevertheless, at the beginning of the Book of Revelation, the author writes, "Blessed is the one who reads the words of this prophecy, and blessed are those who hear it and take to heart what is written in it, because the time is near" (Revelation 1:3). That alone should encourage us to explore this important work in greater detail.

The morning I first composed these words, more than a decade ago, I had read in the paper a quote by one of the great literary and political leaders of our time. He used the same expression, "The time is near. But I probably will not live to see the end." That is the irony of this book: It is compelling and timeless. Revelation is as real as today and as urgent as tomorrow. And while Revelation may be difficult to read, it is nevertheless the only book of Scripture that explicitly promises a blessing to those who read and obey it (Revelation 22:7).

During my study of the Scripture spanning more than fifty years now, I have often been intrigued, inspired, and informed by the words of this dramatic book written under divine inspiration by John on the island of Patmos. Sitting in my study at home in North Carolina, I have read literally thousands of pages from articles and scholarly works on the book. In my personal devotions I have thoroughly immersed myself in the sound and fury of John's language, listening to the voice of God speaking through the apostle. But as I consider all that I have learned about this work, its sinister images, and the actual structure of the Revelation, I am constantly humbled by it. Many great minds have grappled with the meaning of John's visions over the centuries, but in light of the storm I am convinced is coming, I feel compelled to take another look into it to discover its meaning for our age. Perhaps it is because I, like John, am growing older and have a longer perspective on the events of our time. There is something ominous in the air, and I am intrigued by both the horror and hope of what lies just ahead. Of course, John wrote nearly two thousand years ago. His culture and ours are light-years apart, but his message has a signal importance for our time. His visions, dreams, and nightmares were not meant to confound or confuse us. The very word, *apocalypse*, is a Greek word combining the verb *calypto* ("to veil," "to cover," or "to conceal") and the preposition *apo* ("from"). Thus, apocalypse means "to remove the veil," "to uncover," "to reveal," and "to make clear." John's storm warnings were clear to Christians in the first century, and they should be even clearer in the climate of today.

A Sense of Perspective

In the Louvre Museum in Paris some years ago, I stood at arm's length from a large impressionistic painting by Renoir. Globs of paint seemed splattered incoherently across the canvas. I was not much impressed. "What in the world is that?" I wondered aloud. My wife, Ruth, said, "Stand back, Bill, and you will see it." I had been standing too close to the masterpiece and each individual detail, each patch of color, each brush stroke kept me from seeing the effect of the canvas as a whole. I was bogged down in the details. But when I stepped back across the hall, the mystery suddenly disappeared and the beautiful image composed by the artist was clearly visible.

For too long, I suspect, too many of us have examined the Book of Revelation in the same manner. We have turned that great masterpiece into a series of images and brush strokes, and we have tried to outguess each other at the modern meaning of every star, dragon, and number. As a result, we have lost the grand design of the prophet's vision, and we may also have missed the urgency of his warnings.

We cannot afford to lose sight of the big picture, and that is what John's prophecies can do for us. Even though they refer in many places to an unseen time and to future events, they are very real. The words are a true revelation of what lies just ahead.

I have never been banished to a rocky island ten miles long and six miles wide, but I have been banished to an endless itinerary of jet planes, hotels, stadiums, board-rooms, and television studios. I am not surrounded by criminals and political prisoners most of the time, but I am surrounded by ordinary people—businessmen, homemak-ers, teachers, students, laborers, public servants, soldiers, and others. I am not as often alone with the sounds of sea gulls or crashing waves as I would like to be, but I think I understand the texture of John's world and his dilemma as bearer of an earth-shaking message from heaven.

The Man of Vision

Very often I am inundated with the sounds of the city and of men and women in the city drowning in activity and noise. I can stand on a street corner in New York or Paris or London or Tokyo, and I can see hopelessness, fear, and boredom on the faces of the men and women passing by. On the surface, it would seem that John and I have almost nothing in common. Yet I sometimes feel that I can al-most hear the voices he heard. I hear their warnings and, like John, I feel compelled to relay the images I have seen.

Before exploring his imagery, I think it would be appro-priate to review briefly the situation of John himself. Who was this wizened old man—poet, prophet, or pastor? What drove him to write a letter that still boggles the minds of believers and unbelievers alike after all these years? The argument about the identity of the author of Revelation has raged over the centuries. But earliest Christian tradition, preserved by Justin Martyr, Clement, Origen, Irenaeus, Eusebius, Jerome, and other ancient scholars, makes it clear that the author of the Revelation was, in fact, John the apostle, the last living disciple who had known Jesus in the flesh. Modern prophecy schol-ars—from Dr. John Walvoord to Bishop Robinson—agree with their findings, and so do I.

Almost all of that little band who had lived with and learned from Jesus for three years were now dead. Each one, according to early tradition, had been martyred for his faith in the risen Christ.

Many have suggested John's long life, which included the burden of receiving and retelling the mysterious revelations, may actually have been a far greater price for John to pay than merely dying. John was often called the disciple whom Jesus loved (e.g., John 21:20). The great missionary and writer, Amy Carmichael, writes that to John the beloved disciple "was entrusted the long martyrdom of life."

The Suffering Saint

Can you imagine the lightning storm that ignited John's life on that lonely island? Truly the entire revelation he received from heaven was a lightning bolt that struck without warning. That wrinkled old man whose hand trembled as he scratched out countless Greek letters onto scraps of parchment in his prison cave was once the teenage Galilean fisherman who dropped his nets and, filled with hope, followed after Jesus to become a fisher of men. Years later, as an exiled, humiliated, taciturn old man, squinting by candlelight at his growing manuscript, he bears little resemblance to the youth who once stood with Jesus on the Mount of Transfiguration. He hardly remembers a time when, flushed with the aura of Christ's miracles and his own power, he asked to be secretary of state when Jesus set up His kingdom in Jerusalem (Mark 10:35-45). Now he was being struck by the lightning of divine revelation.

The tired old visionary who sprawled exhausted on the rough-hewn table in his cell once stared at a wooden cross upon which the corpse of his Master hung helplessly and alone. Numb with sorrow and inner despair, John saw his dreams die that day. His aching body, roused now by surly guards to begin another day in the quarries, once stood in the empty tomb of Jesus and experienced hope born in him again!

Now John is roughly herded from the prison cave. After breakfasting on a bowl of gruel, he is chained with his fellow exiles and marched by Roman guards up the steep, winding trail to the quarries. Now the cave is empty, but his pile of parchment pages is stacked neatly in a secret hollow beneath his straw sleeping mat. One day those pages will be smuggled off the island. One day Christian volunteers will copy faithfully what John wrote and deliver the Revelation of Jesus Christ to the churches of Asia. And from those churches the Apocalypse of John will spread round the world to you and to me.

Controversy will grow! Great church gatherings will be held to test Revelation's place in the growing body of sacred Christian writings. Is this vision inspired? Is it authoritative? Is it trustworthy? How is it to be interpreted? Some will rise to condemn John's vision to the fire. Others will rise to speak on its behalf. But when the dust settles, the words written by John in his damp island home of Patmos will be given an esteemed place in the canon or approved works of Scripture. In that act, they will be recognized forever as a word not limited in time and space, not limited by language or culture, but a word "God-breathed . . . useful for teaching, rebuking, correcting and training in righteousness, so that the man [and woman] of God may be thoroughly equipped for every good work" (2 Timothy 3:16-17).

It is ironic how the debate has raged. It is even more ironic how the angelic voices anticipated the controversy when speaking to John on Patmos. Twice at the end of Revelation John records the voice as saying, "Write this down, for these words are trustworthy and true" (Revelation 21:5), and again, "The angel said to me, 'These words are trustworthy and true. The Lord, the God of the spirits of the prophets, sent his angel to show his servants the things that must soon take place'" (Revelation 22:6).

Understanding John's Vision

It is one thing to believe that John's words are "trustworthy and true," but it is another thing to understand their full meaning. There are word pictures in Revelation that leave me breathless with their beauty and totally confused as to their exact meaning! I have heard at least a hundred different explanations for one particularly difficult symbol in John's language—none of which seemed adequate, I might add. But that should not permit us to neglect the Book of Revelation or give up trying to understand it. We may not understand *everything*—but that does not mean we can't understand something.

To understand John and the Book of Revelation we need to remember several important things about this remarkable man. First, John was an apocalyptist. That is, he wrote Revelation in a certain type of poetic language known as apocalyptic language. An apocalyptic writer—such as John—was one who used vivid imagery and symbolism to speak about God's judgment and the end of the world. Among the Jewish people in biblical times writers often used an apocalyptic style. Some parts of the Old Testament (such as portions of Daniel and Ezekiel) make use of apocalyptic language.

The difficulty, of course, is that this style of writing, using vivid word pictures and symbols, is quite foreign to us today. Undoubtedly most of John's first readers had little difficulty understanding what his symbols stood for and which of them were symbols and which were not. It takes careful study for us today to understand some of the more obscure parts of his message (much of it quoted from the Old Testament), and some of them we may never understand fully.

Again, this does not mean John's message is lost to us today. The opposite is true. We will be richly rewarded when we take the trouble to dig into the treasures of Revelation. Don't think of John's vivid language as a barrier to understanding; see it instead as the way he painted the picture of God's plan for the future in incredibly vivid colors.

As an apocalyptist John concentrated on one overpowering theme: the end of human history as we know it and the dawn of the glorious messianic age. As such, his message is always one of both warning and hope—warning of the coming judgment and hope of Christ's inevitable triumph over evil and the establishment of His eternal kingdom.

We need that message today—that sin does not go unpunished, that God will judge. We need to know there is hope for the future when we are in Christ. In a battle scene in Francis Ford Coppola's *Apocalypse Now*, a messenger wanders into the front lines, looks at the chaos, and asks, "Who's in charge here?" No one answers his question. Many people today, looking at the chaos and evil of our world, wonder vaguely if anyone is in charge of this universe. John's message in Revelation answers clearly, yes—God is! There is no reason to despair because God is faithful to His promises of salvation and new life through Christ. My prayer as we look at God's message is that God will convict men and women of the reality of His judgment to come and will give them a new hope through the love of Jesus Christ.

The Call to Repentance

Second, John was also a prophet. The apocalyptists despaired of the present and looked to the future expectantly.

The prophets, on the other hand, often held out hope for the present—hope that God's judgment could be delayed if people would repent and turn to God in faith and obedience. That does not mean that the prophets offered an easy way out of all difficulties, as if somehow all problems would vanish if people would just profess their faith in God. Instead, like Winston Churchill standing amidst the bombed ruins of London, the prophets offered "blood, sweat, and tears" for those who would follow God. It would not be easy to serve God and fight against the evil of this present dark and sinful world, and yet the prophets knew that God would be victorious in the end and His people would share in that victory.

So John was a prophet, calling his generation—and ours—to repentance and faith and action. He knew that we could never build the kingdom of God on earth, no matter how hard we might try. Only God can do that—and someday He will, when Christ comes again. But John also knew that God's judgment on this world could be delayed if we would repent and turn to Christ.

That sinewy old man on Patmos, chosen by God to receive and declare His special message, was therefore both apocalyptist and prophet. Why shouldn't he be both? After all, as a young Jew he had heard from the Old Testament of God's eventual judgment on the earth and the coming reign of the Messiah. He also had listened to the call of the prophets—Amos, Isaiah, Jeremiah, and the others—who urged men and women with all their strength to turn back to God. Then one fateful day John had heard the call of Jesus Christ and responded by following Him. In Jesus, he discovered that the message of the apocalyptist and the prophet were united. In Him the apocalyptist's declaration of coming judgment and ultimate victory joined with the prophet's message of repentance and obedience to God in the face of present evil. "In this world you will have trouble," Jesus told His disciples. "But take heart! I have overcome the world" (John 16:33).

Again, we need to hear John's message as that of a prophet, declaring a message not only of the future but of the present. We need to hear his call to repentance and his challenge to live for God, taking our stand for purity and justice and righteousness no matter what others may do.

Third, John was also an evangelist. John's concern was not with a sterile message having no power to influence lives. John was concerned about people. He was concerned with the daily problems they faced as they sought to be faithful to God. He was concerned with the pressures and persecutions many of them encountered as Christians. He was concerned about people because he knew God loved them and had sent His Son to die for them.

The word *evangelist* comes from a Greek word meaning "one who announces good news"—in this case, the good news of the gospel. To some, John's message of the future may have sounded gloomy and depressing. John knew, however, that the worst thing he could do would be to assure people that everything was all right and that there was no need to be concerned about the evil in the world or God's judgment. But John's message is ultimately a message of the good news of salvation in Jesus Christ.

The Gift of Life

Our chaotic, confused world has no greater need than to hear the gospel of Jesus. John's message in Revelation focuses not just on events that will happen in the future, but on what can happen now when Jesus Christ becomes Lord and Savior of our individual lives. John's message focuses supremely on Jesus, the Son of God, who died for our sins and rose again from the dead to give us eternal life. What John declared at the end of his Gospel could also have been applied with equal force to his words in Revelation: "But these are written that you may believe that Jesus is the Christ, the Son of God, and that by believing you may have life in his name" (John 20:31).

John was also a pastor. Revelation was the apostle's last letter to the people he knew and loved best. He began the letter with seven personal notes, one to each of the seven groups of Christians scattered across Asia Minor. As you read through the personal notes, see how well John knew his people and how deeply he loved them. Try to feel his fear for them and for us as well.

It is easy to picture how those first-century Christians began their life in Christ. I have preached in more than eighty nations of the world. I have seen thousands of people listening to the good news of Jesus' life, death, and resurrection. I have watched many literally run to accept Christ as Savior and Lord of their lives. I have witnessed their enthusiasm and been thrilled by their early and rapid growth. Then, just as John did, I have watched first love die. I have seen men and women eagerly embrace the faith, then slowly abandon it, giving in again to immorality, idolatry, and self-destruction. I have witnessed others who accepted Christ and remained faithful to the end but found terrible suffering and sacrifice along the way.

I look back on my many years as an evangelist, and I wonder, Have I made the Christian faith look too easy? Even before I heard the expression, I have constantly borne in mind what Dietrich Bonhoeffer called "cheap grace." Of course it is "by grace you have been saved, through faith . . . not by works, so that no one can boast" (Ephesians 2:8-9). Of course our salvation was a result of what Christ has done for us in His life, death, and resurrection, not what we must do for ourselves. Of course we can trust Him to complete in us what He has begun. But in my eagerness to give away God's great gift, have I been honest about the price He paid in His war with evil? Have I adequately explained the price we must pay in our own war against the evil at work in and around our lives?

A Message of Hope

John worried about his flock as he wrote out his vision of this world (where evil reigns) and of the world to come (where God will restore righteousness and peace again). He wrote of the war between the worlds and of the men and women who fight and die on the battlefield in that war. At the center of his vision, he wrote of Jesus, the Lord of the world to come, who has entered this world to rescue humankind (wherever they find themselves on the battlefield), to guide them through enemy lines, and to deliver them safely home again.

Revelation is not an academic paper produced for some scholarly professional meeting. It is not a poem created by a gifted genius to entertain and divert. It is not the diary of a senile old man driven to wild hallucinations by his isolation and loneliness. Revelation is a pastor's letter to his floundering flock, an urgent telegram bearing a brilliant battle plan for a people at war. It reflects all the realistic horror and heartbreak of a battlefield strewn with the dead. It is frank and it is frightening, but it is a plan for victory—if not for every battle, certainly for the war.

Like John, I have heard that distant thunder. I have seen lightning striking in many places of our world; thus, I know that the coming storm could engulf the whole world. I have seen the storm clouds mounting in the lowering sky. I am still an evangelist whose one goal is to proclaim new life in Christ, but there is serious trouble ahead for our world and for all of us who live in it. In the images of the Apocalypse there is both a storm warning and message of hope for the troubled times yet to come. That is the subject I want to examine next.

5

The One Bright Hope

With so much chaos all about us, there is a crying need for hope in this world. Wherever I look I see strife and conflict—not only on the battlefields of the world but in our neighborhoods and our homes. The traditional safety of the home no longer exists as it did just a few years ago. Too often precious children are violated and abused by their own parents; others are deserted, left home alone, or ignored so that they grow up bitter, angry, and emotionally disturbed. Far too many young men and women coming of age today have no spiritual or emotional roots. They have been deprived of values by an agnostic secular culture. Some are hardly better off than animals.

The actions of some government leaders, public officials, and educators are often outrageous and offensive. The common morality of some people on the street today has fallen to the lowest level in the history of this nation. Many times our society makes heroes and idols of our more publicized moral degenerates. Where is the vision of hope that once sustained us? Where is the faith that gave life meaning?

In my book *Hope for the Troubled Heart*, I dealt with many such issues and offered a practical plan for restoring hope. It is a plan I have used in my own life, and I know it works. But the crisis of faith and hope continues to accelerate with each passing day. In addition to our personal worries, national and global storms threaten to engulf our individual lives, and the dimensions of daily living have grown larger than most of us are able to manage.

In his studies of prophecy, Dr. John Walvoord, who has written many widely read books on various prophetic passages in the Bible, writes that he believes that the world has entered a time of dramatic and ominous change. He says:

> The present world crisis is not a result of any one factor, but a concurrence of causes and effects which combine to set the world stage for a conflict which may quickly bring an end to hundreds of years of progress in western civilization and establish new centers of international power. Whatever the future holds, it is going to be dramatically different than the past. In this dark picture only the Scriptures chart a sure course and give us an intelligent explanation of world-wide confusion as it exists today. (Walvoord, *Nations*, 13.)

Most of the time we are perplexed by the apparent confusion and ignorance we see in the world around us. But according to Dr. Walvoord, conflict and confusion are evidence of the sin and error of the last days. In the light of Scripture, even the most disturbing and mindless acts can be understood. A part of the confusion in the world, however, is in the church itself. Whereas once the church offered a unified standard of values and beliefs to pull the world back from the precipice of self-destruction, too often that standard has been compromised by convenient social theories in place of the Bible's truth and discredited by the moral failures of its leaders.

Apostasy and Disbelief

In numerous churches the Bible is treated as a collection of fairy tales and fables written by half-educated men of an ancient time. While it offers challenging spiritual myths and wholesome encouragement, some "modern" churches seem to feel that no one should go to the Bible expecting to find absolute truth.

Such teaching is an abomination before God. Nothing could be more destructive to true faith and peace on earth. In the face of such a growing storm, the world desperately needs moorings, and God has given us that anchor in His Word, the Bible.

Dr. Walvoord goes on to say:

> The significance of the present world crisis is that it contains practically all the elements which are a natural preparation for the end of the age. . . . The present generation may witness the dramatic close of the "time of the Gentiles" and the establishment of the kingdom of heaven upon the earth, thus bringing to fulfillment one of the great themes of prophecy—the divine program for the nations of the world. (Walvoord, *Nations*, 15.)

A Forbidding Vision

When Ruth and I were in Europe recently, we followed the news in the British, French, and American newspapers. Within a two-week period we clipped a score of articles that used the words *apocalypse* or *armageddon*. Reporters, commentators, editors—the men and women working in all the various modern media—seem hypnotized by the notion of the end of the world as we know it.

I recall an article in the *London Times* a few years ago entitled "The Shadow of Armageddon." The story raised the grim specter of a future race war in Britain. Other columns, editorials, news stories, and letters to the editors were permeated by the common fears of nuclear war, economic chaos, the misuse and the overuse of the earth's nonrenewable resources, runaway crime, violence in the streets, mysterious new killer viruses, terrorism, radically changing weather patterns, earthquakes, floods, famines, destruction, and death. Everywhere I went I found people, both leaders and ordinary individuals, asking one basic question: "Is there any hope?" The answer comes roaring back from the world's press: "There is no hope for planet Earth!"

One morning in the woods near our home I walked with the morning paper in one hand and the Book of Revelation in the other. The lonely exile on Patmos was writing for just such a time as this. His visions ring with hope. Although his letter was addressed to the seven churches in the Roman province of Asia, more accurately to the handful of Christian believers who made up the churches in each town, his letter is written to us as well.

Though his news to them and to us for the long haul of history was hope and good news, his vision for the immediate future was not. He wrote honestly to his Christian friends of the disaster ahead and how they were to face it. We need to take his words to heart. For any way we look at it, the news is both good and bad.

I have spent my lifetime proclaiming one central truth: there is good news for the people of the world. At the heart of that good news is Jesus Christ. He is God in human flesh, and the story of His life, death, and resurrection is the only good news there is to proclaim these days. I have spent fifty years on street corners and in packed coliseums around the world telling people the good news that they can be forgiven. You, too, can be at one with your Creator again. Regardless of your past, you can be guaranteed a future through faith in Jesus as Lord and Savior of your life. I like announcing that good news, but if I am to take John's revelations seriously, I cannot speak only of the good news; for there is bad news as well.

John's Involuntary Vocation

As I indicated earlier, John was many things, but he was an evangelist even as I am. I am sure he would have been content to finish out his last days writing about the past. Imagine the untold stories of Jesus that he might have shared with the people of his day—and ours. After all, John was an old man. The old are supposed to reminisce on the past. He could have added to the books he had already written, including the Gospel of John and the three letters he had sent to some first-century Christians. He might have filled his parchment with memories of those wonderful days with the Master beside the Sea of Galilee and in the hills of Judea.

John was an eyewitness when God walked upon the Earth in human flesh, healing the sick, casting out evil spirits, and raising the dead. What a wonderful, hope-filled book he could have written. But it was not to be. As John lay in his chains there on the isle of Patmos, wondering and struggling under the weight of his too, too human flesh, Jesus Christ came to him through the Spirit of God to share the bad news along with the good, the storm warning along with the calm.

To understand the visions of John, to get hold of both the good news and the bad news at their core, to understand the warning, the hope, and the direction in those visions, we must return to Patmos on a personal pilgrimage. We must walk the beaches with the old man and see his visions again, close up and in living color. We must ask what they meant to John and to that handful of Christian believers scattered across the empire. Then we must ask what John's visions mean to us.

Imagine it. "On the Lord's Day," he wrote to that handful of believers, "I heard behind me a loud voice like a trumpet" (Revelation 1:10). From the text we learn that this revelation by Jesus to John began on "the Lord's Day." Perhaps, in their "benevolence," John's Roman captors allowed this Jewish seer his ancient Old Testament practice of keeping one day out of seven holy. Perhaps that day they had already herded the other grumbling non-Jewish prisoners to their hot quarry labors and left the old man to walk alone along the Aegean Sea. I can imagine him there, praying the ancient prayers, singing the ancient psalms, quoting from memory great portions of the ancient words of wisdom, and remembering the new life and meaning Jesus had given these ancient practices.

A Pastor's Heart

Suddenly, John stands and walks nervously down the beach. He is worried about the Christians on the mainland only miles away. How he longs for this separation from them to end. After all, he had the heart of a pastor. How many men and women, boys and girls sitting in those seven places of worship had probably been led to faith in Christ through John's own preaching? He felt responsible for them and for their spiritual growth. Others, directly and indirectly, had helped raise up those churches, but others (according to early tradition) were dead: Paul, beheaded with a Roman sword; Peter, crucified upside down on a rough wooden cross; John's own brother, James, beheaded by Herod Agrippa; and young Mark, dragged through the streets of Alexandria and burned, his body bruised and still bleeding. Unconfirmed news of the deaths or disappearances of John's close friends and co-workers must have left him lonely and even more fearful for the future of the churches they had planted together.

At first it had seemed safe and rather simple to be a Christian in a world dominated by the Roman Empire. The Caesars had granted special privileges to the Jews, and most of the earliest Christian believers were Jews who shared in those privileges. Under the Pax Romana (the peace Rome built across the world with Roman might and Roman law) the church had spread. Roman authorities had even saved Paul's life in Jerusalem when Caesar's soldiers rescued him from a mob infuriated by his preaching (Acts 21:31-32). Peter had written to the earliest Christians that they were to fear God and "honor the emperor" (1 Peter 2:12-17 RSV)—although the emperor was often evil and persecution was beginning.

Toward the end of the first century all benevolence had ceased. Rome was losing her grip on the world. The emperors and their courts had grown more and more extravagant. The royal treasuries had been drained. New taxes were levied by the Roman senate to help offset their balance-of-trade deficit. When protest and rebellion followed, Rome answered with the sword.

It was no simple task for Rome to maintain an empire made up of so many different races, religions, and cultures. Nationalist movements, political conspiracies, terrorism, and open rebellion grew until the empire was threatened from within and from without. Out of the emperor's growing paranoia to maintain Rome's power and keep her subjects in check, one simple test of loyalty evolved. On certain feasts and holidays, row upon row of subjects lined up to walk past the area's Roman magistrate, toss a pinch of incense into a fire in the golden bowl at his feet, and mutter, "Caesar is Lord."

Jesus or Caesar?

Most citizens of the empire were glad to pay tribute to the emperor and to the empire that had brought them this period of peace. But for Christians, another loyalty oath was at the center of their faith: "Jesus is Lord," not Caesar.

In spite of their gratitude to the empire and to the emperor, in spite of the admonitions of Paul and Peter to worship God and honor the emperor, this act of Caesar worship was impossible. Because of their refusal to put Caesar before Christ, Christians began to be persecuted.

William Barclay writes, "This worship [of Caesar] was never intended to . . . wipe out other religions. Rome was essentially tolerant. A man might worship Caesar *and* his own god. But more and more Caesar worship became a test of political loyalty; it became . . . the recognition of the dominion of Caesar over a man's life, and . . . soul" (*The Revelation of John*, 1:21-22).

Imagine a village in the suburbs of Ephesus or Laodicea. Christian believers are at work tanning leather, dyeing cloth, harvesting crops, raising families, studying math and history—at worship, at work, or at play. Then, suddenly, hoofbeats are heard clattering up the nearby cobbled streets. The horses are reined in by a Roman centurion and his honor guard. A leather camp table is unfolded. An incense burner is placed upon the table. A flame is lit. Heralds sound the trumpets. There is no place to hide, no time to decide.

Believers must join their neighbors in that line. Just ahead the village mayor tosses his incense into the flames and exclaims proudly, "Caesar is Lord." Others follow. The line ahead grows shorter. The moment of decision draws near. Will the Christians avoid the conflict and protect their lives and security with the simple act of obedience? Will they mutter "Caesar is Lord" and sneak back home to safety? Or will they recognize that act as a symbol of a wider disobedience, refuse the incense, proclaim "Jesus is Lord" and pay the price for their disloyalty to the state?

Did John wander up and down the beach at Patmos that Sabbath remembering the centurion, the incense, and the terrible decision of ultimate loyalty each believer had to make? Who knows? Perhaps it was in just such a line, surrounded by his neighbors and friends, that John himself failed the emperor's test and, as punishment, was exiled to the island prison. We don't know the charges leveled against the apostle that led to his exile, but we do know why John said he was there: "I, John, your brother and companion in the suffering and kingdom and patient endurance that are ours in Jesus, was on the island of Patmos because of the word of God and the testimony of Jesus" (Revelation 1:9).

It was not easy to be a Christian then. It is not easy now. Late in the first century, during the time of John's exile, the persecutions of the Christian church by the Roman Empire had begun in earnest. It was difficult to keep the faith then. It is now. There are grand and awful moments before a centurion's blazing fire. There are little, awful moments almost daily when one longs to give in to the values of this world, to give up the high standards of our Lord, to give way to the various temptations that pressure every man, woman, or young person who believes. Even Christians are tempted to surrender to the passions or the pleasures that pursue us all.

A Daily Decision

We think of modern Christians living under atheistic or totalitarian regimes as being the only ones who must daily decide their ultimate loyalties. It is not true. Every Christian in every nation—totalitarian, democratic, or somewhere in between—decides daily to be loyal to Christ and the kingdom He is building or to give in to this age and its values. In the United States we can see the clear evidence of a growing intolerance toward Christians and Christian values. It is no longer as easy to profess Christ as it once was in this nation. We must each take up our cross daily or, in fear, compromise to the world's standard.

No wonder John was anxious. The believers then had (and now have) a constant and confounding choice. Those infant Christians in the churches of Asia lived in a world (not unlike our own) where their belief in Christ often left them at odds with the political powers, the economic realities, and the social norms. The day-by-day choices were difficult and demanding. Great suffering lay ahead. Would they keep the faith? Would they stand firm, or would they give up under the pressure and the pain of following Jesus? Every day today—as then—Christians will face many decisions. Will they give in to the materialism, the selfish pleasures, the dishonest practices of this present age? What do you do when you face these decisions? Is your steadfast desire to do God's will, or do you give in to the steady pressures of those around you? The Bible says, "Don't let the world around you squeeze you into its own mold, but let God remold your minds from within, so that you may prove in practice that the plan of God for you is good, meets all his demands and moves toward the goal of true maturity" (Romans 12:2 PHILLIPS).

Suddenly, John heard the voice "like a trumpet." We are dealing with mystery here. I can't tell you how the visions came or in what real or symbolic form they appeared to the seer. When I read the beginning of John's revelation on Patmos (Revelation 1:12-20), I try to picture it in my mind. We don't know if John, "in the Spirit," simply sat quietly on the Patmos beach and saw the visions in his mind's eye. There is a tradition that the Spirit of God came to John in a dark cave and lifted him up from that cave to four different locations just as Jesus was led by Satan to the mountaintop in His desert temptations. It is even possible that the visions all took real form and substance to John—more real than the holograms in Disneyland's Haunted House where specters dance through walls and young and old watch open-mouthed at the lifelike apparitions before them.

A Picture of Patmos

I do believe, however, that John saw vividly what he describes, that everything he saw was from God, and that each vision is as important and as full of meaning and application today to you and to me, as it was to those seven churches in Asia. Come with me to Patmos. Picture John praying desperately for the churches in his care. Suddenly he hears a voice, trumpet clear, speaking to him.

The biblical account ignores the first words of the speaker. Perhaps it was a simple greeting, not unlike the angel greeting Mary before giving her the good news of Jesus' birth. Perhaps it was the glory of the Lord shining round about or a host of angels from heaven, not unlike those that caused the shepherds to shake with fear before hearing their good news. We don't know what the figure said, but we do know the first response of John to his "good news." He was terrified.

As he whirled to "see the voice," his eyes were blinded by the light from seven great lamps. Standing in the light was a man, his eyes blazing, his head and hair "white like wool." The figure's feet were "like bronze glowing in a furnace, and his voice was like the sound of rushing waters." The figure held seven stars in his right hand. Out of his mouth came a sharp double-edged sword and his face was "like the sun shining in all its brilliance" (Revelation 1:12-16).

John fell before the figure "as though dead," stunned and awed by what he saw. That man (standing in the light with a robe "reaching down to his feet" and "with a golden sash around his chest") was Jesus. Yet John did not recognize his Master. It was the very same Jesus who had first appeared to John by the Sea of Galilee. Three years they had been together; still John did not recognize the Savior. This was the very same Jesus who had appeared to John and the others in a locked upper room, His resurrected body changed yet still bearing open wounds on hands, feet, and side from the nails of the cross and a cruelly thrust Roman spear. This was the very same Jesus who had taken on the powerlessness of a human being to share humanity's suffering, to feel humanity's weaknesses and temptation, and to deliver mankind from evil. Yet John, longtime disciple, close personal friend, and intimate associate, had no idea that this giant, glowing figure was his risen Lord.

Then, gently, as a mother wakens a child from night terrors, the figure leaned over the panic-stricken John, touched his shoulder, and said, "Do not be afraid. I am the First and the Last. I am the Living One; I was dead, and behold I am alive for ever and ever! And I hold the keys of death and Hades" (Revelation 1:17-18).

Spectral Imagery

What is going on here? Well, imagine what was going on in John's mind. Had he, only moments before this mysterious encounter, been fearing for the future of the church? Then suddenly the risen Christ Himself appears to deliver the word that is needed as desperately now as it was almost twenty centuries past. Had the seer been wondering if in fact there was sufficient power available to him and to his flock to withstand the dangers of that evil day, when suddenly the Creator and Sustainer of the universe reveals Himself as the One who holds the key, the One who holds the power over the very worst fears that plague humankind—death and eternal lostness?

"Write, John!" commanded the Lord of power. Then He clearly specified to whom the letter should be sent: to the leaders of the churches ("the angels of the seven churches," which literally means "pastors") and to the members of the churches from which this light would shine to brighten the entire world ("the seven lampstands"). "Write . . . what you have seen," commanded the figure bright as the sun. "Write . . . what is now and what will take place later" (Revelation 1:19).

This is the good news. Imagine how you would feel if you were John. At one moment, John was worrying about his Christian friends struggling to survive in those awful times of hard choices and bloody persecutions. The very next moment, he was standing before the Lord of history who assures him by His very presence that He is still in control of this world. He still has plans for His people, and He is about to tell us what we can do to participate in His plan for the redemption and the renewal of planet Earth. Perhaps right now you are facing some particular problem, and you even are at the point of despair. But Christ comes to you and says, "I am Lord! There is no circumstance beyond My power, and you can trust Me."

Then, almost immediately, there is bad news with the good. The irony of what follows, the words John was instructed to write, reminds me of a disaster that hit the state of California a few years ago. In the past three years, the West Coast has been through a long and desperate period of drought, punctuated by torrential rains and sudden flooding. Just a few years earlier the state suffered through the worst winter in memory. Winds had howled, felling power lines and plunging cities into darkness. Seas had bashed and buffeted beachside communities, swallowing houses, piers, parks, and highways in a powerful, murky tide. So much rain had fallen, the rivers came up and drowned people and animals, swamping whole towns and croplands. It was a terrible time and the media were filled with stories on how to cope with the present storm.

The front-page news in the *Los Angeles Times* warned that worse times were coming. Scientists at the California Institute of Technology told people across the entire state to prepare for an earthquake of major proportions. The instructions were clear. Lists of emergency supplies were recommended.

How they should react was described in detail. Get away from buildings with glass windows. Stand in a strong archway or rush into an open space. Don't exit your houses without guarding against heavy tiles and pieces of plaster falling from above. Turn to the emergency radio station. Gather your medical supplies and help your neighbor—for the roads will be closed and emergency vehicles will be stranded. You may have to wait for help for several days.

Picture the poor Californian, wading through the flooded ruins of his beachfront home, being warned that soon an earthquake will tumble what remains into the sea. That is the double-edged predicament that faced the Christian believers in the seven churches of Asia. This is the bad news with the good. They are already facing terrible trouble. That reality is acknowledged and warning given in the seven individual letters to the churches (Revelation 2-3). But worse trouble is coming. That second warning echoes in the calm before the storm even as the seals are opened and the future revealed.

It is good news to know that God has a plan for the redemption of the world. But first, the prophet warns his people to set their lives in order. That's his immediate, short-term advice, complete with specific directions as to how it might be accomplished. John catalogs their sins and warns them of the consequences. He exhorts them to overcome. (In the next chapter we will look at these seven letters of advice to the first-century Christians and see how relevant they are to you and me.)

Signposts of Hope

But the prophet also warns that there are even worse storms ahead. We are to prepare to meet them. That's the long-range warning of the four horsemen of death and destruction already riding in their direction and in ours. There's good news in knowing that we can overcome the present sin, weakness, and suffering in our lives and in so doing grow tough enough to overcome the sin, weakness, and suffering that lies ahead. The most important signpost of hope is God's Word, which warns of imminent disaster and clearly marks the detour route to safety.

My wife, Ruth, and I know that God can prepare a plan to rescue His people. We have seen Him do it time and time again. Ruth was born and raised as the daughter of missionary parents in China. She witnessed firsthand how God prepared His church there during times of trouble to withstand the even greater troubled times ahead. The Christians in China not only survived the years of crises and conflict, but today they are growing and multiplying and becoming stronger under difficult times. So, in the midst of the storm, there is one bright hope for the future. God has a plan for His people, and He gladly shares it with all who will believe. Through John's visions on the island of Patmos we are given clear and prominent signposts that will lead us all along the way.

6

He Who Overcomes

Revelation 2-3

T he Book of Revelation has long been described as a book of mysteries. Its arcane and provocative language, like ancient hieroglyphs, challenges the imagination. Many times John's narrative elicits more questions than answers. One reason is because John gives us a glimpse of the unseen—but real—world of spiritual reality.

Among the various mysteries discussed by the apostle Paul in his letters to the church was the idea that our world, the world of the visible, is an unreal and impermanent place. The real world, he said, is the unseen world. "We do not look at the things which are seen, but at the things which are not seen. For the things which are seen are temporary, but the things which are not seen are eternal" (2 Corinthians 4:18 NKJV). By this, Paul meant that the spiritual world exists in our very midst, around us and unseen, but he also meant that the consequences of our daily lives and decisions in this physical world have eternal consequences in the life to come. The reality of this understanding of our world has taken on new meaning and urgency in this storm-tossed age. But John must have been overwhelmed by the blazing reality of the unseen world that appeared before him on Patmos.

When the Spirit of the risen Christ came to John in his barren cell, the aging apostle must have been in awe, for the unseen world burst upon him with fearsome reality. As a Roman prisoner, half-starved, sometimes beaten, constantly harassed and abused, his life on that barren, rock-strewn island in the Aegean Sea was as real and unmysterious as the cold ground upon which he slept, as real as bread and water. The life he lived was as physical and tangible as the pain in his aching joints and the burns and blisters on his hands and feet.

Tradition tells us that John's face was wrinkled and blackened by the sun. His arms were lean and muscular, and his hands were rough with calluses. As a political prisoner, exiled to a rock off the coast of what is now modern Turkey, John was forced to carry stones chipped from granite cliffs above the sea to a cargo dock below the Roman citadel. The fortress guarded the narrow isthmus between the Bay of Scala and the Bay of Merika. The gravel John carried on his back was used to build the foundations for the temples and palaces of the Emperor Domitian and to pave Roman roads, which always led to Rome.

We can imagine that John, stumbling under the loaded straw basket strapped to his forehead, used both hands to grasp his staff and pick his way painfully down the treacherous path. Even the Roman guards must have wondered at the determination of this gray-bearded Christian Jew who worked alongside the other prisoners by day and then spent his evenings writing stories no one could understand.

But John was not doing what he wanted to do; he was under the compulsion of a mystery. He was writing at the direction of the Holy Spirit of God, Who came to him in waking dreams and vision. At the beginning of his book, John wrote, "On the Lord's Day I was in the Spirit, and I heard behind me a loud voice like a trumpet, which said: 'Write on a scroll what you see and send it to the seven churches: to Ephesus, Smyrna, Pergamum, Thyatira, Sardis, Philadelphia and Laodicea'" (Revelation 1:10-11).

So, in his cavelike prison cell, John, the seer of the unseen world, spent every free moment recording the seismographic warnings of a world bulging and buckling just beneath the surface. I often have the feeling that in many ways John's ancient world was much like our own.

The Vision of John

These stories of urgency and warning, probably written over several harrowing months, were copied and sent as instructed to the seven churches in Asia. Eventually, the Apocalypse of John was titled by its opening line, "The Revelation of Jesus Christ," or simply "Revelation" and became the last and perhaps most controversial book in the New Testament.

We don't know the details of what happened when the Spirit appeared to John. In other places, the Bible describes the way God appeared to Moses, Abraham, Jacob, and Paul. The accounts in the first three books of the New Testament of the appearance of Moses and Elijah to Jesus and His transfiguration in a brilliant cloud of light gives us a vivid image of how God's presence was experienced. But these reports also tell us how mortals responded: They fell on their faces in terror before a Holy God.

The apostle John was affected in much the same way. He fell prostrate before the mighty presence of the risen Lord. Perhaps he shielded his eyes against the blinding light. The great figure whose own eyes shone like fire, the seven lamps blazing around Him, and the sun reflecting off the surf smashed together in a stunning spectacle of light. John must have rubbed his eyes in wonder as he tried to focus on the scene and grasp its meaning.

Perhaps Jesus moved out of the light, reached down for John's gnarled hand and gently lifted the old man to his feet. Maybe their eyes met for a moment as they had met a half-century earlier. In that flash of recognition, John must have seen past the blinding splendor and recognized the risen Lord—the same Jesus who had walked beside him on a Galilean beach and in the streets of Jerusalem. Possibly John felt the same compelling love of Jesus he had known as they walked the trails and hillsides of Judea. Perhaps he felt Jesus' arm on his shoulder as the Lord led him up the shoreline and past the grove of palm trees to his prison cave. Maybe John stumbled in the darkness of his cell searching for the oil lamp and lighting it, flattening out a new piece of parchment and inking the end of a freshly shaved quill. He sat for a moment before the driftwood slab that served as his desk and altar, waiting for the Lord to speak the Revelation.

Reality and Beyond

You may imagine the details of John's dream in another way. The details aren't important. But it helps me to see John there with the risen Lord. For whatever form the vision took—whether it was a very private, personal revelation by our Lord in John's mind's eye, or a very literal experience on a Patmos beach—to get a feeling for this moment, to see what actually happened on that island that day, is to realize the wonder and hope of Christ's revelation, both the good news and the bad.

We have been talking about John's vision of Jesus. But are we necessarily to expect God to give us a vision like that? No. God has given us His Word, the Bible, and that is all we need. Do you want to know God more deeply, more intimately? Do you want to discover His will for your life? Then read and study the Scriptures daily. They are a personal and compelling revelation for all time—whatever storms may come.

We don't know the details, but this one thing we know. The risen Lord spoke to John and told him to write. "Write," He said. "Write. . . . the mystery of the seven stars that you saw in my right hand and of the seven golden lampstands. . . . The seven stars are the angels [leaders or pastors] of the seven churches, and the seven lampstands are the seven churches" (Revelation 1:19-20). Then He began the series of short letters to the seven churches in the Roman province of Asia. "To the angel of the church in Ephesus," commands the risen Lord, "write!" (Revelation 2:1).

The events of that day elevate the words of those seven short letters into God's eternal Word, as trustworthy and authoritative for our times as they were in John's. What we learn from these words grows beyond the words themselves into profound lessons about God.

First, we see that God cares about each of us as individuals. He knows us by name. Our risen Lord cares about each of us personally. I invite you to look at the details in these letters. God named names. He described events. He commended the churches for their successes. He scolded them for their failures. He gave them warm, loving, confronting counsel. That alone gives me a tremendous sense of hope. He knows us as a mother knows her child. The risen Lord did not withdraw to some distant corner of the universe; He is present in the spirit of every believer. When we search His Word, when we stop to hear His voice, He will be as specific now as He was then.

Second, He sees us as sharing our lives with other believers in the church. He was concerned about each of those individual churches in the cities and towns of Asia. He didn't dictate those letters to key leaders across the world or to official gatherings of bishops or clergy. He wrote to individual churches, small clusters of believers, leaders and followers together. At the heart of these letters is God's assumption that we belong together at work and at worship in a local church.

He cared about each of their individual churches then as He cares about each of our individual churches now. He cares deeply about how we relate to Him, to each other, to our communities and to our world. He wants to stand with us through the storms of life. That should give us great hope!

Third, the issues to which the risen Lord spoke then are the very same issues about which He would speak to us now. Our problems are not unique. Our sins, our temptations, our weaknesses, our needs are no different from theirs. That, too, gives me hope; for Jesus anticipated the struggles we would face, and the call He gave them is the call we must hear today.

Fourth, although the form of each letter is practically the same, the content of each is unique. He knew that every church was facing unique struggles, so He addressed each individually. Jesus does not mass-produce advice. We can gain hope from this. His words to them are His words to us, but we too face our own struggles; therefore, as we search these letters, we can be assured of finding exactly the right word at the right time to suit our particular struggles.

The letters to the churches show that Christ knew what the future held. He knew the price they would have to pay for their stand against evil. But He also knew those churches were not yet prepared to pay that price; they were not yet strong enough to face their storms alone. He knew that unless they spent time and energy preparing themselves, they would not survive the winds of destruction. He knew that unless they learned how to overcome, they might themselves be overcome by the on-coming tempest.

There are clues in the letters that we must also follow as we face the hurricane bearing down on us. The letters are His words of power that will help us survive the evil day to come.

Ephesus and Laodicea:
The Call to Holy Passion

Ephesus was a large seaport city on the Aegean Sea. The apostle Paul helped found the church in this great commercial and religious center. At the heart of the city was the temple to Artemis (Diana), one of the seven wonders of the ancient world, a temple four times the size of the Parthenon in Athens. Paul almost lost his life in his courageous stand against the idolatrous worship of Artemis (Acts 19). He invested two years of his life in the people of Ephesus and the growing young church there, and that investment paid rich dividends for the kingdom of God. Ephesus became the center from which the good news of Christ spread throughout Asia.

There is a wonderful moment in the Book of Acts when the elders from the church in Ephesus met Paul in Miletus to say their last good-byes to him. He was on his final journey to Jerusalem. From there he would go on to Rome where he would meet his death. The elders held onto the apostle and wept as he shared his final thoughts with them. At the heart of his advice that last day were these words: "After I leave, savage wolves will come in among you and will not spare the flock. . . . So be on your guard" (Acts 20:29, 31).

Apparently, they had taken Paul's words to heart. More than half a century later, Christ's letter to them in the Revelation indicated that He was pleased that they had "tested those who claim to be apostles but are not, and . . . found them false" (Revelation 2:2). At Miletus Paul had instructed them "to help the weak," and in Revelation Christ commended them for "your deeds, your hard work and your perseverance" (Revelation 2:2). Still, in spite of their obedience and their endurance, something had gone wrong. "You have forsaken your first love," He warned them. "Remember the height from which you have fallen! Repent and do the things you did at first" (Revelation 2:4-5).

Four miles from the Maeander River in Asia Minor, along a major tributary, lies the city of Laodicea. This, too, was a prosperous town in the time of John's exile. On the road between Rome and the southern provinces, Laodicea became a center of banking and exchange. A prestigious medical center known around the world for its healing eye salve was another Laodicean claim to fame. Sheep grazed on the hills around the city, and their pure black wool was renowned. The most expensive, stylish clothing of the empire was made from the rich, black fabrics woven here. How ironic (and how perfect an example of our risen Lord's attention to detail) that He would say to the church in Laodicea, "you are . . . poor, blind and naked" (Revelation 3:17).

We don't know the early history of the young Christian church in Laodicea, but we know how highly Christ must have valued their potential in kingdom building, for this church felt His wrath in the words of John with a white-hot intensity. "You are lukewarm—neither hot nor cold—I am about to spit you out of my mouth," Christ warned them (Revelation 3:16). Then, in an almost immediate counterpoint, Christ continues with one of the best-known and most poignant invitations in biblical literature: "Those whom I love I rebuke and discipline. So be earnest, and repent. Here I am! I stand at the door and knock. If anyone hears my voice and opens the door, I will come in and eat with him, and he with me" (Revelation 3:19-20).

Both the Ephesian and the Laodicean Christians had lost their holy passion. The same thing had happened to Jerusalem in Jeremiah's day when he wrote, "The word of the LORD came to me . . . 'I remember the devotion of your youth, how as a bride you loved me and followed me through the desert, through a land not sown'" (Jeremiah 2:1-2). In other words, the people of that day had also lost their first love, and God had rebuked them.

The "first love" of the Ephesians had settled into a kind of faithfulness to doctrinal purity. They could probably spot a heresy or a heretic a mile upriver. They probably knew the creeds by heart and passed them on faithfully from generation to generation. But Christ's letter says, "Repent!" Repent of the coldness of your hearts and your lack of zeal. Repent of your lovelessness and your lack of concern for others.

Apparently the first passionate prayers of the Laodiceans had settled into comfortable prayers of gratitude. Christ mocked their prayers: "You say, 'I am rich; I have acquired wealth and do not need a thing.' But you do not realize," He warned, "that you are wretched, pitiful, poor, blind and naked" (Revelation 3:17).

One vacation, Ruth and I had been invited to the home of some wealthy socialites. They had gathered together a large group of their neighboring vacationers for a party and asked me if I would say a few words. I explained the gospel simply and briefly, reminding them that pleasure and possessions are not lasting—that only the person who knows Jesus Christ as Savior can know true happiness. As I concluded, an attractive woman known for her casual morals and high lifestyle, young and smartly dressed, laughed gaily. "But, Billy," she protested, "what about those of us who are perfectly happy?"

From God's point of view, that woman was spiritually wretched, pitiful, poor, blind, and naked, as the years ahead were soon to prove. Christ says to people like her, "Repent!"

The Problem of Spiritual Passion

For the churches in Ephesus and Laodicea, the problem was the problem of spiritual passion. "You have forsaken your first love," John wrote the Ephesians. "You are neither cold nor hot," he said to the Laodiceans. What began as a wholehearted commitment to Christ and His work had gradually cooled. We don't have any of the details, only these fragments of history from Revelation, but we can picture it from our own experience.

I remember the first time I saw Ruth. It was love at first sight. I can still remember the excitement I felt. I remember the first time I held her hand. I remember the thrill of our first kiss, our eyes shining with love for each other. I remember my stomach churning, heart pumping, blood boiling during our honeymoon and for years afterward. First love is wonderful. But the first flames of that first physical passion inevitably cool.

We are still very much in love today, but it is not the passion of our youth; today our love centers around sharing and commitment. I think it is interesting that the word *love* is an active, not a passive, verb. Love must have an object. To truly love, we must love someone or something. Love should not be confined to the physical. It comes with a lifetime of commitment. Ruth and I can sit on our front porch on a summer's evening without saying a word, but we are communing with each other and communicating. The passion is even deeper because the relationship and the commitment are deeper. Over the years we have known so many people who did not have that spiritual commitment to each other. In some cases, their love was only physical. The flames of the honeymoon faded, then the day-to-day routine settled in. When the passion of their first love died, the practices associated with it died as well.

If you are a Christian, perhaps you will remember the moment you first heard of Jesus Christ and believed in Him as Savior and Lord of your life. Perhaps you remember kneeling at your parents' bedside, at a church altar, or around the campground at a retreat. Perhaps you came forward in an evangelistic crusade. Do you remember joining the church and feeling the loving arms of other Christians reaching out to you? Can you recall your baptism and the joy you felt in that act of faith?

When I accepted Christ someone handed me a booklet entitled *Biblical Treasures.* It had Scripture memory verses and even hymns. I can remember milking the cows on my father's dairy farm, singing those hymns and memorizing those Scriptures as I worked. Do you remember the time you made your first generous pledge to the church, or joining a small group of brothers and sisters in Christ to sing "Amazing Grace" or to work for the poor and oppressed in your town? Do your remember your "first love" and all those acts of worship, witness, work, or fellowship that flowed spontaneously from the time of your "first love"? That's what John needed to relate.

Christ was calling the Ephesians and the Laodiceans away from respectable, comfortable, passionless, lukewarm religion. He wanted them totally committed to Him, wholeheartedly available. He called them back to the holy passion and the joy of their first love. They had settled instead for mere theological respectability and material comfort. He wanted them alive, depending, risking, passionate again. For it is in that "first love" commitment that they would find the strength to face the storms.

The Act of Acceptance

John was addressing the believers in Ephesus and Laodicea, but his words touch our hearts today. Perhaps you have never known Christ personally as your Savior and Lord, never loved Him that way. Perhaps you have never experienced the wonder of Christ's forgiveness for your sins. Before going any further in reading this book, you can know all of this right now.

You may ask, "What do I have to do?" First: Admit your need. Confess, "I am a sinner." Second: Be willing to turn away from your sins (repent). Third: Believe that Jesus Christ died for you on the cross and rose from the grave. Fourth: Through prayer, invite Jesus Christ to come in and take control of your life. When you receive Him as Savior and Lord in this way, you enter into the promise of His love and the joy of eternal life with Him. It's just that simple! God loves you. Christ died for you. You repent of your sin. You receive forgiveness. And you, too, discover the joy of that "first love."

Recently I met a well-known attorney on an airplane. He was drinking everything the stewardess served to drown his pain. It wasn't working. He told me that he was a church member in good standing, but, he said, "I need to clean up my act. I really would like to serve God." I immediately recognized that he did not even know the Lord. Sitting across the aisle was my associate T. W. Wilson. I was studying and preparing for an important engagement at the end of our flight, so I asked T.W. to share the way of salvation with this man.

Later, I heard that the man went back to his home church and asked if he could say a few words on a Sunday evening. He admitted to the whole church what a hypocrite he had been. Then he looked out over the congregation and said, "A lot of you are the same kind of hypocrite I've been. I've cleaned up my act and made my peace with God." Recently he has been giving his testimony in other churches. Even though he had been a longtime church member, he finally found his "first love."

For those of us for whom that "first love" stage is long past, John has some very specific advice. "Remember therefore from where you have fallen; repent and do the first works, or else I will come to you quickly and remove your lampstand from its place—unless you repent" (Revelation 2:5 NKJV). The Old Testament is full of ardent expressions describing God's relationship with His people as a relationship of love. In New Testament terms, the church is the "bride of Christ." He expects us to be faithful to our vows.

In this modern age, we need to be reminded that love is more than *feeling*. Love is a commitment; it is *doing*. "For God so loved the world he gave," John had written years earlier (John 3:16). "Dear children, let us not love with words or tongue but with actions and in truth" (1 John 3:18). You can do the works of first love again and in the process rekindle the intensity of that love.

The Acts of Love

When we are truly in love, we want above all to be with the ones we love. We enjoy talking with the ones we love, and listening to them. Many times I have gone off to a quiet place just to talk with God alone, to actually walk with Him. Many times before some of our crusades, I have wandered into the woods or the mountains to pray, to talk, and to think with God in private.

I remember that before the London Crusade in 1954 I spent a great deal of time on the front porch of what we at Montreat call the "Chapman Home." It was the old

home of one of the great evangelists of another generation, J. Wilbur Chapman, and the place where the famous
hymn, "Ivory Palaces," was written. I used to sit on that
front porch and pour out my heart to the Lord—and I
would hear Him speak and give me assurance that He was
going to be with us in that crusade. We were still young
and inexperienced in those days, but we were trying to
reach one of the great cities of the world for Christ. The
London Crusade was supposed to be a month-long crusade. We ended up staying three months, and by the end
of it tens of thousands had found Christ. The crusade
made news all over the world and encouraged Christians
everywhere.

I also remember the New York Crusade where we
stayed sixteen weeks at Madison Square Garden. I can't
tell you how many problems we faced! How many crises
came even before the crusade began! How I used to walk
the trails around my home and pour out my heart to the
Lord. In some of the darkest hours, I could feel the touch
of His hand on mine as I reached up through the darkness.

When was the last time you set an afternoon aside simply to be alone with the Lord, to walk and talk with Him
as you might your very best friend? From my earliest days
of faith, I loved to read, study, and memorize the Word. I
was eager to learn what Jesus Christ wanted from me; I was
eager to know His will. When was the last time you turned
off the noises that drown out His still, small voice and
took time to read and memorize those Bible passages that
give life such meaning and hope?

I remember how I loved to be with the members of my
church for worship and fellowship. It's so easy to drop out
of regular worship, to move from your hometown and
your home church and never find a new community of
believers to replace it. How quickly, alone and cut off from

worship, our interest dries up and our "first love" cools. Perhaps you remember the joy of sharing your faith in those early days, or working in the streets to help the poor, or teaching, or giving—how easy it is to stop those works that spring spontaneously out of "first love." How easy it is to let your "first love" die!

"Remember the height from which you have fallen!" John writes in the Spirit. "Repent and do the things you did at first." You may not feel like working at first love. It may seem like drudgery to read and memorize the Word. It may be inconvenient to take time out regularly to be alone and pray. It may feel awkward to find and join a church in your neighborhood. You may resist getting involved again. It's easier to hide out and not be asked to give or teach or work or lead. But beware; you have been warned. Unless you get about the business God called you to, you are in danger of "being removed." This storm warning is for you. Even now the storms are raging around us.

Pergamum, Thyatira, and Sardis: The Call to Righteousness

North of Ephesus, clustered about the Hermus River Valley, lie the three cities in the next group of letters from Revelation. Pergamum, a coastal city, was the capital of the Roman province of Asia. It was a city crowded with heathen temples and the home of the first temple of the imperial cult of Rome, the place where Caesar was worshiped as a god. Thyatira was inland on the Lycus River, a commercial center on an important trade route. Many trade guilds had their headquarters in Thyatira. Membership in the guilds was necessary to work, and the immorality of the guild banquet orgies was widely known and fully accepted. Sardis, a wealthy commercial city, was also known for its loose, luxurious lifestyle. The city had twice been captured by enemies as a result of its slackness in spite of its well-fortified, hilltop citadel built to guard the city from invasion.

While the Christians at Ephesus and Laodicea were orthodox and comfortable, the churches at Pergamum, Thyatira, and Sardis were apparently victims of their runaway physical passions that led to idolatry and immorality.

In each case, the Lord first commended the churches before He chastised them. To those at Thyatira, He said, "These are the words of the Son of God, whose eyes are like blazing fire and whose feet are like burnished bronze. I know your deeds, your love and faith, your service and perseverance, and that you are now doing more than you did at first" (Revelation 2:18-19). To Pergamum, although He had very little good to say, He did promise, "To him who overcomes, I will give some of the hidden manna. I will also give him a white stone with a new name written on it, known only to him who receives it" (Revelation 2:17). In other words, there was a small minority in Pergamum who held on to their first love. He said the same about Sardis: "You have a few people . . . who have not soiled their clothes" (Revelation 3:4).

Christ found something or someone in all three churches to commend. Many people who have studied these passages tend to think of these three churches as being fallen and sinful, unlike our churches in every way. But that wasn't the case. There was much about these churches that was commendable. Still they were in serious trouble—especially in light of what lay ahead—and they didn't even know it. The parallels between the churches of that day and our own may actually be much too close for comfort.

To the Christians in Pergamum, John writes, "I have a few things against you: You have people there who hold to the teaching of Balaam, who taught Balak to entice the

Israelites to sin by eating food sacrificed to idols and by committing sexual immorality. Likewise you also have those who hold to the teaching of the Nicolaitans" (Revelation 2:14-15).

To the people in Thyatira, he writes, "I have this against you: You tolerate that woman Jezebel, who calls herself a prophetess. By her teaching she misleads my servants into sexual immorality and the eating of food sacrificed to idols" (Revelation 2:20).

To those in Sardis, he writes, "You are dead. Wake up! Strengthen what remains . . . for I have not found your deeds complete in the sight of my God" (Revelation 3:1-2).

What is going on here? What is so seriously wrong in Pergamum that the risen Lord Himself threatens that unless they "repent," He will fight against them with the sword in His mouth? What is happening in Thyatira that causes our Lord to warn, "I will strike her children [the followers of the false teacher in that church] dead. Then all the churches will know that I am he who searches hearts and minds, and I will repay each of you according to your deeds" (Revelation 2:23)? Or what's happened in Sardis that He says to them, "If you do not wake up, I will come like a thief, and you will not know at what time I will come to you" (Revelation 3:3)?

There are clues in John's short letters that will solve the mystery of Christ's anger at these three churches. Balaam was an Old Testament prophet who led God's people off their trail to the Promised Land and into the towns and practices of God's enemy, the Moabites (see Numbers 22:21, 24, 31). One commentator describes Balaam as an example of compromise with false religion. The Nicolaitans were first-century followers of a similar false prophet who taught the Christians to give in to the practices of tipping their hats to the false gods of the city (and their immoral sexual practices) so that the gospel might be more acceptable to the people.

Jezebel had been a foreigner (a Phoenician princess) who centuries before had married a king of Israel and insisted on practicing her sacrifices to the idol, Baal, alongside the worship of the God of Israel. She had dared to encourage the people of Israel to worship her false god and practice his immoral ways. Now someone in Thyatira whom John nicknamed "Jezebel" was teaching those first-century Christians to give in to the worship of the gods of the city and to their immoral sexual practices. The people were standing by, allowing, even obeying her.

Imagine the predicament of those first-century believers. They lived in towns where many different gods were worshiped. Their neighbors' homes had shrines to various deities; in little nooks and in grand temples stood statues and symbols of family gods, ancestral gods, ancient mythical gods, and the modern god of Rome—Caesar himself. A Christian couldn't walk through a neighbor's house without passing a pagan shrine. He could hardly buy meat that hadn't first been sacrificed to a pagan god. He couldn't conduct business without walking through the temple of the patron gods of his union or guild. In the market or at business, he couldn't avoid the devout throngs of people before the temples of Diana or Isis. He couldn't cross the city without passing the sentries and the priests who tended the place of worship set aside to worship Caesar.

Why offend neighbors by ignoring—or worse, by condemning—their religious beliefs? It would only mean a token offering, an orange placed at a neighbor family's shrine or a pinch of incense at the feet of Caesar's giant marble form. It would only mean standing at the pledge of allegiance or bowing at the prayer or unobtrusively joining in the hymn to the deities of friends, neighbors, and co-workers at a social, political, or commercial event. Why be so rigid? Why not worship the one true God in private while simply nodding good-naturedly in the direction of the false gods on every corner? Was this really so bad?

Why all the fuss about sexual immorality? There was a beautiful parklike sanctuary called Daphne just outside Antioch, that town where the first Gentile church was established (Acts 11:19ff.). The temples of Diana and Apollo were surrounded by lush green lawns, flower gardens, fountains, and cypress groves. Leading citizens from the business, professional, and political worlds met there to rest, to conduct business, and to worship. Temple prostitutes were provided as a courtesy. What John called sexual immorality was a common practice of the first century— even part of worship for the unbeliever. Men had wives and concubines. The wives were for raising families. The concubines were for sexual pleasure.

So what was the problem? Why was the risen Christ, through John, so angry at their occasional adultery? It kept their sexual needs satisfied. It kept Christian tradesmen from looking like fanatics—or worse, like fools—during guild parties and initiations. Why were the sexual standards of Christ's revelation to those early Christians so tough, so rigid, and so demanding? Why is idolatry (worshiping the values of this world) so often tied together with immorality (giving in to our sexual passions)?

Review the up-and-down history of the people of Israel and you will see how God rescued a motley crowd of Jewish slaves and started them toward the Promised Land. Filled with gratitude to God, they "believed his promises and sang his praise" (Psalm 106:12). But almost immediately their gratitude turned into grumbling.

Grumbling and gratitude are, for the child of God, mutually exclusive. Be grateful and you won't grumble.

Grumble and you won't be grateful. The psalmist writes, "They soon forgot what he had done and did not wait for his counsel. In the desert they gave in to their craving; in the wasteland they put God to the test" (Psalm 106:13-14).

When Israel felt passionately about God and His great mercies to them, when they sought His guidance and obeyed His commands, they were victorious over their enemies. But when their holy passion for God and His will died, they were defeated. When Moses disappeared on the top of Mount Sinai and was gone for so long, they immediately reverted to idolatry and had Aaron make a golden calf from the jewels they had taken from Egypt. When Moses came down from the mountain, he found them in an orgy of idolatry and immorality.

There is only one passion that can help us control the many other passions which plague us; that is the passion to know and obey God. When this primary passion grows cold, we give in to our lower passions. When we get out of contact with Christ, we try to fill the void with other things. We read about it every day in the newspaper and watch it on our television screens.

It is like the prodigal son who tried to fill his stomach with the husks that the pigs were eating. I meet people constantly who are going to one round of parties after another: gambling, drinking, abusing drugs, partaking of a thousand and one things that this world has to offer. But nothing satisfies the hunger of the soul.

Today there are many people, even in so-called Christian countries, who are turning to Satan worship to try to fill the longings that only God can satisfy. Not even human love can satisfy the longing for God's love that we feel. Instead of turning back to the Father's love, we begin a mad, promiscuous search for the perfect human lover. Idolatry is closely connected to immorality: When the natural love of God is perverted, men and women seek substitutes—any substitute.

On Patmos, the risen Christ sounded His warning to the churches of Asia. He ordered them to stop giving in to the pressures to conform to the values of the people around them. "Repent!" commands John. "Wake up!" he warns them. "Hold on!" he cries. His cry echoes down through the ages to you and me.

Look at the condition of marriage within the context of today's Christian homes and churches. The divorce rate is almost as high among believers as among unbelievers. Almost every day a new rumor crosses my path of another leader in the church whose marriage is in shambles. All too often, in both the spiritual and in the marital dimensions of life, it is simply a matter of letting "first love" grow cold (the problem of the Ephesians and the Laodiceans) and of giving in to the values of this age and to its immoral practices (the problem of the Christians in Pergamum, Thyatira, and Sardis).

The Test of Passion

It is an interesting, if not frightening, test to compare the current levels of our holy passion to know Christ and His will in our life with our current practices. Inevitably, I find the person who is passionately following the Master will be better able to master his or her passions than the person whose "first love" has died. Invariably, I find the person who is involved in irresponsible, destructive, and debasing practices is the person who is falling out of love with Christ and is trying to fill the empty space with other things, even trying to fill the spiritual emptiness with sexual excitement. It will not work! Only God's love can fill the empty space. Human love will always fall short and fail; sex or materialism alone will not even come close to filling it. The Scripture makes it clear that our "first love" is always to be our Lord.

For those who would worship the one true God, the command is clear: "You shall have *no other* gods before me" (Exodus 20:3, italics added). God's instructions regarding sexual morality are equally clear. Old and New Testament literature both cry out for sexual purity. Hebrews 13:4 says, "Marriage should be honored by all, and the marriage bed kept pure, for God will judge the adulterer and all the sexually immoral." In 1 Corinthians 6, Paul writes, "Flee from sexual immorality. . . . He who sins sexually sins against his own body. Do you not know that your body is a temple of the Holy Spirit . . . ? You are not your own; you were bought at a price. Therefore honor God with your body" (verses 18-20).

Adultery (sexual relations with anyone but your own spouse) and fornication (sexual relations apart from the loving, lifelong commitment of marriage) are expressly forbidden for they are inevitably destructive, dehumanizing, and demeaning to God's creation. God's Word promises that sexual immorality, though a short-term source of physical pleasure and emotional escape, in the long run will lead to disappointment, heartbreak, and even death. The Bible is clear: "You shall not commit adultery" (Exodus 20:14).

It seems that almost all entertainment and even advertisements give just the opposite message. They tell us to enjoy ourselves now, take care of this life and ignore the next. We've become used to such expressions as "You only live once," or "You only go around once." Richard Pryor, the comedian, said, "Enjoy as much as you can. Even if you live to be ninety that's not as long as you're going to be dead."

In our fallen world, satanic influences are everywhere pushing us toward idolatry and sexual immorality. Right moral living is not easy. It demands difficult choices. It requires selflessness. At times it may create tension between what we want to be for God and what we crave for ourselves. In that awful struggle to overcome, friends and family may come to our aid. Pastors and counselors and fellow Christians may assist us. Setting goals, practicing disciplines, building new interests and diversions, creating systems of reward to modify our behavior, all of these may help. But in the struggle for righteousness, there is nothing more helpful than being passionately related to Christ through His Spirit and being passionately committed to finding and doing His will in our lives.

Those children of Israel who got off the trail, who let their "first love" die, who gave in to the values of this world, never reached the Promised Land. The Bible says "their bodies were scattered over the desert" (1 Corinthians 10:5).

The price we pay in broken lives and shattered dreams when we let that "first love" die goes far beyond what we can imagine when we begin giving in to pagan values and practices. As you read these words, you may know that you have sinned against God and need His forgiveness. Perhaps you have fallen into sexual sin, or you have allowed worldly desires and pleasures to fill your heart and mind. Whatever your sin, you need to repent and turn to Jesus Christ in faith for forgiveness and new life.

Smyrna, Philadelphia:
The Problem of Suffering

Smyrna, now the city of Izmir, Turkey, was and is one of the great business and trade centers of the Near East. Almost two centuries before Christ, Smyrna welcomed Rome and served Caesar with unquestioning loyalty. The city was perhaps the most beautiful in the entire region. Many religious cults were headquartered there, including the cult of Caesar worship. Although eleven cities bid for it, the Roman senate built a temple to the Emperor Tiberius in Smyrna. A great and powerful Jewish minority also lived there and joined with Rome in making life tempestuous for Christians of both Gentile and Jewish background.

Philadelphia, due east from Smyrna, was built on a plateau looking out across the valley of the River Cogamus. This prosperous city was called the "gateway to the East," and through its gates passed caravans to and from Rome, the capital of the empire. To them, John writes, "I have placed before you an open door" (Revelation 3:8). Here, too, the Jewish synagogue was strong and hostile toward the young Christian church. We know almost nothing about either of the Christian churches in Smyrna or Philadelphia except for these two short letters dictated to John by the risen Christ on the island of Patmos.

We do know that both churches were faithful. There is not one word of criticism in the letters to the Christians in either church. John writes to Smyrna, "I know your afflictions and your poverty—yet you are rich!" (Revelation 2:9). To Philadelphia, he writes, "I know that you have little strength, yet you have kept my word and have not denied my name" (Revelation 3:8). Apparently, both churches were small; both had few economic resources; both faced hostile environments (John—a Jew himself—scathingly refers in both letters to the "synagogue of Satan"). For both churches, more troubled times lay ahead.

The irony of these two letters is immediately apparent. In the stormy times to come—or, as John writes to Philadelphia, in "the hour of trial that is going to come upon the whole world to test those who live on the earth"— one church (Smyrna) will face terrible suffering. The other church (Philadelphia) will escape unscathed. All the assumptions we can make about suffering are tested by these two short letters. Both churches seem equally faithful. Yet one will suffer "even unto death." The other will not suffer at all.

But this seeming inequality has precedent in the Scripture. In Hebrews 11 we have a long list of people whom God delivered. But in verse 35 the writer says, "Others were tortured and refused to be released." In the Book of Acts, for example, James was beheaded, while Peter was delivered.

In these passages and others we are reminded that suffering has a mysterious, unknown component. John, too, assumes that suffering is a natural part of Christian faith. He doesn't question why one church suffers and another does not. He doesn't even expect God to rescue Smyrna from suffering, yet he credits God with protecting Philadelphia from the suffering that lies ahead.

John simply delivers the bad news to Smyrna—"the devil will put some of you in prison to test you, and you will suffer persecution for ten days. Be faithful, even to the point of death." He gives good news to Philadelphia—"I will also keep you from the hour of trial" (Revelation 2:10; 3:10). Suffering is simply a fact. To both churches Christ's advice is simple. To Smyrna: "Be faithful, even to the point of death, and I will give you the crown of life" (Revelation 2:10). To Philadelphia: "Hold on to what you have, so that no one will take your crown" (Revelation 3:11).

There are several applications here that we must not overlook in our own times of trouble. First, expect suffering. Don't feel surprised, put upon, proud, or afraid. Suffering is part and parcel of the Christian life. Second, don't look at anyone else and what he or she does or doesn't have to bear; comparisons are demoralizing either way.

Third, recognize that it doesn't take great wealth or social influence to be faithful (note how few resources these two churches had), but it does take patience and endurance. Remember, one aspect of the fruit of the Spirit is patience (Galatians 5:22). So, fourth, remember that one day all earthly suffering will end and the second death, the eternal death of the spirit, will not touch us. Fifth, keep in mind that, when one bears suffering faithfully, God is glorified and honored. The suffering servants of Christ will be honored in a special way and will be given a new name which "no man knows except he that receives it." Christ said to the church at Philadelphia, "Him who overcomes I will make a pillar in the temple of my God. Never again will he leave it. I will write on him the name of my God" (Revelation 3:12).

Some years ago the great Canadian photographer, Yousuf Karsh, sent me a book of his photographs. On the wrapping paper the customs official had stamped the words, "Value of Contents." Under that had been written, "Autographed by the author." Inside, it was autographed to me. I thought that was very interesting; while the book alone would have been worth perhaps forty or fifty dollars, with the autograph it became much more valuable. As believers in Jesus Christ, our value is the fact that we are going to be autographed by the Author.

I don't understand the reasons for suffering and persecution. I don't know why the churches in one part of the world endure terrible pain and deprivation while other churches are fat and rich and almost pain free. I don't know why some of the young evangelists who gathered in Amsterdam in 1983 and 1986 carry scars from burnings and beatings they suffered for Christ's sake while my life has been free from that sort of persecution. I don't know why Corrie ten Boom had to watch her sister die in a Nazi prison camp, or why Joni Eareckson Tada is paralyzed from the neck down.

Perhaps you have faced pain or suffering you did not understand. You may even have become angry at God for allowing it to happen while others have escaped such problems. Don't let the acids of bitterness eat away inside of you. Instead, learn the secret of trusting Christ in *every* circumstance. Learn to say with Paul: "I have learned to be content whatever the circumstances. I know what it is to be in need, and I know what it is to have plenty. I have learned the secret of being content in any and every situation, whether well fed or hungry, whether living in plenty or in want. I can do everything through him who gives me strength" (Philippians 4:11-13).

Enduring to the End

Several years ago, while traveling in an Eastern European Communist country, an Orthodox priest who accompanied me made the statement, "Every believer has a cross. I know what ours is. But I wondered what yours was." Then looking out over the crowd of reporters standing before me, he said simply, "Now I know!"

All I know from the short letters in Revelation is this: Christ commands us to "Overcome!" in the strength He alone can supply as we turn to Him in faith, trusting His promises.

"Overcome!" cries the risen Savior from the island of Patmos. "Overcome!" writes John at the end of each letter to the seven churches and to us who, like them, will soon be asked to suffer outrageously for Christ and His kingdom's sake. "Overcome!" cried the leaders of each of the seven churches to their flocks, who then went on to join the saints and martyrs known and unknown through the ages. These have heard the call to suffering and have taken it seriously.

"Overcome!" echoes the Word directly to us to join with those who have been laughed at or ignored, humiliated, stripped, tried unfairly, imprisoned, beaten, tortured, and killed. To everyone who endures the storm, there awaits a crown of victory.

7

Standing Before God

Revelation 4-5

One of the most moving moments in my life as an evangelist is the moment when I stand before thousands of people and invite them to come forward to receive Christ as Savior and Lord. I can see the struggle on their faces as the Spirit of God touches their hearts and, one by one, moves them down the aisle to the place of public commitment. I can often see the tears of emotion on their faces as they stand with a counselor in front of the platform. Sometimes I see their joy as they stand forgiven by their loving Savior, reborn and redirected. But I can also see the relief on most of those faces.

On some occasions the people who come forward to surrender their lives to Jesus embrace their counselor and waiting friends, and they walk from the auditorium or stadium as infant members of Christ's body, the church. On the other hand, I see some faces that indicate that they are confused and doubting and even wondering why they came forward. Many of these people actually find Christ in the extensive follow-up system we have.

I believe our Lord was thinking of those new believers when He spoke to John on Patmos. Christ knew the horror and the heartbreak that lay ahead for the faithful in the churches of Asia and in every faithful church around the globe for centuries to come. Christ knew the price they would pay to "overcome." He knew they would need His power in the present struggle and His promise for that day ahead when He would wipe away their tears and they would live with Him forever. So, as He ends the seven letters to the churches, He gives an invitation not to unbelievers, as I do, but to Christians. This invitation from Revelation is, I think, the most beautiful and powerful invitation in the entire biblical account.

As John was writing those strong words from his Lord to the churches, he knew what each of them had suffered in their struggle to be faithful. He also knew that trials and testing would build stamina, and testing would build character. In his letter to the Romans, the apostle Paul had written, "we also glory in tribulations, knowing that tribulation produces perseverance; and perseverance, character; and character, hope" (Romans 5:3-4 NKJV). Christ's word to John was, "Those whom I love I rebuke and discipline. So be earnest, and repent" (Revelation 3:19). But the reward of earnest repentance is splendid. Christ continues, "Behold, I stand at the door and knock. If anyone hears my voice and opens the door, I will come in to him and dine with him, and he with Me" (Revelation 3:20 NKJV).

The Promise of His Presence

This promise of Christ's presence in those future times of trouble is a promise to every believer. Most often we hear these words as an invitation to unbelievers, but here they are spoken to *believers* in those struggling churches of Asia. We have the assurance that in the storms of life today, Jesus Himself will be standing just outside the door waiting to be invited in. He is waiting to share a meal with us, waiting to share our sorrows, to renew our courage, to come in and talk intimately.

We are not alone. We never shall be. He has to be there; all we need do is open the door to Him. What is your need today? Do you need comfort in your personal trials? Christ is waiting. Do you need forgiveness for your sins? He is knocking. Do you need to make a new commitment to serve God with your life? Whatever your spiritual need, right now Christ is knocking at the door of your heart. He is Lord of the universe, and He wants to be Lord of your life as well.

When Jesus was on trial in Jerusalem, the Roman governor turned to the crowd and asked, "What shall I do, then, with Jesus who is called Christ?" (Matthew 27:22). I would suggest that this may well be the most important question that has ever been asked. It is also the question you must ask yourself. No one else can answer it for you. Unless you have made the decision to accept Jesus Christ and follow Him as Lord of your life, you will not share in the promises that follow. Jesus said, "To him who overcomes I will grant to sit with Me on My throne, as I also overcame and sat down with My Father on His throne. He who has an ear, let him hear what the Spirit says to the churches" (Revelation 3:21-22 NKJV).

What happened next staggers the imagination. "After this I looked," John writes, "and there before me was a door standing open in heaven. And the voice I had first heard speaking to me like a trumpet said, 'Come up here, and I will show you what must take place after this.' At once I was in the Spirit." We don't know what "in the Spirit" meant to John, but what he saw is clear. Our task is to prayerfully consider the meaning of his vision.

The Throne of Glory

Nestled into the two chapters between the practical orders to the churches and the terrible warning of the four horsemen of the Apocalypse is the vision that lies at the center of the believer's hope and at the heart of the entire Revelation. If John was worried about the world and its condition, if he was concerned about the future and how his flock could overcome it, and if he was perplexed about the power of evil and the apparent weakness of good on this planet, the next vision made all the difference. It offers equally great promise for our time.

"There before me was a throne in heaven with someone sitting on it," wrote John. He was hard pressed to describe the person he saw sitting on the throne. He described his appearance as jasper, a transparent crystal-like stone, and carnelian, a fiery red stone. Apparently, John was nearly blinded by the glory surrounding the throne. An emerald rainbow encircled it. "From the throne came flashes of lightning, rumblings and peals of thunder," and before the throne, reflecting back the entire incredible scene, was what looked like a sea of glass as clear as crystal (Revelation 4:2-6).

Surrounding the throne were twenty-four other thrones. Seated on them were twenty-four elders dressed in white and wearing crowns of gold. Around the throne were four living creatures. The first was like a lion, the second like an ox, the third had a face like a man, and the fourth was like a flying eagle (Revelation 4:7). Each of the four living creatures had six wings and was covered with eyes all around. The visual impact of that moment must have been overwhelming. For nineteen centuries Bible commentators have analyzed that scene, describing in detail the names of the elders (usually assumed to be the twelve Old Testament patriarchs and the twelve New Testament apostles) and the living creatures (usually seen as seraphim and cherubim, angelic beings created to carry out God's commands).

John didn't bother to analyze what he saw. But what he heard he reported in detail. Those strong, angelic creatures never stopped chanting these words:

> Holy, holy, holy
> is the Lord God Almighty,
> who was, and is, and is to come.
> Revelation 4:8

Whenever the living creatures gave "glory, honor and thanks to him who [sat] on the throne and who lives for ever and ever," the twenty-four elders fell down before Him and worshiped Him and lay their crowns before Him, saying,

> You are worthy, our Lord and God,
> to receive glory and honor and
> power,
> for you created all things,
> and by your will they were created
> and have their being.
> Revelation 4:11

The Mystery and the Majesty

For this one moment in time, the old apostle was ushered into the presence of the Mystery behind the universe. There is no way to describe God. John could only describe the response to God by both the angelic and the human beings before him. Yes, there was a description of color and beauty, of majesty and power, but even as he stood before Him, God remained a mystery to John and to us—the Mystery who was and is and will always be, the Mystery behind our creation and our preservation, the Mystery worthy of our glory and honor and power.

The risen Christ had called John into the presence of God so that the old man could know, and through him we could know, this fact: Behind the universe there is a Power and a Person worthy of our praise and of our trust. In spite of rumors to the contrary, we are not creatures abandoned on a planet spinning madly through the universe, lost in galaxies upon galaxies of gaseous flaming suns or burnt-out cinder moons. We are the children of a great and wonderful God who even now sits in power accomplishing His purposes in His creation.

At the heart of this mystery is great hope. The national powers that we see hell-bent for destruction—amassing weapons, killing, and being killed—are not the ultimate power. Nor are the individual figures who rule in our lives the ultimate powers; mothers, fathers, teachers, pastors, counselors, politicians, diplomats, bankers, police officers, social workers, wardens and jailers, probation officers, tax collectors, dictators and their soldiers, kings and presidents will all one day stand powerless before this God of John's vision.

The Revelation is carefully calculated to restore and renew hope in John and in each of us. I'm not sure how John beheld that vision, but I am certain of the truth it represents. There is a God behind creation, and though in many ways He remains a mystery, I am confident that He has created the planet on which we live, that He has created me, and that what He has created He loves and has a plan to save. If He didn't, He wouldn't be worthy of our praise.

George Ladd wrote about this scene: "However fearful or uncontrolled the forces of evil on earth may seem to be, they cannot annul or eclipse the greater fact that behind the scenes God is on his throne governing the universe" (*A Commentary on the Revelation of John*, 70). God is in control! That awesome truth penetrates every chapter John writes, and it can make the difference for you if it penetrates every area of your life. You can trust your life and your future to God, because He alone knows the future. You can trust Him, because He loves you and because He is ultimately in control of this universe.

How do I know He loves you and me? I know that He sent His only Son to die on the cross for our sins. "For God so loved the world that he gave his one and only Son, that whoever believes in him shall not perish but have eternal life" (John 3:16). How do I know He is in control of the universe? I know that Jesus Christ broke the power of evil and sin through His resurrection from the dead. Christ is alive!

John stood staring in awe and wonder as God suddenly held out a scroll "with writing on both sides and sealed with seven seals." A mighty angelic voice trumpeted out the question, "Who is worthy to break the seals and open the scroll?" Apparently what followed in the silence of that awful moment left John weeping, for there was "no one . . . worthy to open the scroll or look inside" (Revelation 5:4).

Why the tears? At that very moment, God Himself was holding out a communique, a letter, a news flash, a story, a list, and no one was worthy to open it. So John wept. Is there no one who can tell us what is written on the scroll? Is there no one worthy to bear God's message to us?

Suddenly, one of the elders approached John and said, "Do not weep! See, the Lion of the tribe of Judah, the Root of David, has triumphed. He is able to open the scroll and its seven seals" (Revelation 5:5). Immediately, John turned in the direction the elder was pointing. What did he expect to see? A lion, of course, the traditional Jewish symbol of the conquering Messiah who would come to deliver His people from evil. Instead, John writes, "I saw a Lamb, looking as if it had been slain, standing in the center of the throne" (Revelation 5:6).

Again, John beheld a mystery. Who was the Lamb standing on the throne? Years before, John himself had transcribed the words of John the Baptist when he identified Christ as the Messiah, saying, "Look, the Lamb of God, who takes away the sin of the world" (John 1:29). The Lamb was Jesus, the Messiah, God's anointed One, His only begotten Son. Christ had two roles to play in the redemption of this earth. First, He came in the humble form of a man. In that form He suffered and died. Through His sacrifice the penalty for mankind's sinfulness was paid. Second, He would reign as Lord, the promised Messiah, the Lion of David in splendor and in power.

Now John was watching a vision of that perfect sacrifice, the Lamb of God "in the center of the throne." Suddenly he saw—as in the strange but perfect logic of a dream—the Lamb reach out and take from the hand of God the scroll no one dared to open. Suddenly, the elders and the angelic forms all fell down before the Lamb in a chorus of praise. The universe echoed in "a new song":

> You are worthy to take the scroll
>   and to open its seals,
> because you were slain,
>   and with your blood you
>   purchased men for God
>   from every tribe and language and
>   people and nation.
> You have made them to be a kingdom and
>   priests to serve our God,
>   and they will reign on the earth.
>
> Revelation 5:9-10

Then John heard "ten thousand times ten thousand" angels all encircling the throne and joining in that song of praise to the Lamb who was bridging the gap of silence between God and His creation:

> Worthy is the Lamb, who was slain,
> to receive power and wealth and wisdom and
> strength
> and honor and glory and praise!
>
> Revelation 5:12

The vision widened. The song swelled. John says in wonder,

> I heard every creature in heaven and on earth
> and under the earth and on the sea, and all that is
> in them, singing:
>
> To him who sits on the throne and to the Lamb
> be praise and honor and glory and power,
> for ever and ever!
>
> Revelation 5:13

And again, the elders all fell down before the throne and worshiped, and the four angelic creatures lifted their voices in a solemn "Amen!"

The Mystery of the Trinity

The vision of Revelation 4 and 5 offers two great spiritual truths. First, there is a powerful God at the center of creation who is worthy of our trust and praise in the stormy days ahead. Second, the mediator between God and man is Jesus, our Savior and Lord. The presence of God in His glorious splendor blinds us. Without Jesus as our guide, we cannot fully grasp who God is. But in Jesus, the Lamb of God, we see all of God we need to see. Jesus said to Philip, "Anyone who has seen me has seen the Father"

(John 14:9). From Jesus we learn all of God we need to know.

This two-sided vision is an all-important source of hope we can cling to. It would be a mistake only to see God isolated, high and lifted up on a throne surrounded by thunder and lightning. What hope would we have in that kind of powerful but impersonal God? That would be about as comforting as the turbines in a hydroelectric dam. But it would be an equally great mistake to see Jesus only as a wonderful man who suffered and died, who gave us an example of what human life should be: a good man assassinated by villains, as Lincoln and Gandhi were slain. Jesus was not just a good man. He is God and the Son of God. He is that same powerful God revealing Himself in weakness and in love. In John's vision we see the Father through the life, death, and resurrection of the Son, and the Third Person of the Trinity, the Holy Spirit of God, makes all of this known to us. Who can explain such a mystery?

John isn't asking us to put our brains aside. But for this one shining moment he would simply have us join that great throng around the throne. He would have us bend our knees in praise. He would have us lift our voices in song. For what we see is a colorful picture of a truth almost beyond expressing: Jesus, the slain Lamb of God, is the only one worthy to open God's scroll, to speak God's Word to us. Jesus, the risen Lord, is the only one powerful enough to lead us through the future that this scroll reveals.

The Truth of His Coming

In the summer of 1989 I was interviewed by a London newspaper reporter who asked if I thought the world would recognize Jesus the next time He comes to earth. I have heard people say that Christ would no doubt be crucified even quicker by today's pagan culture if He were to come now. But I didn't hesitate in my reply. "Yes," I said, "because He's not going to come riding on a donkey the next time. He's coming as King of kings and Lord of lords." No matter what you think of Jesus Christ, you should know that He is not coming back as the suffering servant. He is coming as king.

When we read John's attempts in these early chapters of Revelation to describe the glory and majesty of the glorified Christ and the indescribable reality of His great throne of judgment, we know that words are simply not adequate to capture the vision. The majesty of our God is beyond anything our finite minds can conceive. Even the most surreal imagery does not do it justice. This is the Christ of power, dominion, and glory Who is coming back to this world. In the language of today, He is *totally awesome!*

A rabbi in Israel said to a group of visiting Christians not long ago, "You know, our two religions are not all that far apart. When the Messiah comes back, we'll just ask him, 'Is this your first or second visit?'" But the humor of that remark cannot disguise the terrible consequences it entails. For when Christ returns, that slight difference will make all the difference in the world.

Jesus Christ the Messiah has identified Himself time and time again as the Redeemer of the world. He said, "Behold, I stand at the door and knock." For twenty centuries He has sent His prophets, apostles, saints, martyrs, and ordinary believers like you and me into the world to proclaim His name before all generations, and He demands that we hear His voice and recognize Him *by faith* and that we accept Him as Lord of our lives. When we see Him next, face to face, it will be too late to decide.

Matthew records Jesus' words, "Not everyone who says to Me, 'Lord, Lord,' shall enter the kingdom of heaven, but he who does the will of My Father in heaven" (Matthew 7:21 NKJV). In the Gospel of the Greek physician, Luke, Jesus says,

> For many . . . will seek to enter and will not be able. When once the Master of the house has risen up and shut the door, and you begin to stand outside and knock at the door, saying, "Lord, Lord, open for us," and He will answer and say to you, "I do not know you, where you are from," then you will begin to say, "We ate and drank in Your presence, and You taught in our streets." But He will say, "I tell you I do not know you, where you are from. Depart from Me, all you workers of iniquity." There will be weeping and gnashing of teeth, when you see Abraham and Isaac and Jacob and all the prophets in the kingdom of God, and yourselves thrust out.
>
> Luke 13:24-28 NKJV

What a bleak and heartrending scene that will be. How tragic for those who have been blinded by their personal pride, or intellect, or ideas of tolerance, or by their doubt into believing that Christ's words are meaningless. For two thousand years His words have been proclaimed over and over again. I myself have proclaimed them thousands of times over the last fifty years. No one in the civilized world can claim He has not heard the news that Jesus Christ wants to be Lord of his or her life. No one can claim ignorance.

The Holy Bible is the bestselling book in the history of the world. Even today it outsells every other book in the world. In the newly liberated countries of Eastern Europe, there aren't enough copies to satisfy their hunger for God.

The International Bible Society, the American Bible Society, and other groups have given away millions of copies, and they haven't even scratched the surface of the demand. No thriller or novel or romance or spy-chaser or cult book or anything else outsells the Bible. It's not as if the Truth were out of reach. What other excuses can you find?

One of the problems, of course, is that Satan is alive and well on planet Earth. He is a liar and a deceiver who stands behind us, mocking, scoffing, laughing at the Word of God, convincing people that the Bible is just another self-righteous book. It is so judgmental, he says; it's full of holes, he says. But Satan "is a liar and the father of lies" (John 8:44). I agree with Peter de Parrie, a young author, who says he finds it odd that the same people who never think to question the instructions that come with their VCR or microwave "instantly bristle with questions about God's instructions on the most important issues in all of life." If the handbook on their Japanese camcorder warns them to keep it away from water, they do it, but if the Bible, which comes with much greater authority and a much longer warranty, tells them to "flee fornication," they recoil in horror!

A Word for the Nations

Some years ago I was in Washington, D.C., in the office of a very powerful and well-known politician. I suddenly looked in his eyes and said, "Sir, have you ever received Christ as your Savior?" He hung his head and didn't say anything. After at least a full minute, he said, "You know, no one has ever asked me that question before." I asked him if he wouldn't like to receive Christ right now and have the confidence of eternal security. As I held out my hand, I said, "It means repentance." I explained that it means faith in Christ and Christ alone. He was silent for two or three minutes, and I didn't say any more. Then he held out his hand and said, "I'll receive Him now," and we prayed. He was a church member. He had been around Christianity all his life, but he had never made that personal commitment. Nothing on earth is more important. Nothing.

My mother used to look out the window every morning and say, "Maybe this will be the day when Christ comes again." She lived with that daily anticipation, but the signs of His imminent return have never been greater than now. Everyone outside the family of Christ is under the judgment of God. To share in the rewards of eternal life and security in the presence of the God of Revelation, we must first acknowledge His Son. That is not optional, no matter what your instinct or your tradition or your faith may tell you.

In his first letter, John wrote, "He who has the Son has life; he who does not have the Son of God does not have life (1 John 5:12). It's as simple as that. Without a personal knowledge of Christ as Lord, the possibility of peace with God ends suddenly when the time clock of your life runs out.

In Revelation, John issues Christ's challenge to "overcome." In his letters, he writes, "Who is he who overcomes the world, but he who believes that Jesus is the Son of God?" (1 John 5:5 NKJV). Then he added, "He who believes in the Son of God has the witness in himself; he who does not believe God has made Him a liar, because he has not believed the testimony that God has given of His Son" (1 John 5:10 NKJV).

Furthermore, anyone who denies the reality of Jesus Christ as the glorified Son of God is, by definition, *against* Christ. John says that such a person is an *antichrist.* "Who is a liar," he says, "but he who denies that Jesus is the Christ? He is antichrist who denies the Father and the Son.

Whoever denies the Son does not have the Father either; he who acknowledges the Son has the Father also" (1 John 2:22-23 NKJV). The logic is simple and irrefutable. The Word of God is clear.

Then John calls for each of us to be faithful to what we have been taught by Scripture over all these years. He says, "Therefore let that abide in you which you heard from the beginning. If what you heard from the beginning abides in you, you also will abide in the Son and in the Father" (1 John 2:24 NKJV).

The reward for faithfulness to the teachings of Scripture, John says in the very next verse, is eternal life. Christ is coming for the church. Just as it was my mother's hope until she went at last to be with Him, it should also be our hope. What greater glory can we anticipate than to stand before the throne of God, to humble ourselves before His great and incomparable majesty, and to hear Him say, "Well done, good and faithful servant!" (Matthew 25:21).

Part 3

In the Midst of the Tempest

8

Escape from Paradise

> I looked, and there before me was a white horse!
> Its rider held a bow, and he was given a crown, and
> he rode out as a conqueror bent on conquest.
>
> Revelation 6:2

In the beginning God created the heavens and the earth"
(Genesis 1:1). By His very nature, God creates. He is the
Creator, and we discover the essence of Who God is in His
creation. We see Him everywhere in it. The apostle Paul
said, "For since the creation of the world His invisible
attributes are clearly seen, being understood by the
things that are made, even His eternal power and Godhead"
(Romans 1:20 NKJV). If we know anything about His creation, we know something of God. For creating is what
God does.

In the Book of Genesis, the book of beginnings, we see
how God made the earth and all that is in it. He made it
beautiful beyond expression: the seas, the mountains, the
rolling prairies, the mighty forests, and the infinitely var-
ied life forms that populate every part of this planet. He
made all these and the universe that surrounds us were
made by God: it is all His creation.

Ruth and I live in the mountains of North Carolina.
Every day we experience the wonder of sunrise and sun-
set as if for the very first time. The world around us

abounds with wonders. David, the psalmist, sang, "The heavens declare the glory of God; And the firmament shows His handiwork" (Psalms 19:1 NKJV). If you have ever walked in a forest glade on a misty summer morning anywhere along the Blue Ridge Parkway, you know something of God's handiwork.

Since men first scratched out their rough drawings on hides or papyrus or, as at Altamira and Aurignac, on the walls of caves, they celebrated the beauty and wonder of God's creation—even if they did not know it. The world created by God was perfectly designed for human life, with food and game, sparkling mountain streams, and every pleasant thing. It was made to order by a loving God for the enjoyment of the only living beings made in His own image, the man Adam and the woman Eve.

The image we see of paradise in the Book of Genesis is brief, but it is beautiful. Moses writes,

> The LORD God planted a garden eastward in Eden, and there He put the man whom He had formed. And out of the ground the LORD God made every tree grow that is pleasant to the sight and good for food. The tree of life was also in the midst of the garden, and the tree of the knowledge of good and evil. . . .
>
> Then the LORD God took the man and put him in the garden of Eden to tend and keep it.

Genesis 2:8-9, 15

That was the life God wanted us to enjoy forever, but He did something only a loving and benevolent Creator would do: He gave us minds and wills of our own. The Bible teaches that God desires to have fellowship with us, to have dialogue with us. He did not make us as robots or mindless creatures but as beings capable of choosing or not choosing, of loving or not loving. What has become of the human race since the creation is the result of the choices we have made through our own free will. Since Adam and Eve were enticed by Satan's charms in the Garden of Eden, believing that they might "be as gods," humanity has had to scrape out a living in a world less desirable and more threatening than Eden. We are guilty of sinning against our Creator.

For All Have Sinned

By choosing not to obey the Creator, Adam and Eve sinned. What is sin? Theologian and author Dr. Myron Augsburger says,

> Sin is the perversion of the good; it is the cheaper form of something better. Sin is not just things that we have done; rather, it is a perversion at the very core of our being that causes us to deify self and demand our own way. In this self-centeredness, we are persons formed in our own image, rather than what we were created to be—persons created in God's image.
>
> The answer to our sin is not simply restitution for a few bad things that we have done. The answer is to turn to God and open ourselves to Him. All sin is ultimately against God. (*The Christ-Shaped Conscience*, 29.)

As we move one step closer to the heart of John's revelation, and the ominous work to be done by the four horsemen of the Apocalypse, it is important to pause long enough to grasp where the human race has come from and how far it has fallen. The very image of the horsemen indicates the seriousness of the consequences of our sin. Through arrogance, willfulness, and conceit, the world has earned its punishment. In our escape from paradise, we sank deep in the mire of the humanist dilemma.

It is sad and ironic that two centuries of scientific and technological achievements seem to have convinced humanity that God has no part in the creation. Through study and genius, the greatest minds who have ever lived have touched the very edges of God's creation, and some have apparently decided there is no God. I think of a child so absorbed with his paper airplane that he is oblivious to the 747 taking him around the world.

The ultimate statement of the humanist view is the phrase credited to the existentialist writer, Jean-Paul Sartre, that "man invents himself." That is the ultimate silly notion. The concentration camp survivor and psychiatrist Viktor Frankl responded to Sartre in his influential book, *Man's Search for Meaning:* "I think the meaning of our existence is not invented by ourselves, but rather detected." Frankl said that the importance and meaning of life is not in who we are but in what we do with all that we have been given by God.

The problem in the world today is that people do not do what they know to be right. They seek after their own wills, contrary to the will of God, and in the words of the prophet Hosea, "They sow the wind and reap the whirlwind" (Hosea 8:7). Paul wrote in his letter to the Romans, "For all have sinned and fall short of the glory of God" (Romans 3:23). The other half of this equation, Paul says, is that "the wages of sin is death" (Romans 6:23). The cause is our willfulness; the price is separation from God for all eternity.

The One Who Deceives

The first horseman described by John in the Book of Revelation is the rider of the white horse. Over the centuries Bible scholars have argued about the identity of this rider. The text says he is wearing a crown and carrying a bow of great destruction in his hand. In Revelation 19, Christ is pictured on a white horse wearing many crowns, and this has led some to believe that the rider on the white horse here in Revelation 6 is also Christ. I do not believe this to be the case. In the Greek text the crown worn by the rider of the white horse is called *stephanos*, which would refer to the crown of victory worn by a conqueror. The crowns Christ wears in Revelation 19, on the other hand, are *diadema*, or the crowns of royalty. Although the rider on the white horse bears a resemblance to Christ, his appearance is actually (and no doubt deliberately) deceptive. A closer look reveals his true nature. He is "a conqueror bent on conquest," greedily riding roughshod over all who stand in his way—the rider of the white horse is characterized by his lust for power.

Who, therefore, is the rider on the white horse? He is not Christ, but a deceiver who seeks to capture the hearts and minds of all mankind. He is one who seeks to have people acknowledge him as Lord instead of the true Christ.

We should always remember that one of the Bible's strongest indictments of Satan is that he is a deceiver, implacably opposed to the truth of God. Jesus said concerning Satan, "He was a murderer from the beginning, not holding to the truth, for there is no truth in him. When he lies, he speaks his native language, for he is a liar and the father of lies" (John 8:44). In Revelation 20, John speaks of God's final judgment on "the devil, who deceived" (verse 10).

The rider who deceives has been at work in the world since the dawn of human history. He was at work in the Garden of Eden when Satan accosted Adam and Eve and by his diabolical power of deception convinced them to turn their backs on God and disobey His clear command.

As a result, the human race fell from its sinless glory, bringing death and despair in its wake.

From Eden to Armageddon, there is a worldwide battle raging between the forces of God and the forces of Satan, between light and darkness, between good and evil. Every man, woman, and child alive today is caught in the crossfire. Satan stalks the earth seeking to dominate and to destroy God's creation. At the same time our Creator, in His love and mercy, works to save that which He has created. The Garden of Eden was "round one" of that battle. It has since escalated into what Dr. Arno C. Gaebelein referred to as "the conflict of the ages." Some day Satan and his works will be completely destroyed and Christ will be victorious, but until that time the battle still rages.

The one who deceives was at work in the animosity between Cain and Abel. He sowed dissent among the Israelites as they fled from slavery in Egypt, persuading them that a golden calf could save them or that they should return to the fleshpots of Egypt. He roamed the Sinai wilderness, spreading lies among the children of Israel to make them doubt God's promises and to prevent them from entering the Promised Land. Back and forth the battle has raged: God urging humanity to follow Him to peace and safety; evil darting in and out of the ranks on his white horse, waylaying, luring, lying, and deceiving the careless, and bringing death to those who follow him.

The horseman who deceives rode up to Samson, the herculean Hebrew judge, and subtly seduced him through the arms of Delilah. He rode up to David, the king of all Israel, and promised him undisturbed pleasure through the murder of Bathsheba's husband. Then David's royal scepter was plagued by a sword that wouldn't go away. The horseman rode up to Judas and promised him power through the betrayal of God's only Son, but Judas soon discovered that he was putting a hangman's rope around his own neck.

The Work of Betrayal

The first horseman storms into our lives today as he has throughout history. The thunder of his coming can be heard growing louder and louder on the horizon of this troubled world. He promises us whatever it takes to persuade us to disobey God and join his tragic train of captives plodding to their doom. But if we believe in Jesus Christ, we must do all we can, through God's strength, to resist his alluring deceits.

One of the biggest problems confronting our world is the fact that, through years of manipulation and deceit, morality and traditional values are no longer in vogue. The deceiver has betrayed our culture and convinced leaders in government, the media, the universities, and even in the churches that black is white and wrong is right. A 1985 Gallup survey reported that 90 percent of all Americans claim some religious affiliation, and all but 2 percent of those claim to be in the Judeo-Christian tradition. But the reality of daily life in America and throughout the West shows that biblical morality has little place in the lives of most people. By and large, the secular culture will accept any set of values or beliefs and any sort of behavior, so long as it is not noticeably Christian.

In her informative and perceptive article entitled "Naming Good and Evil" in the journal, *First Things*, Professor Joyce A. Little writes:

> Unwilling to be God's image in the world and unable, whatever claims some may make to the contrary, to become God in any serious sense of the word, modern man seeks high and low for something, almost anything, to inform him, to give

him an identity; the cosmic consciousness of the New Age, the magic and witchcraft of goddess mythology, the archetypes of Jungian psychology, Joseph Campbell's hero of a thousand faces, Carl Sagan's voyage through the Cosmos, the cults of Elvis, Marilyn, and Madonna, Robin Leach's visits with the rich and famous, 1-900 psychic counselors and personal astrologers, even in alarming numbers the demonic powers promised by satanic cults. Virtually no stone is left unturned in this frenetic search for some hint or clue as to where to go from here. (*First Things*, May 1992, 29.)

Where does that leave us? Secular culture militates against Christian virtues. How many times have we heard "fundamentalists" and "Bible thumpers" attacked or mocked in the popular press? As principles and values are shattered in the world around us, even some Christian leaders are charmed by sin's allure and some have fallen from grace. To each one of us the apostle Peter warned, "Be sober, be vigilant; because your adversary the devil walks about like a roaring lion, seeking whom he may devour. Resist him, steadfast in the faith, knowing that the same sufferings are experienced by your brotherhood in the world" (1 Peter 5:8-9 NKJV). The deceiver on his white horse is already loose in the world. He has succeeded in perverting a huge segment of the population, and he is sporting the victor's crown.

God's Certain Judgment

In some ways God's judgment is like pain in our physical bodies. Whenever we experience pain or discomfort, we generally wait for a while to see if it will go away. But if the pain continues and becomes intense, we go to a doctor to find out what's causing it. At that point, the doctor can generally deal with our problem and relieve the pain.

In the beginning, the pain is like an alarm, warning of potential danger. The purpose of the pain was *corrective*—to let us know something was wrong so we could take action to correct it.

God's judgment is often meant to be *corrective* in much the same way. It is meant to remind us of our need to get right with God before more serious complications appear. God can use trials and difficulties to teach us and help us to become better people for His glory. The writer of Hebrews said, "My son, do not make light of the Lord's discipline, and do not lose heart when he rebukes you, because the Lord disciplines those he loves. . . . No discipline seems pleasant at the time, but painful. Later on, however, it produces a harvest of righteousness and peace for those who have been trained by it" (Hebrews 12:5-6, 11).

The four horsemen of the Apocalypse point inevitably to deeper moral and spiritual problems that affect our lives. But each is unique. Each carries his own agenda. In the following chapters we will look at them closely to see what God is saying to us. In every age we have seen precursors of the horsemen riding over the earth. They had a very specific agenda for those first-century churches in Asia, but they have an equally precise program for us today.

Somewhere above Patmos, the seal was broken. The four horsemen were ready to mount their steeds. Then John heard one of the four creatures who served God at His seat of power cry impatiently, "Come!" Then the text reports that the rider of the white horse "was given a crown" (Revelation 6:2). As suddenly as he appeared, the rider kicked the flanks of the pure white stallion and raced toward the earth "as a conqueror bent on conquest."

For John, this image must have been unmistakably clear. He had perhaps watched the invading legions of Rome enter Jerusalem with the conquering centurion riding a prancing white steed and carrying in his hand the bow, a sign of victory and of power. Perhaps this is even a subtle flashback to an event that happened in the Roman Empire just before John's exile on Patmos.

The Romans were dauntless and fierce, but they feared their Parthian neighbors who threatened the far eastern borders of the empire. The Parthians rode swift white horses and were deadly accurate archers. In A.D. 62 a large Roman army had been overrun by the Parthians and forced to surrender. Apparently the Parthians were such skilled bowmen that even from a galloping horse, bow held waist high, an archer could pierce an enemy on another moving horse across the battlefield. William Barclay says that there is still an old English expression, a "Parthian shot," which means "a final, devastating blow to which there is no possible answer."

The Coming Storm

As I review various commentaries on the Book of Revelation, I keep coming back to one basic question: Are the judgments that John foresees inevitable? Will they definitely happen, or can they somehow be delayed or even completely averted? In other words, are they *conditional* so that they may be avoided by repentance or faith, or are they *unconditional* and will happen no matter what?

This is not an easy question to answer, and I am aware sincere students of the Bible may not all agree. However, after careful study I have come to the conclusion that the answer is *both!* At a time known only to God, the thunderous hooves of the four horsemen will storm across the stage of human history, bringing deception, war, hunger, and death on a scale so massive that it will stagger the imagination. God will use the four horsemen in an awesome act of judgment on the earth, and like a tremendous tidal wave smashing on the shore, nothing will be able to stand against it. The Bible makes it perfectly clear that God's judgment is certain, and it is coming: "For he has set a day when he will judge the world with justice by the man he has appointed" (Acts 17:31).

Looking at the evidence of judgment already visible in the world, I have to say that I believe that time may be very near. Perhaps in its early stages it is already upon us. But even if that is the case, I believe there is hope for a reprieve if God's people react in time and come before Him in humility and prayer. Throughout history there have been many occasions when God delayed or averted His hand of judgment for a period of time because men and women have repented and turned to Him in faith and obedience. But I believe sincere repentance is our only hope.

Throughout the centuries cries of anguish have echoed through the streets of our troubled world. Time and time again we have seen disaster in the pages of history—times of deception, war, hunger, and death. Violent strife and conflict have haunted the human race to one degree or another since the day Adam and Eve first chose to rebel against God.

At those times, death rides through every city and town bringing suffering and death. But sometimes, just as suddenly, we enter a time of peace and relative calm. Why? I believe it is because there are times when God withholds His judgments, possibly even for several generations, because many have listened to His message of warning and turned to Him in repentance and faith.

A good example of this is seen in God's dealings with the people of the ancient Assyrian capital of Nineveh. They were an evil, pagan people who worshiped idols and often fought against God's people. God sent the prophet Jonah to Nineveh to proclaim His coming judgment to them: "Go to the great city of Nineveh and proclaim to it the message I give you. . . . Forty more days and Nineveh will be overturned" (Jonah 3:2, 4). But when the king of Nineveh heard Jonah's message, he repented and ordered the whole people to repent as well. As a result God's judgment was averted. Only later, when evil increased in the generations after Jonah and the people failed to repent, did God's judgment finally fall on Nineveh. God's judgment is often this way. Some day it will come in all its fullness and finality, but in the meantime it may be that God's hand of judgment will pause when we repent, just as this first horse pauses before being let loose on the world in full measure.

The Call to Arms

As we approach our study of the four horsemen and their judgments, we must not feel that we are to sit back and do nothing to fight evil just because some day the four horsemen will come with full and final force upon the earth. Yes, God's final judgment is inevitable, but He alone knows when it is, and until that time we are to learn the lessons of the horsemen and act in such a way that God may be pleased to delay His judgment and allow our world the time to hear His Word and turn to Him.

Perhaps I can expand on the illustration about pain above to make the point. We know that death is inevitable for each of us. But when we get sick we don't say, "Oh, well, I'm going to die eventually anyway so I might as well do nothing about my illness." No! We seek the best medical help we can obtain, because we hope we will get over our illness and live for many more years. In the same manner, God's ultimate judgment on this world is inevitable. But when we hear the hoofbeats of the four horsemen approaching, God expects us to listen to their warning and repent before it is too late. In His grace He may be pleased to turn aside His judgment for a time, just as He has done in the past.

The first step to overcoming the deceiver is to acknowledge that he exists. The second step is to recognize that he works through deception. The rider's method, first and always, is deception. He promises peace to the world, but he gives only false peace. He will be a superman imposing a supersystem with an iron fist. Jesus said, "I have come in my Father's name, and you do not accept me; but if someone else comes in his own name, you will accept him" (John 5:43). The world that has rejected Jesus Christ will readily receive the devil's antichrist.

The Bible teaches that some time in the future there will be a great superman, called *the* antichrist. As we read in 1 John (2:18) "the antichrist is coming." On the other hand, John prophesied that previous to the actual antichrist's coming, there would be "the spirit of the antichrist" (1 John 4:3), and there would be "many antichrists" (1 John 2:18). In the following chapter we will examine some of the deceptions and manifestations of antichrist in the world today.

9

Spiritual Deception

One afternoon in Paris, Ruth answered a knock on our hotel room door. Two men stood there. One explained in broken English that the other was "the Messiah" who had come to see me on a "divine errand." After a brief, pathetic encounter with another of the deranged people who have come my way claiming to be the Messiah, Ruth remarked to me, "He claimed to be Christ, but he couldn't even speak to us in our own language." There is a vast menagerie of masquerading messiahs in the world today—both men and women claiming to be the Christ. Some of them are mental or emotional cripples. Others scheme and dream with ever more menacing motives and powers. But all of them are counterfeits.

The Bible promises that this line of false christs will grow longer and longer until the final embodiment of antichrist appears at the head of the procession. He will be Satan's man. Imitating Christ, he offers peace, but he is as false as the peace he offers. His golden age will be short-lived.

Some of the deceivers around us are more obviously in league with Satan and the satanic than others. Some make no overt attempts to deceive; they speak directly of the tempting powers of evil and call men and women to worship at the feet of Satan himself. Overt Satan worship is perhaps the easiest deception to see through.

With nearly a million copies in print today, *The Satanist Bible* declares the aims, purposes, and practices of Satan worshipers. Under the guidance of leaders such as Anton LaVey and Michael Aquino, the satanists persuade thousands of deluded men, women, and especially teenagers, to follow them in their hellish practices. As the author of books such as *Satanic Rituals* and *The Complete Witch*, LaVey is perhaps the best-known, most persuasive satanist priest in America.

Perversion of the Good

Jerry Johnston's book, *The Edge of Evil: The Rise of Satanism in North America*, gives a startling portrait of the real dangers of Satanism and other "black arts" in our society. Johnston describes the way young people are recruited, introduced to the bizarre rituals and practices of Satanism, and even included in evil sacrifices. The book shows how innocent "seekers" are systematically led into a life in the occult.

What is the danger in such beliefs? In his classic book, *Those Curious New Cults*, William J. Petersen, former editor of *Eternity* magazine, says, "The most infamous blasphemy of Satanist ritual is the Black Mass" (p. 80). Petersen describes how, in the Black Mass, the participants try to reverse everything they know about Christianity. The crucifix is hung upside down. The altar is covered in black instead of white. Hymns are sung backward. The rite is performed by a defrocked priest, and whenever the Lord or Christ is mentioned, the priest spits on the altar or worse. To make the blasphemy even more despicable, sexual rites are added. Sometimes a child is even slain. During the ceremony, the worshipers renounce their faith, acknowledge Satan as Lord, and, when the ritual concludes, the high priest closes with a curse rather than a blessing.

Regardless of how obviously evil or repulsive all this may seem, you should remember that it is not fiction. It is not even rare any more. There are thousands of satanists in the world today. In my travels throughout the world I have seen innumerable varieties of Satan worshipers. One night in Nuremberg, Germany, we were holding a crusade in the same stadium in which Hitler used to stage his infamous rallies. It was difficult to sit in that place and hear in the echoes of memory the masses shouting, "Sieg, Heil!" We realized that from this place the Third Reich had marched out to wage war on the world and, in the pursuit of its pagan ideologies, to exterminate millions of Jews and other prisoners held for political, religious, and psychological reasons. But we were reaching sixty thousand people a night in that open arena. They were singing Christ's praises, and I was preaching the Word of God. Thousands were coming to accept Jesus Christ as Savior and Lord. The presence of God's people there seemed to exorcise the old demons that had stalked those aisles so many years before.

Then one night, as I sat on the platform, Satan worshipers dressed in black assembled just outside the stadium doors. Using ancient, evil rites, they tried to put a hex on the meeting. The rumor of their presence spread, Christians prayed, and in answer to those prayers, nothing came of the incident.

The Power of Prayer

Another night in Chicago, three hundred Satan worshipers approached McCormick Place with the specific intent of taking over the platform and stopping the crusade service that was in progress. They announced their plan in advance, but I didn't dream they would actually try to storm the platform. We had just sung the second hymn of the evening. George Beverly Shea had sung a gospel song, and Cliff Barrows was about to lead a massed choir in a great anthem of praise. At that moment a policeman rushed to the stage and whispered something to the mayor, who was present that night to welcome us.

At the same moment, the Satan worshipers forced their way past the ushers at the rear of that spacious auditorium and were proceeding down the back aisles toward the platform. There were more than thirty thousand young people in our Youth Night service. Only those seated near the back saw the Satan worshipers enter. The mayor of Chicago turned to me and said, "Dr. Graham, we'll let the police handle these intruders."

We never call in the police for crusade duty if we can help it. "Let me try it another way, Mr. Mayor," I suggested. I then interrupted the choir's song and addressed the thirty thousand young people there in McCormick Place. I explained, "There are about three hundred Satan worshipers now entering the auditorium. They say they're going to take over the platform. You can hear them coming now."

The crowd could hear the rising chant of the Satan worshipers. Everyone turned to see them moving with determination down the aisles, past the ushers who were working to restrain them. They were causing a considerable disturbance by that time. I continued addressing the crowd. "I'm going to ask you Christian young people to surround these Satan worshipers," I exhorted. "Love them. Pray for them. Sing to them. And gradually ease them back toward the entrances through which they have come."

I will never forget that moment! Hundreds of young Christians stood to their feet and did exactly as I had asked. Some grabbed hands and began to sing. Others put their arms around the Satan worshipers and began to pray for them. Others calmly shared their faith with them. Everyone else in McCormick Place sat praying as God's Spirit moved through His people to confound the work of Satan in our midst. I stood watching in silence. I waited and prayed until peace was restored and the service could resume.

It happened again in Oakland, California, in the football stadium. Hundreds of Satan worshipers again invaded the meeting to distract and disturb thousands who had come to hear of Christ and His plan of salvation. We did the same thing we had done in Chicago. Again, hundreds of Christians stood and gently led the worshipers of Satan from the stadium. I asked the young people to surround them and to love them. They did! Later that week I received a letter from one of the leaders of the satanist group thanking me for what I had done. He wrote, "I think you saved our lives." The power of those Christian young people came not in the impact of evil and violent force, but in their quiet, loving, prayerful resolution.

A Storm of Discord

In recent years we have seen some encouraging signs within the churches. Many are growing dramatically, with a surge in Christian megachurches and theologically sound "branch churches" and related parachurch ministries. Evangelical seminaries are bulging at the seams. Countless thousands of small-group Bible studies have sprung up all over the nation. But other reports say that at the same time, there is growing dissatisfaction in recent years—especially among "young urban professionals"—with "traditional Christianity." These people, between the ages of twenty-five and forty, have grown up in an age of discontent and distrust. They have a schooled distrust of "fundamentalism." But they have also witnessed the scandals in the highly visible media church, including promiscuity and the misuse of funds by some television preachers. According to some reports, much of this generation has been "turned off to religion" by the predominantly hedonistic secular culture.

In their bestseller, *Megatrends 2000*, John Naisbitt and Patricia Aburdene reported that religion is on the rise in this generation. They cited a 1987 Gallup poll which showed that 94 percent of Americans believe in God, but they asked, "are Americans 'religious' or 'spiritual'?" (John Naisbitt and Patricia Aburdene, *Megatrends 2000*, 295). Approximately 70 percent of the baby boomers, they say, believe in "a positive, active spiritual force." While the authors say that conservative, Bible-believing churches are growing steadily, they also show that the New Age movement and other "nontraditional" movements are still booming. These authors also relate that, according to the *Encyclopedia of American Religions*, four hundred new religious groups were formed in the United States between 1987 and 1989.

Do such statistics indicate deception or discontent? Again, I would have to say both. Young people and young adults are experimenting with exotic practices and beliefs in the effort to find "unity" with "the force." Millions have been deceived, and where deception exists, disillusionment follows. Disillusionment and deception are the two primary alternatives to true faith in God, and they are the handiwork of the first horseman of the Apocalypse.

The deceiver has many options in his bag of tricks; the first is leading susceptible people to ignore religion altogether. When we feel alienated, isolated, unloved, lonely, and adrift in a cold dark universe, we need God. But the deceiver tells us "there is no God." The nineteenth-century philosopher Friedrich Nietzsche said "God is dead." Do not seek God or Jesus Christ, he whispers, seek escape. I would suggest that this is the real reason why drugs are such an epidemic in America today. This is why promiscuous sex runs rampant, why alcohol abuse is commonplace. Without faith in God, men and women are alone. They will do anything to fill the void in their lives, but short of Christ, nothing works. Augustine said, "Thou madest us for Thyself, and our heart is restless, until it repose in Thee" (*The Confessions of Saint Augustine*, 1:1).

The New Age

A second form of deception is the substitution of false religions. The rise of the so-called New Age movement over the past twenty-five or thirty years is the best modern example. The New Age is, in fact, another storm warning indicating man's search for "transcendence" without regard for righteousness. Whether it's Dianetics, est, Unity, Gaea, Transcendental Meditation, Taoism, ufology, crystalology, goddess worship, reincarnation, harmonics, numerology, astrology, holistic healing, positive thinking, or any of a hundred "consciousness raising" techniques of our day, the modern age is on a search for some mystical "divine unity," a search which actually testifies to the failure of modern secular humanism to satisfy the spiritual hunger of the soul.

Humanity was designed for a relationship with God. As the body craves oxygen, so the spirit craves God. We all have a passionate desire to know God and to communicate with Him, but ever since Eden we have been guilty of sin, and nothing but repentance—by humbling ourselves before the cross of Christ—will ever bring us back into fellowship with Him.

The real disaster of the cult of humanism and its New Age and other expressions is not just the foolishness of placing one's trust in such a frail, finite, and limited creature but that it separates man from the authentic source of power and meaning. David's lament in Psalm 10 has never been truer than today: "The wicked in his proud countenance does not seek God; God is in none of his thoughts" (Psalm 10:4 NKJV).

Many people have decided that there is no room for God in their lives, no need of Him. The God of Jacob is too confining. The problem, however, is that denying the existence of God cannot make Him go away any more than denying the existence of the Internal Revenue Service makes the tax man go away. Many people who have imagined a god of their own choosing will be horrified when they have to stand before the true God of heaven. For God is, and His is the kingdom and the power and the glory forever. No pious idealism, no New Age fantasy, and no amount of denial can ever change that fact.

Still another ploy of the New Age is to transform God into something else, or to come to the conclusion, as many have done, that we are gods. On the last page of her book, *Out on a Limb*, actress Shirley MacLaine attempts to make herself equal with God when she writes:

> I know that I exist, therefore I AM.
> I know that the God source exists. Therefore IT IS.
> Since I am a part of that force, then I AM that I AM.

In the eyes of a righteous God, there is no greater blasphemy, but such "abomination" has become common heresy in our day. It is one more evidence of the rider on the white horse "going out conquering and to conquer" through his deceptions.

The Work of the Deceiver

In this age of humanism, man wants to believe he can become his own god. The remark attributed to Protagoras, that "Man is the measure of all things," is the central tenet of humanist ideology. But it is the ultimate deception of

Satan: to rob men of their relationship with the God of the universe through a lie as old as Eden, that "You will be like God" (Genesis 3:5).

Because it springs from false theology, and especially because it is inspired by the deceiver himself, the New Age movement will not bow before God. Rather, it tries to manufacture its own infinitely forgiving and fallible god designed on the pantheistic concept of the oneness of man with the universe. When a Hollywood actress claims to be God, she is simply denying that she has sinned and fallen short of the glory of God. New Agers are terrified by their own mortality, and they want to believe that somehow the soul will survive. Of course it will, but not as they imagine.

Someday the New Age gurus will die, even as we all must die, and their bodies will return to the earth from which God made it. Then what remains, their eternal spirits, will stand before the true and righteous and all-knowing God of creation and explain why they felt compelled to run so hard to escape the God who loved them and gave His Son as a sacrifice. They can explain why, instead, they publicized beliefs which are an abomination in the eyes of a jealous God, and they will hear His reply.

On that day, sincerity will mean nothing; hard work will mean nothing; good intentions will mean nothing. God judges every man, woman, and child by the standard of the only God-Man who ever lived, Jesus Christ. Jesus, the innocent Lamb of God, pledged His innocence for us, to stand between our sin and the judgment of God the Father. Without that holy Shield, no one is worthy. That is the lesson of the fourth chapter of Revelation.

The sin nature is born within each of us; we are not born noble, as Rousseau and the philosophers of the Enlightenment declared. The horseman who brings war testifies to the evil and deceit in our human natures; the terror of war and the storm clouds of holocaust prove that. Left to our own devices, we will destroy the world around us.

Author and writer Russell Chandler, in his book *Understanding the New Age*, reports that dozens of American companies (perhaps unintentionally) are indoctrinating men and women into the New Age movement through "consciousness raising" techniques and required "self-improvement" courses. Many Fortune 500 companies regularly send their executives off to remote training centers and retreats to "get in touch with their inner person." In plain language, that means they are being introduced to such New Age practices as meditation, visual imaging, Zen, yoga, chanting, and even Tarot cards. All this is done in the name of "success enhancement." What it amounts to is opening up the human spirit to the ultimate source of deception: the father of lies.

How Deception Takes Hold

Why are the cults and the New Age movement so successful today? Why are so many people willing to be swept away by false teaching and thereby are turning their backs on God's truth? There are many reasons, but I am afraid we Christians must confess that at times we have been part of the problem because we are not examples of Christ's love and purity as we should be. Many people—especially young people—have become disillusioned with the Christian faith and the church, and have therefore been open to deception.

This is not a new phenomenon. Throughout history there have been examples of Christian believers becoming unwitting allies of the horseman who deceives. Rather than standing against the symbol of the white horse whose hoofbeats we can hear, unknowingly we can assist him. Sometimes it is in word and action. For example, some churchmen in Nazi Germany gave their official blessing to Hitler's Third Reich as it wreaked havoc on Europe (although others, like Dietrich Bonhoeffer, courageously spoke out and even paid for their courage with their lives). Sometimes our sin comes as a result of our silence and inaction: sins of omission.

Today, too, Christian believers are in danger of helping the rider on the white horse to deceive. In his book, *Unholy Devotion: Why Cults Lure Christians*, Harold Busséll says: "In our fervor to point out [the cult's] errors of doctrine, we have virtually ignored our own shortcomings and vulnerabilities." I will briefly illustrate some of the ways too many people assist in the deception of others through: (1) half-truths, easy answers, and lies, (2) maintaining double standards (saying one thing but doing another), (3) discriminating against certain sins while approving or ignoring other sins, (4) inadequate practical teaching on "the inward journey," and (5) inadequate practical teaching about the "outward journey."

The Need for Caution

One of the primary reasons young people reject Christ and follow after the rider who deceives and his New Age and cultic allies are the half-truths, easy answers, and lies we Christians have sometimes told in our attempts to "sell the faith." I have listened to too many sermons, read too many Christian books, and seen too many Christian films with happily-ever-after endings. Some even declare that if you become a Christian you will get rich or always be successful. That is simply false teaching.

In our attempts to share the faith, some have given the impression that, once a person has accepted Christ as Savior and Lord, his or her problems will be over. That is not true; in fact, it is often quite the opposite. Becoming "new" in Christ is a wonderful beginning, but it isn't the end of pain or problems in our lives. It is the beginning of our facing up to them. Being a Christian involves a lifetime of hard work, dedicated study, and difficult decisions. Christ did not teach that a life of faith would be easy, but that the reward for endurance would be great.

After the apostle Paul's dramatic conversion on the road to Damascus, I doubt if he ever dreamed what hardship and suffering lay ahead. Even though God had told Ananias, who was to disciple Paul, "I will show him how much he must suffer for my name" (Acts 9:16), he could not have known what lay ahead in not only living the Christian life, but in serving Christ. In 2 Corinthians 6, he recounts some of his sufferings, not in discouragement and complaining, but in joy and victory:

> In great endurance; in troubles, hardships and distresses; in beatings, imprisonments and riots; in hard work, sleepless nights and hunger; . . . through glory and dishonor, bad report and good report; genuine, yet regarded as impostors; known, yet regarded as unknown; dying, and yet we live on; beaten, and yet not killed; sorrowful, yet always rejoicing; poor, yet making many rich; having nothing, and yet possessing everything.

> 2 Corinthians 6:4–5, 8–10

Then the apostle gives even more specific detail. He says:

> Three times I was beaten with rods, once I was stoned, three times I was shipwrecked, I spent a night and a day in the open sea, I have been constantly on the move. I have been in danger from rivers, in danger from bandits, in danger from my own countrymen, in danger from Gentiles; in danger in the city, in danger in the country, in danger at sea; and in danger from false brothers. I have labored

and toiled and have often gone without sleep; I
have known hunger and thirst and have often gone
without food; I have been cold and naked. Besides
everything else, I face daily the pressure of my concern for all the churches. Who is weak, and I do not
feel weak? Who is led into sin, and I do not in-
wardly burn?

If I must boast, I will boast of the things that
show my weakness.

2 Corinthians 11:25–30

For Paul the Christian life was one of suffering. The
same could be said of a multitude of Christ's followers,
many of whom were killed for their faith. So when Christ
said time after time that one must "deny himself and take
up his cross daily and follow me" (Luke 9:23), He was indicating that it will not always be easy to be His follower.
The apostle Paul warned, "Everyone who wants to live a
godly life in Christ Jesus will be persecuted" (2 Timothy
3:12). He offers no cheap grace, no easy life. He did not
call for what has been called "easy believism." As someone else has said, "Salvation is free but not cheap."

Charles T. Studd was a famous sportsman in England,
captain of the Cambridge XI cricket team. A century ago
he gave away his vast wealth to needy causes and led the
Cambridge Seven to China. His slogan was, "If Jesus
Christ be God and died for me, then no sacrifice can be
too great for me to make for Him."

During the first decade of this century, Bill Borden left
one of America's greatest family fortunes to be a missionary in China. He only got as far as Egypt where, still in his
twenties, he died of typhoid fever. Before his death he
said, "No reserves, no retreats, no regrets!"

A generation ago, Jim Elliot went from Wheaton College
to become a missionary to the Aucas in Ecuador. Before

he was killed, he wrote, "He is no fool who gives up what he cannot keep to gain what he cannot lose." In some parts of the world it is still very hard to be a Christian. In many places men and women are martyred for their faith. At this moment Coptic and Orthodox Christians in the Middle East are undergoing great trials and sufferings. In Latin America, Asia, and in many places in Western Europe, the price of faithful service to Jesus Christ can be humiliation, torture, and death. A 1991 report by Barrett and Johnson shows that more than 40 million Christians have died as martyrs since A.D. 33, including an average of 290,000 Christian martyrs worldwide per year in the 1990s.

In North America it may be just as hard to stand up against the ridicule of secularism and its humanist values. Materialism and self-centeredness are the great vices of our age. But whatever comes your way, know that Christ is in your struggles with you. He knows what it means to suffer, for He, the sinless Son of God, suffered the pangs of death and hell for you. He knows what it means to be tempted, and "Because he himself suffered when he was tempted, he is able to help those who are being tempted" (Hebrews 2:18). In the midst of every situation of life He can give an inner calm and strength that you could never imagine apart from Him. "Peace I leave with you," He said, "my peace I give you. I do not give to you as the world gives. Do not let your hearts be troubled and do not be afraid" (John 14:27). The storms of life will come, but Jesus will be there with you.

The benefits of Christianity are tremendous, but the trials may sometimes seem just as great. So when any preacher or teacher of the Christian gospel oversells either the material or the spiritual benefits of the faith, he is actually aiding the work of the horseman who deceives.

Double Standards

Another reason the rider who deceives is having a field day in our society is the double standard practiced within some Christian churches. I like the little bumper sticker that reads, "Christians aren't perfect, just forgiven." Christian leaders point their finger at cults and cult leaders and accuse them of deceiving their members. "They say one thing and practice another," the cultists complain.

But perhaps we need to examine our own history as Christian believers. How many Christians today are guilty of the same sin? Too often our Christianity is in our mouths and not in our minds. Which of us cannot identify with the words of the apostle Paul who said, "For the good that I will to do, I do not do; but the evil I will not to do, that I practice" (Romans 7:19 NKJV).

Often the outsider can see through our facades; he calls it hypocrisy. He has heard the stories of Christian churches that have been divided by anger and hatred. He knows about the deacon who left his wife to run away with the church organist. He knows how some of the Sunday morning faithful spend Saturday night. He knows that Christian believers, too, are human. Yet how we work to keep that secret hidden!

We sometimes see Christian books about celebrities who are supposedly converted to the faith. All too often, after the book is released, our celebrity Christian is caught in a front-page scandal. We produce films about the wonderful change Christ makes in a couple facing tragedy. Then, as has happened on occasion, just as the film is released that same couple announces their divorce. Ministers, deacons, Christian leaders, and celebrities are all vulnerable to sin. Why can't we simply face up to these problems openly and deal with them—without excusing them?

As long as we remain in these mortal bodies, none of us will ever be perfect. None of us lives without occasional sin and failure, and it is hypocritical to pretend otherwise. At the same time, however, we must never grow complacent about sin or simply say, "Oh well, everyone else is doing it too." The Bible commands, "But just as he who called you is holy, so be holy in all you do" (1 Peter 1:15). It also tells us that there is forgiveness and new life when we repent and confess our sins to Christ.

Washed Whiter Than Snow

My wife told me a story about the early mountain people in the area where we live who used to have a wooden cradle with slatted sides to put their laundry in. The cradle was placed crossways in a rushing creek, and as the water flowed through the slats, the laundry was continuously cleansed. Ruth laughed, this was probably the first automatic washing machine in North Carolina. One day a bootlegger in our area was converted. When he was taken down to the stream to be baptized, he asked if he could please be put crossways to the current so that he would "get washed the cleaner!"

When sin and failure come in our lives, as they most certainly will, we still have the wonderful promise that "the blood of Jesus, his Son, purifies us from all sin" (1 John 1:7). That promise was written to believers. And the word used here, *purifies* (or, in the King James Version *cleanseth*), means "continuous cleansing."

The greatest thing you can do when you have sinned is to go immediately to the Scriptures and claim the many promises of God. Memorize some of them. Psalm 119:11 (KJV) says, "Thy word have I hid in mine heart, that I might not sin against thee." Because it was inspired by God for imperfect human beings, Scripture has the remedy for sinfulness.

Another thing I have found helpful is to confide in a very close Christian friend who can share your burden, problem, or failure in confidence. I would add a word of caution here, however. There are some believers in whom you may confide who cannot wait to tell someone else. Use caution in choosing friends, counselors, and confidants, but don't let fear be an excuse for hiding your secrets from a Christian brother or sister. Just be sure you can trust the one to whom you talk. Then ask that person to read the Scripture and pray with you.

Why must we pretend with each other? Why should we wear assumed smiles of victory in our public gatherings and weep tears of loneliness and anger when we are alone? If your business fails and bankruptcy threatens, let your brother and sister in Christ be aware of your struggle. If your marriage is coming apart at the seams, find at least one or two trustworthy believers to share your pain and help you deal in practical ways with the problems you face. The Bible says, "Carry each other's burdens, and in this way you will fulfill the law of Christ" (Galatians 6:2).

It only takes one act of repentance to receive Christ as Lord and Savior. But repentance is not a one-time act. All Christians are guilty of individual and corporate sin. Corporate sin is participating in a group's sin, whether it's a family that ignores a neighbor in need, a church that ignores the needs of its neighborhood, or a nation that ignores the demands of a holy and righteous God.

Freedom in Forgiveness

Once we confess the fact that we Christians, too, still sin, we see unbelievers in a new light, and they will see us in a new light. We do not look down on their sinfulness from any position of arrogance. We simply reach out in understanding and in love, offering to our fellow sinners the forgiveness and new life that we were freely given in Christ. When we admit that we are not perfect, just forgiven, and share the Scriptures, we drive away the rider who deceives. But as long as we pretend to be perfect and live behind the double standard, we give him room to ride.

Let us pray that God will make us sensitive to sin wherever it is found. We must reach out in Christian love to those whose lives are battered and bruised by sin, point them to the only One who can bring healing and new life, and welcome them into our fellowship. "For it is God's will that by doing good you should silence the ignorant talk of foolish men. Live as free men, but do not use your freedom as a cover-up for evil; live as servants of God" (1 Peter 2:15-16).

The inward journey is that lifelong pilgrimage of spiritual growth and maturity in the life of the believer. Many times pastors and Christian leaders tend to see conversion as the end rather than the beginning of life's struggle to know God and to do His will. Going forward in a crusade or church to receive Jesus Christ as Lord and Savior is really just the first step of the inward journey.

Ultimately this journey should include such things as daily study of God's Word, the practice of prayer, the reading of Christian books and articles, memorization of Bible verses, gathering together with other believers in a sound Bible-believing church, participation in small mentoring or Bible study groups, and building intimate and honest Christian friendships. All of these activities are necessary if we are to grow in the Christian faith. We must not assume that people understand and practice these disciplines on their own. They need direction and encouragement, and in many cases they need leadership.

I'll never forget a pastor's telling me the story of one of his most faithful members who did not know how to pray.

She had been a hard-working, committed member of the church since her conversion in a crusade. She had taught Sunday school and pledged her financial support. She had even brought neighbors and friends to church. One Wednesday evening the pastor asked the woman to lead in a closing prayer. After a long, embarrassing silence she ran from the room in tears. For a while the woman disappeared. She wouldn't answer her phone. She didn't return to church. Finally, she called the pastor and made an appointment to see him. In his study, the woman confessed that she didn't know how to pray. She didn't know what to say or how to say it. Everyone had just assumed that she could pray, but she honestly didn't know how.

The pastor told me that teaching this person from a totally secular background how to pray was one of the most difficult and rewarding tasks of his ministry. By walking her through the elements of a simple, heartfelt prayer, he helped her gain new and intimate access to the very throne of God. The experience gave new meaning to the disciples' request directed to Jesus, "Lord, teach us to pray, just as John taught his disciples" (Luke 11:1).

The Moment of Innocence

Each evening in our crusades, I give the invitation for people to commit themselves to Christ. Afterward I talk to them about four important things that must be part of their lives if they are to develop and mature. One of those is prayer. I tell them that they may not be able to pray like a clergyman in the beginning, but they can start with just a simple sentence. "Lord, I love you." That's a prayer. Or, "God, help me." That's a prayer. Since the disciples had to be taught to pray, we, too, ought to study the Scriptures and learn to pray.

Christian leaders would do well to recognize that the term "babes in Christ" has a very specific meaning. There is an innocence and vulnerability in many new believers that the deceiver will exploit if we allow him. If we do not continue to teach Christian principles to the new believers, we run the risk of simply opening their eyes to spiritual issues so that cults or other influences can take over. In contrast, cult leaders sweep down upon their converts and offer them rigorous spiritual discipline. While we are taking for granted that all is well with the new converts, cults assume that their new members know nothing. They start from scratch and build into the newcomer all the skills he or she needs to feel a part of that particular cultic system.

By assuming too much, we can leave these infant believers open and vulnerable to New Age spiritualism with its sophisticated systems and pat answers or to other kinds of modern "isms" that can quickly overcome the truth they have so newly gained. It is important for local church leaders to keep in touch with the spiritual state of their members, to discuss their level of biblical knowledge, or to determine how well and how often people pray.

A recent survey showed that 85 percent of the seminaries of this country had no classes on prayer. How many local churches offer classes on developing the skill and practice of prayer? One church had a "week of waiting," an *entire week for prayer!* The rider who deceives gloats when we assume our people are alive and growing. He is all too free to ride into our ranks and to make victims of us all if and when our inward journey, our spiritual growth and maturity, are not a primary concern to us all.

The Outward Journey

The outward journey is an expression that I think originated with Elizabeth O'Connor, the historian of the Church of the Savior in Washington, D.C. To grow on an inward journey, the journey to know God, is not enough. We are also called to follow Christ onto our streets and into our neighborhoods. We are called to serve Christ in bringing His message of redemption to the world. The outward journey, which takes us beyond our own small world to the world in need, is the inevitable outworking of a genuine inward journey. The Great Commission of Christ points in two directions: toward God and toward our neighbors.

The Church of the Savior requires that each member be actively working in some sort of outreach project, whether it be evangelism through a Bible study; a retreat ministry; rebuilding houses or feeding the poor; caring for orphans, widows, and transients; being involved in the primary concerns of education; public housing; or environment. That is an exceptional requirement for membership, but to require people to be effective ambassadors of Christ is not at all unrealistic. I wish more churches would consider this option. Sometimes we act as if attending church on Sunday morning and putting an offering in the basket is all that God requires of us. That sort of church is little more than a picnic or an amusement. It makes the faith seem like an empty ritual; "It makes me feel good." We forget Jesus standing before the rich young man saying, "Sell everything you have and give to the poor. . . . Then come, follow me" (Mark 10:21).

The rider who deceives revels when we make faith seem too easy. Faith involves trust and commitment. The crowd at the fringe of the cross is easily led away. But those who mix their blood and sweat with the tears of the martyrs are not easily deceived. The more involved a believer is in a daily devotional life and in the lives and needs of others, the more he or she will grow in faith and in practice. The less involved, the more likely he or she is to be deceived.

Many sincere people leave the church and join the cults because the cults make demands. When committing their lives to a belief or cause, people expect a challenge. People respond to the call to hardship. The cults offer practical ways that the followers can serve others, while churches often talk about "cross bearing" but never give their members the sorts of practical, sometimes difficult tasks, that make Christian service practical and rewarding. It may seem ironic, but if we don't make demands, the rider who deceives will rein in and provide practical programs of caring as the first step of deception.

10

The Material World

Christians who are actively growing in their faith and their understanding of the nature of God experience a fulfillment in life that is truly indescribable. Through times of both joy and sorrow, the reality of the Spirit of Christ living within brings a peace and dynamic vitality which gives life great meaning and purpose. It was with a sense of this reality that the psalmist sang, "How awesome is the LORD Most High, the great King over all the earth!" (Psalm 47:2).

I have traveled in parts of Europe, Asia, and the Third World where there is no joy. No one smiles; there is no happiness or celebration. Everything is grim and depressing, without hope; it is what some have described as "life in the abyss." For me it is the perfect image of life without God.

Thanks to the events of the past few years, God has opened up many opportunities for me to preach in those places, and we are seeing hope and vitality restored because the people in those lands are hungry for meaning and they want to know Jesus Christ. In our own nation, however, there is an even greater danger: men and women who know the truth—who have benefited from a Christian tradition—have traded God for gadgets. They have departed from eternal truth for momentary self-gratification, and they worship the false gods of materialism and humanism.

A generation ago, Western society had a somewhat more modest opinion of itself. Despite reasonable pride in our technology and industry, most Americans lived simple lives. Our fathers and mothers all worked hard so we could have it better than they did, but most were "just plain folks."

We had been taught that "pride cometh before a fall." Furthermore, both tradition and religion made it clear that self-centeredness was anti-social and unacceptable. Teachers warned that "rights" were always accompanied by "responsibilities." Democracy showed us that in American society each person may rise to his level of competence, but nobody owes you a living.

I sometimes wonder if the ovens of Auschwitz and the cloud over Nagasaki didn't give us a somber warning about the dangers of human potential. No doubt the immense power of modern weapons and the capacity of a civilized nation to condone hideous atrocities, like those at Auschwitz, caused us to view the awesome complexity of human nature with caution. We learned something about our capacity for inhumanity and ruthlessness. What the Western world learned on the battlefields of two world wars helped teach us compassion, and it gave us a remarkable depth of character. For a moment at least, the world seemed deeply grateful to God for a return to peace on earth, and all over this land there was a sense of genuine humility—but it was short-lived.

By the mid-1950s, America was absorbed with "modernism." From the fins of our automobiles to the shrinking swimsuits of Hollywood models, it was apparent that America was making a deliberate turn toward the new, the modern, the materialistic, and the shocking. The music, the movies, and the media of the day reveal the degree to which this change was taking place in the popular imagination. Hot jazz, rhythm and blues, and the early rock-and-roll hits were slightly off color, and young people took a mischievous pleasure in scandalizing their elders.

As GIs, Army nurses, and others returned to the campuses, the relatively new discipline of psychology became a major topic of interest. By the mid-1960s, psychology was the hottest major in American universities. Many of psychology's insights into the reasons behind human behavior are of value, and some of them confirm what the Bible had said long ago. However, today we can see that some of the founders of that science—like early astronauts of the mind—were among the leading contributors to the shift in values taking place in American attitudes. Unfortunately, that was not all good news.

The principle which made secular psychology so radical was that it introduced a break with much that had gone before. Just as the theories of Charles Darwin had undermined belief in God as the Creator, modern psychology also tended to turn people against belief in God. It taught that there was hidden depth and substance within each individual. The outer person was a compromise; the inner person was profound and important. Psychology thus concluded that the true self, buried under a false covering of social conditioning and religious prejudice, was struggling to be set free. For some psychologists, therefore, religion was seen as a hindrance rather than a help to human personality.

I am happy to say that recently we have seen the rise of new forms of Christ-centered and Bible-based psychology that attempt to deal with emotional issues in the context of Christian faith and belief. A number of well-known Christian psychologists have helped develop the foundational principles of this discipline, and many excellent books on the subject are available. Today there are also some very helpful Christian counselors and clinics. Much modern secular psychology, on the other hand, preaches individual self-interest as the ultimate reality at the expense of compassion, concern for others, and devotion to a higher purpose in life—as in our relation to God and our fellow man. "Pop psychology" has contributed in no small way to the chaos of hedonism, secularism, and nihilism in modern culture.

Over the years America has been characterized as a nation of rugged individualists, so the language of self-reliance and self-interest did not, at first blush, arouse concern. However, as Floyd McClung points out in his book, *Holiness and the Spirit of the Age*, we have taken a giant step beyond the context of the frontier spirit into something much uglier. He writes:

> Modern individualism, which is divorced from the moral foundations of Christianity and surrounded by a hedonistic society, has produced a way of life that is neither beneficial to individuals nor productive to society at large. Individualism used to be expressed positively within the context of the family, the community, the church, and the government. Personal rights were subjected to the overall good of society. But individualism today no longer observes such boundaries. The cry is, "I want what I want when I want it!" Such selfish individualism weakens the very underpinnings of a nation built on strong moral foundations. (*Holiness and the Spirit of the Age*, 78.)

From high school on, young people are indoctrinated with the secular definitions of self-esteem, self-image, self-realization, and self-actualization propagated by the prophets of selfism. Today the ideas and principles of Carl Jung, Alfred Adler, Carl Rogers, Abraham Maslow, Gordon

Allport, Erich Fromm, and not least, Sigmund Freud, are better known on college and university campuses than those of Moses, Samuel, Isaiah, Jesus, or Paul.

The focus on self, auto-centrism, and behaviorism has led our society into a fascination with pleasure, emotional and sexual stimulation, and "personal fulfillment." What Freud described as the liberation of the id was the first step toward the cult of the self.

America's compulsion for "maximum personhood" is in evidence everywhere. Legitimate recreations, from racquetball to golf, have become obsessions for some people. Athletics, running, health fadism, even muscle building among both men and women have taken on the aura and discipline of cultic and mystical rites. The focus of our activity is no longer on the heart, the soul, or the mind, but on the body. Feeling good is the ultimate success. The executive's t-shirt says, "No Pain, No Gain!" as he runs wind sprints on his lunch hour. Why? Certainly I believe in health and physical fitness. Because of my own travel schedule and frequently exhausting speaking requirements, I am a firm believer in the value of conditioning. I enjoy walking, swimming, and physical exercise within reason; it's very important for old and young alike. I also believe God expects us to take care of our bodies. The Bible says, "Do you not know that your body is a temple of the Holy Spirit?" (1 Corinthians 6:19). But at the same time we are not to turn our natural concern for health into an unnatural quest for eternal youth. The Bible says, "For physical training is of some value, but godliness has value for all things" (1 Timothy 4:8).

The cult of self has become an addiction. Some analysts have suggested that self-absorption is actually a defensive reaction against the loneliness and sterility of today's depersonalized modern lifestyles. We have become urbanized and disconnected. Some people lack family or roots, or any reference to our heritage of faith. Consequently, without the old connections and dependencies that gave life meaning, many have lost their sense of belonging, and many, if not most, have lost all sense of community. Floyd McClung writes: "To most Americans the world is a fragmented place that presents them with a multitude of choices and offers little meaning or comfort. They believe they are basically alone and have to answer only to themselves. Thus they find it very difficult to commit themselves to others. Left without God, the individual's pursuit of happiness and security is the only source of meaning" (*Holiness and the Spirit of the Age*, 79).

Ultimately, I believe, even child abuse is a sign of the selfishness and disregard for others such thinking encourages. When anyone places his own gratification ahead of everything else, there are no limits to what he or she will do. This is a tragedy. To injure, ignore, disrespect, and violate the innocence of a child are among the greatest evils known to man, but it is no longer uncommon in this society. Jesus said it would be better for a man to be thrown into the sea with a millstone tied around his neck than to face God's wrath for child abuse (Luke 17:2). I wish more people took that threat seriously.

The press has publicized some of the more shocking and graphic aspects of child abuse—especially the physical abuse which makes good headlines—but they have almost entirely ignored the psychological and emotional abuse caused by modern social trends. Today we are experiencing an epidemic of parental neglect, mothers and fathers absent from home, children exploited by advertising and mass media, immature sensibilities bombarded by erotic and vulgar programming specifically aimed at vulnerable young minds, and the encouraging of excessive, even pathological, self-interest and self-absorption. Where are these stories in the secular media?

There is a serious question of exploitation and abuse in the way the media themselves use children. At a time when busy, self-absorbed parents lubricate their consciences by lavishing expensive playthings and electronic components on their children, the media take full advantage of the situation. Advertising exploits children, creating the desire for things children can easily blackmail their parents into buying. Entire ad budgets are built on the strategy that children determine the buying habits of their parents: "If you love me, buy me this."

The Hollow Men

As I suggested earlier, we are not yet free of the legacy of the free-thinking sixties. The spirit of revolt which blossomed in the 1960s, partly as a result of the Vietnam War, convinced a generation that "turning off and spacing out" was a legitimate "lifestyle" option, even a legitimate form of revolution. While the "yuppies" and the "uppies" of the eighties and nineties have plugged back into the cash flow, accumulating possessions and accolades on their way to the top, there is a pervasive sense of coldness, heartlessness, and aloofness in their manner.

Music lyrics and visual imagery are growing increasingly erotic, violent, and anti-social and are the common idiom of youth today. The television and stereo have trespassed the innocence of America's children, while preoccupied mothers and dispassionate fathers stare aghast wondering what went wrong. Rock videos, R-rated movies, and prime-time vulgarity posing as comedy have seared the souls of our children. These electronic babysitters have become violators. America's children are growing up wild and rank like weeds in a moral wasteland.

Fortunately, there are signs of a moral groundswell. Articles and books with the courage to name names and document sources are appearing with greater frequency. David Elkind's *The Hurried Child: Growing Up Too Fast Too Soon* describes the dangers of a culture that places adult responsibilities, rights, desires, and entitlements within the easy grasp of children.

Dr. James Dobson and Gary Bauer's *Children at Risk* describes the moral crisis in this nation in great depth, calling it a civil war of values. Focus on the Family, the Colorado-based ministry headed by Dobson, regularly targets the exploitation and abuse of children. With his co-author, a former Reagan administration adviser, Dobson gives a chilling résumé of the rise of anti-Christian secularism and the value-neutral morality being perpetrated on the family. In a chapter entitled "Love and Sex," Dr. Dobson offers this assessment:

> Robbed of sexual standards, society will unravel like a ball of twine. That is the lesson of history. That is the legacy of Rome and more than two thousand civilizations that have come and gone on this earth. The family is the basic unit of society on which all human activity rests. If you tamper with the sexual nature of familial relationships, you necessarily threaten the entire superstructure. Indeed, ours is swaying like a drunken sailor from the folly of our cultural engineers. (*Children at Risk*, 55.)

It is vitally important that preachers, authors, speakers, commentators, and broadcasters speak out about destructive behaviors and vividly portray the dangers that confront both young and old in our society. The pressure from the other side is so intense, only a mammoth reaction can ever hope to counter the trend. But my greatest fear is that the books and articles and the emotional reactions behind them will pass and nothing much will change for the better for America's children. Four decades of re-programming by permissive educators and social agencies have perverted and corrupted the foundations of moral discipline in this nation. Can such a culture survive, or has the crisis of deception already taken us much too far toward the Apocalypse?

Consider the crises of promiscuity, teen pregnancy, and abortion raging through the land. Consider the growing problems of date rape, drug use, alcoholism, pornography, and sadomasochism even among elementary-age children. I recently read the report of an eleven-year-old boy who was being charged with the sexual abuse and sodomy of a four-year-old girl. He learned about such things through a dial-a-porn number given him by a friend in Sunday school.

I have also heard reliable reports that immorality is as epidemic in our churches as in the secular world at large. One recent poll claimed that 40 percent of the young people in Bible-believing evangelical churches are sexually active. Furthermore, 60 percent of single adults, including those who attend church regularly and participate in Bible studies, are not only sexually active, but half reported having sex with multiple partners. No wonder the world is in crisis. No wonder teenagers are confused. No wonder there is danger in the streets. No wonder gang violence is at an all-time high. No wonder teen suicide has reached epidemic proportions. No wonder the dropout rate in high schools all over America is astronomical. No wonder young adults fail in life and come home to live with mom and dad. No wonder there is nothing for young people to believe in. No wonder the soul of America is in peril. No wonder we fear for tomorrow. Satan, the deceiver and corrupter, is riding roughshod throughout the land.

Who stands for truth? Does anybody care anymore? At the bitter end of an era of liberation—women's lib, kids' lib, animal lib, and everything-but-ethics lib—America has apparently been liberated from its moral foundations. But for too many, the good life has become a living hell.

The Lowest Common Denominator

You cannot watch television or read a newspaper anymore without realizing the dangerous implications of these trends. National newsmagazines have dedicated entire issues to the topics of fear and panic in our neighborhoods. In a May 1992 editorial in *USA Today*, entitled "The Decay of Morality," Gerald F. Kreyche examined the values perpetrated by the popularizers of immorality. He writes:

> Shacking up; having babies out of wedlock, with the man bearing no fiscal or moral responsibilities; single parenthood—all seem almost *de rigueur*. (A recent news report cited the doubling of births by teens during a two-year period. Among black teenage mothers, just one in ten is married. Nationwide, one out of four babies is born to an unwed mother.) Lesbians and gays are unabashed in their relationships. The new head of the National Organization of Women (NOW) admits to having both a husband and a female "companion." Welfare, instead of being a temporary help to overcome a momentary hardship, has become a generations-old "entitlement," making the American "work ethic" a hollow term. Throughout all of this, we are told by society to be tolerant, understanding, accepting, and, above all, nonjudgmental.

Kreyche suggests that any Rip Van Winkle waking up in the 1990s after a long sleep would go into a "value culture shock that would push the needle off the Richter scale." I have to agree. Poll after poll reveals that more than 90 percent of this country claims some kind of moral and ethical value system based on a belief in God, yet those values apparently have little or no influence on their lives. Not only have the Christian roots of this nation been banished from the universities and other institutions, but the Word of God is commonly scorned as misogynous, manipulative, and mythical.

I am grieved to see how some churches have compromised on basic principles. In many cases, they have deserted the truths of Scripture in favor of a lie. But this falling away in our culture and our churches is but another sign that we have entered the "time of troubles" Jesus foretold. He described the coming storm in the parable of the sower, saying that there would be a time when the people would leave the truth and seek after their own lusts. Later, the apostle Paul offered a further glimpse of the Apocalypse in his instructions to young Timothy, when he wrote:

> But know this, that in the last days perilous times will come: for men will be lovers of themselves, lovers of money, boasters, proud, blasphemers, disobedient to parents, unthankful, unholy, unloving, unforgiving, slanderers, without self-control, brutal, despisers of good, traitors, headstrong, haughty, lovers of pleasure rather than lovers of God, having a form of godliness but denying its power. And from such people turn away! For of this sort are those who creep into households and make captives of gullible women loaded down with sins, led away by various lusts, always learning and never able to come to the knowledge of the truth.
>
> 2 Timothy 3:1-7 NKJV

Paul describes desperate times which, even forty years ago, would have seemed impossible and fantastic; yet, this is the world we live in today. How could such times ever come on earth?

For the benefit of Timothy, his disciple, and the church the young pastor was going to lead, Paul's letter told him to live in obedience to the principles he knew to be correct and not to be influenced by the sinful world around him. In his letter to Timothy, Paul said:

> But as for you, continue in the things which you have learned and been assured of, knowing from whom you have learned them, and that from childhood you have known the Holy Scriptures, which are able to make you wise for salvation through faith which is in Christ Jesus.
>
> 2 Timothy 3:14-15 NKJV

Hard times had already come to Christians in the Roman Empire. Persecution and death were common. For the faint-hearted there was greater justification for falling away than there is today, but Paul told Timothy to stand fast. He reminded him that "All Scripture is given by inspiration of God, and is profitable for doctrine, for reproof, for correction, for instruction in righteousness" (2 Timothy 3:16 NKJV). In this statement was the central truth of the authority of God's Word that is often disputed in today's world.

American courts of law have been deprived of much of their authority, both domestic and divine. There is little judgment for crime in our time. By the same token, sinners have denied the authority of the ultimate moral authority, the Bible, in order to condone their sin. But much worse, some men and women in the church who should faithfully uphold the authority of Scripture, instead, defame and deny it. This, too, is the work of the deceiver. The writer of Hebrews warned:

For it is impossible for those who were once enlightened, and have tasted the heavenly gift, and
have become partakers of the Holy Spirit, and have
tasted the good word of God and the powers of the
age to come, if they fall away, to renew them again to
repentance, since they crucify again for themselves
the Son of God, and put Him to an open shame.

Hebrews 6:4-6 NKJV

But we can have new life in Christ, and this is our
greatest need as individuals and as a society. In his letter to the Romans, Paul wrote, "Do not be conformed to
this world, but be transformed by the renewing of your
mind" (Romans 12:2 NKJV). The power of the Holy Spirit
to defeat the natural inclination to sin within us is available to everyone who will accept Christ as Savior and
Lord. Paul also said,

Our old man was crucified with Him, that the body
of sin might be done away with, that we should no
longer be slaves of sin. For he who has died has
been freed from sin. Now if we died with Christ, we
believe that we shall also live with Him, knowing
that Christ, having been raised from the dead, dies
no more. Death no longer has dominion over Him.
For the death that He died, He died to sin once for
all; but the life that He lives, He lives to God.

Romans 6:6-10 NKJV

In the letter to Timothy, the apostle said, "For God has
not given us a spirit of fear, but of power and of love and
of a sound mind" (2 Timothy 1:7 NKJV). So why do we fight
against the God who loves us? Why do so many work so
hard for something they can have so freely? What a tragedy that those who follow modern secular philosophies
choose to turn away from the God of heaven to serve false
and fallible idols in their own flesh.

180

Judgment of the Church

The Bible teaches that there will be false teachers and prophets in the church as the age draws toward its end. As the apostle Peter said,

> But there were also false prophets among the people, even as there will be false teachers among you, who will secretly bring in destructive heresies, even denying the Lord who bought them, and bring on themselves swift destruction. And many will follow their destructive ways, because of whom the way of truth will be blasphemed. By covetousness they will exploit you with deceptive words; for a long time their judgment has not been idle, and their destruction does not slumber.
>
> 2 Peter 2:1-3 NKJV

Satan does not have to build a church and call it The First Church of Satan in order to seduce modern society. He can do better than that. He wants to take charge of our schools and social institutions, the thoughts and attitudes of influential leaders, the media, and the policies of our government.

The apostle Paul warned that many will follow the false teachers, not knowing that in feeding upon what these people say they are taking the devil's poison into their own lives. Thousands of people in every walk of life are being deceived today. False teachers use high-sounding words that seem like the height of logic, scholarship, and sophistication. They are intellectually clever and crafty in their sophistry. They are adept at beguiling men and women whose spiritual foundations are weak.

These false teachers have departed from the faith of God revealed in the Scripture. The Bible states plainly that the reason for their turning away is that they gave heed to Satan's lies and deliberately chose to accept the doctrine of the devil rather than the truth of God. So they themselves became the mouthpieces of Satan.

Writing to Timothy, the apostle Paul warned, "Now the Spirit expressly says that in latter times some will depart from the faith, giving heed to deceiving spirits and doctrines of demons, speaking lies in hypocrisy, having their own conscience seared with a hot iron" (1 Timothy 4:1-2 NKJV).

Paul later wrote to Timothy, "For the time will come when they will not endure sound doctrine, but according to their own desires, because they have itching ears, they will heap up for themselves teachers; and they will turn their ears away from the truth, and be turned aside to fables" (2 Timothy 4:3-4 NKJV). Doesn't this sound familiar today?

Satan is a liar, a deceiver, and a great imitator. As far back as the Garden of Eden, Satan's purpose was not necessarily to make mankind as ungodly as possible but to make it as godlike as possible, but without God. Satan's method has often been to imitate God. The Scripture says, "For Satan himself transforms himself into an angel of light. Therefore it is no great thing if his ministers also transform themselves into ministers of righteousness, whose end will be according to their works" (2 Corinthians 11:14-15 NKJV).

Satan is still using this form of deception, and often his representatives are being disguised as ministers of righteousness. While propagating that which brings death and darkness to the mind and heart of the sinner, they profess to be representatives of enlightened living. This is satanic deception. By the time the storm of spiritual and moral deception unleashed by the first horseman disappears over the horizon, the full power of the antichrist will have come upon the earth, bringing its dreadful curse.

But after this happens in John's Revelation, the horror the world fears more than any other follows: the second horseman, the rider on the red horse who brings war and destruction.

Part 4

The Eye of the Hurricane

11

The Bringer of War

> Then another horse came out, a fiery red one. Its
> rider was given power to take peace from the earth
> and to make men slay each other. To him was given
> a large sword.
>
> Revelation 6:4

Fears of the Apocalypse are as old as civilization. War,
anarchy, brother against brother, neighbor against
neighbor, nation against nation—the complete breakdown
of sane human relationships has characterized human history. Every society since the dawn of time has known
great evil and destruction, but the holocaust to come will
surpass anything the human mind can imagine.

In Revelation 6, John tells of the red horse of the
Apocalypse—the bringer of war. This second horseman
will spark unprecedented violence and storms of destruction until the final hour when the Messiah Himself will
intervene and crush the allies of Satan and the evils of
Armageddon. You recall that Jesus told His disciples: "For
then there will be great tribulation, such as has not been
since the beginning of the world until this time, no, nor
ever shall be. And unless those days were shortened, no
flesh would be saved; but for the elect's sake those days
will be shortened" (Matthew 24:21-22 NKJV).

It would be naive for anyone to ignore the fact that
this ominous rider who brings war is, even now, riding

relentlessly in our direction. Some say the earth has become a global village. We are all neighbors, especially now that the Cold War is over. The West won the war many contend. But we cannot afford to celebrate prematurely; the post-Cold War stockpiles of nuclear weapons still give mankind the power to destroy the earth seventeen times over in flames reaching 130 million degrees. No United Nations resolution, no peacekeeping force, no new world order can stop it when the appointed time arrives. While we all should work and pray for peace, we know that the danger is still great.

Furthermore, the number of aggressive Third World nations with dreams of glory constantly seems to be growing. There are several military dictators who would think nothing of lobbing a nuclear missile into Tel Aviv or Jerusalem if they had the capacity. So long as men live by the laws of self-sufficiency and expediency, there will be tyrants who can bring calamity upon the world.

In these tempestuous times, no one can speak of war with confident detachment. Each of us has a vision of nuclear destruction etched permanently in our mind. Before the final days of World War II, wars were more or less limited to battlefields and sea lanes. Supplies were transported over vast distances. Oceans, mountainous terrain, snow-covered highways, arid deserts, and fast-moving rivers all created natural barriers to limit war and give combatants at least the illusion of distance and safety. Especially for North Americans, wars have been something fought "over there" or "overseas."

But the warning bell that rang in the newsroom of the Japanese Broadcasting Corporation at 8:45 on the morning of August 6, 1945, signaled an alert that changed all that. The announcer rushed in to read the bulletin he had just received from the Chugoku District Army Headquarters:

"Three enemy aircraft have been spotted over the Saijo area," he said. Suddenly there was a blinding blue flash of light over Hiroshima . . . and a moment of absolute unearthly silence. In the wake of the mind-boggling eruption that followed, an ominous mushroom cloud of boiling gases rose above the incinerated mass where a city once stood. This was to be the symbol of a new era for the decades to follow.

The newsman was vaporized and the entire radio station with him. The consecutive bombings of Hiroshima and Nagasaki had the intended effect: They brought an abrupt end to that terrible war, but they also changed the course of history and taught the entire world the new dangers of war. In the aftermath of those deadly events, we sometimes forget that the nuclear bombing of Japan also saved lives. Many Japanese leaders today, even in those two cities, will tell you that the bombs probably saved millions of Japanese as well as Allied lives; for had the war not ended then, abruptly, the Japanese would certainly have fought to their last breath to protect their homeland. But the cities of Hiroshima and Nagasaki have become part of the new definition of war for all time to come.

The trouble is, too many of us who were not alive that day stubbornly refuse to change our antiquated definitions of war. We refuse to believe the truth about the horrible power we have unleashed. We prefer to remain in a fool's paradise: War is something that happens somewhere else.

Historians tell us that the world has seen more than four thousand wars during the last five thousand years, most of them lasting for years at a time. Some, like the Thirty Years War in Europe, lasted for decades and drained the lifeblood and the youth of a dozen nations. We know that more than 60 million people died in the two world wars of the first half of this century.

Since the harrowing moments of the arms buildup of the 1960s and 1970s—in the anxious days of the East-West nuclear arms confrontation—we understand the potential for political intimidation. Each side imagines the other more powerful than itself, and each demands ever more powerful and inhuman weapons. In the Persian Gulf War we saw the incredible accuracy and destructiveness of modern conventional firepower; we can only begin to imagine what all-out thermonuclear war would unleash.

Almost any petty tyrant can become a nuclear or bio-chemical bully in the present world situation. Even though the total devastation of nuclear war should make such a prospect unthinkable, unpredictable hotheads such as Saddam Hussein or Mohamar Qaddafi could rock the world with a surprise attack. The change from conventional to nuclear and biochemical weapons has made the task of international diplomacy immensely more complicated.

The Madness of War

The very existence of nuclear armaments has changed the character of conflict. War is not what it used to be. Author and researcher George Segal wrote, "The fundamental change was that whereas previous wars could be conceived of as useful instruments of policy, a nuclear war would only result in the death of the planet. We would be left with a 'republic of insects'" (*World Affairs Companion*, 90).

When it became clear that even simple nuclear weapons possessed the capacity to annihilate everything in their killing zone, war strategy had to change. Stealth and craftiness were added. To the world's arsenal of intercontinental ballistic missiles, submarine-launched warheads, silo-based missiles, and even satellite-launched weaponry, we suddenly found nuclear missiles hidden on constantly moving, subterranean railroad cars. With all this motion and commotion, the threat of massive destruction was greatly increased. In fact, most analysts said that total destruction was "assured," and the acronym of the 1970s became MAD, Mutually Assured Destruction.

All about us today there are wars and rumors of wars. In addition to the recent war in the Persian Gulf, there are more than forty wars raging in the world at this moment.

It is mind-boggling to think that as many as fifteen nations (or more) now have nuclear technologies of one kind or another, and more than half of those possess nuclear armaments. Despite the loudly proclaimed end of the Cold War, as many as twenty-five nations are scrambling to join the nuclear fraternity. If we add all the nuclear weapons stockpiled by the former Soviet Union, the United States, Great Britain, France, India, Israel, China, and other smaller nations, then we get an idea of the massive destructive potential the nations of the world now possess.

One thing becomes clearer with each passing day: War is no longer something that is necessarily limited to "over there." The rider of the red horse has closed the distance. The red horse's hoofbeats bring a deafening sound of war up and down the streets of our hometowns. The winds of war may have subsided, but the storm is not out of sight. We cannot yet put away the warning flags.

By nature we all want peace. Our leaders promise peace, but the best peace has never been more than a restless calm. The world is in such desperate chaos so much of the time, I have to wonder, is peace just an illusion? Does the current calm indicate imminent peace or perhaps a storm more dreadful than we could ever imagine? I cannot help but believe that today we are in the eye of the hurricane and that the breathless vacuum since the fall of Communism and the collapse of the Soviet Union could

189

be but a fragile pause before a more sinister storm. It is a feeling I cannot deny, but I pray that it will not be so.

A Reasonable Hope

For centuries legislatures and parliaments have attempted to keep the peace. In times past, mighty leaders such as Caesar, Constantine, Charlemagne, Napoleon, the czars of the East, and the kings of the West each, in turn, promised lasting peace. But they all failed. Today bold schemes for global unity and brotherhood are being proclaimed in Brussels, New York, Geneva, Tokyo, and Washington, D.C. Yet there is no universal peace, and the world is growing weary of empty promises.

As we witness the various events unfolding in Eastern Europe, Latin America, the Middle East, and here in the United States, there is cause for optimism. From many perspectives we seem to have entered a period of calm. But there are many reasons to remain on our guard.

The world economy is in serious trouble, and the federal deficit is terrifying. In 1992, the United States government faced a $400 billion debt it has virtually no prospect of paying or even paying down. Rising debt is a serious problem both for families and corporations. Growing crime and violence make even clean, well-lighted places unsafe in the middle of the day. In addition, we have an ongoing disintegration of morals, collapse of the family and traditional family values, and increasing prejudice against religious expression by a growing number of secular organizations. Most observers today believe that America is living in a post-Christian era.

How does the situation of the world today accord with God's plan for peace on earth? I have to ask again, as I did at the very beginning, will there ever be peace on earth, or is peace an illusion? Will the impending storm destroy the world?

Before answering that question we need to stop and consider for a moment something that is easy to forget in our contemplation of the terror of a nuclear war. We forget the infinitely greater horror of an eternity apart from God. The horrors of a nuclear war will be transitory as far as eternity is concerned. The horrors that are ahead for all who reject God's offer of mercy, grace, and salvation in Christ are too terrible to imagine.

Remember that moment just before Jesus' betrayal and crucifixion? As Christ was walking away from the temple in Jerusalem, He spoke this warning: "You will hear of wars and rumors of wars, but see to it that you are not alarmed. Such things must happen, but the end is still to come. Nation will rise against nation, and kingdom against kingdom" (Matthew 24:6-7).

Even while He was uttering these words, the most hideous and horrendous deed of all time and eternity was about to be carried out: Men were about to crucify the Prince of Peace. However, it is important for us to remember that though Christ warned us there would constantly be wars and rumors of war, it does not follow that we should sit by silently while the peoples of the world destroy each other. We must not allow our silence to give approval to such devastation with weapons of mass destruction. We must warn the nations of the world that they must repent and turn to God while there is yet time. We must also proclaim that there is forgiveness and peace in knowing Jesus Christ as Savior and Lord.

An End to Evil

We have to ask ourselves: Is this the end times that the Bible describes so graphically? Is this the final storm that will sweep away everything in its path? The Scriptures definitely teach that there will be an end to human history as we know it, and most biblical scholars believe that it is coming soon. It will not be the end of the world, but it will be the end of the present world system that has been dominated by evil.

The Bible teaches that Satan is actually "the prince of this world" (John 12:31) and "the ruler of the kingdom of the air, the spirit who is now at work in those who are disobedient" (Ephesians 2:2). As long as he is still at large, in constant conflict with God and pursuing his deadly plan, be assured that wars will continue and death and disaster will multiply. Without God there will be no hope for humanity.

The Scripture also shows that a number of easily discernible signs will occur as we approach the end of the age. These signs seem to be coming into focus even now. Jesus said in Matthew 24 that there would be famines, pestilences, and earthquakes, but He also said that these would only be the beginning. He said that people "will betray and hate each other, and many false prophets will appear and deceive many people. Because of the increase of wickedness, the love of most will grow cold" (Matthew 24:10-12). But He added, "This gospel of the kingdom will be preached in the whole world as a testimony to all nations, and then the end will come" (Matthew 24:14). In this sign alone we see the possibility of reaching the entire world with the gospel through revolutionary new technologies before the end of this century. This will be an unprecedented opportunity that could never before have come about, but it is a very real possibility today.

During our London Crusade in 1989 we were able to reach 230 cities throughout Britain and 33 African nations by live satellite during prime-time viewing hours. We have even larger plans for the future. In 1993, during our all-European crusade from Essen, Germany, we plan to install a satellite setup that will enable us to reach all of Europe. No one evangelist or ministry can fulfill Christ's prophecy alone—that is not our intent, and I would never make a pretense of attempting to do so—but every outreach, every good work, every time the gospel is presented and every broadcast that carries the good news of Christ to another lost soul is a fulfillment of Christ's promise. That is the work I rejoice in doing.

The Coming of the Beast

Another major sign that Christ foretold was the steadily increasing intensity of warfare. Some people would quickly point out that the world of the 1990s seems to be growing calmer, not more dangerous. I would quickly caution that we do not yet know what to make of the political changes of the last few years. Nothing is certain, and there is a great potential for chaos, collapse, and war. Already we are seeing signs of this in Yugoslavia and elsewhere. We know that there is always calm before the storm. We cannot yet rule out the likelihood that this is indeed what we are experiencing at this moment.

Nevertheless, Daniel, whom Jesus quoted concerning the final age, prophesied: "And the people of the prince who is to come shall destroy the city and the sanctuary. The end of it shall be with a flood, and till the end of the war desolations are determined" (Daniel 9:26 NKJV).

Revelation 11, 13, and 16 detail the devastations to come. In chapter 11, John describes the coming of the antichrist, saying, "the beast that ascends out of the bottomless pit will make war against them, overcome them, and kill them. And their dead bodies will lie in the street of the great city which spiritually is called Sodom and Egypt, where also our Lord was crucified" (Revelation 11:7-8 NKJV). The people of the world will cry out in awe and wonder, "'Who is like the beast? Who is able to make war with him?'" (Revelation 13:4 NKJV). Ultimately, no one will stand against the beast.

Jesus indicated that there would be many wars, perhaps thousands, before the last great war and before His return. In the context of the increasing intensity of warfare, He said, "See that you are not troubled; for all these things must come to pass, but the end is not yet" (Matthew 24:6 NKJV). For nearly two thousand years since He spoke those words there have been alternating cycles of war and peace—wars big and small, domestic and foreign. But modern technology has dramatically changed the rules of the game. The war to come will likely be a single world war in which the triple terror of nuclear, biological, and chemical weapons will be used in the utter destruction of the world.

Jesus indicated that when such a war does come to pass, "If those days had not been cut short, no one would survive" (Matthew 24:22). This means total war, with the annihilation of all humanity as a probable outcome, barring divine intervention. Never before has total cosmocide—meaning the destruction of the entire planet—been at our fingertips. There are no precedents in political science or human history to guide the people who command such power. The world has been at war since the time of Adam, but never on the scale that Jesus predicted in Matthew 24 and Revelation 6. Never before has the world had the potential to obliterate the entire human race.

This is the situation and these are quite possibly the weapons of the second horseman of Revelation 6. In verse 4 we see that he has the power to take peace from the earth. This surely means world war, not just civil wars or even conventional conflicts. At this moment, the political and military polarization seems to have vanished, but we must not presume on the future.

Power blocs in Europe, Asia, and North America are already being formed that could eventually clash over economic and trade issues, over immigration and population, or in some other scenario that might lead to the most devastating war in human history. Whatever the provocation, and whoever the participants may be, it will be a war so intense and destructive that, unless God intervenes miraculously to stop it, all of humanity will die.

How many will die? Albert Einstein predicted that a full-scale nuclear exchange would incinerate at least a third of the world's population. This is the same proportion the Bible indicates: "'One-third of you shall die of the pestilence, and be consumed with famine in your midst; and one-third shall fall by the sword all around you; and I will scatter another third to all the winds, and I will draw out a sword after them'" (Ezekiel 5:12 NKJV).

Is it possible that we could have even a century of peace, or possibly more? Yes. War is not inevitable. If the human race would turn from its evil ways and return to God, putting behind its sins of disobedience, idolatry, pride, greed, and belligerence, and all the various aberrations that lead to war, the possibility of peace does exist. But when we see the way things are in our society, with all the anger and violence around us, who can anticipate such a transformation? To turn away from its habits of vice and animosity, the world would need to come to God through humility and repentance, on a global scale. Can that really happen?

Yes, I still believe that there is hope. The world, however, has never known total peace. We may know peace for a generation perhaps, but through sin and through the work of Satan in our world, we are incapable of living in lasting peace. Think of the innumerable crises that confront us: recession, economic collapse, AIDS, drug abuse, violent crime, and racism. The human heart without God is depraved, and the deceiver exploits our weaknesses to his own ends. Already storm clouds are gathering. When they unleash their fury, nothing will stand in their way.

Unreasonable Fears?

I was interviewed in 1986 in Paris by a very agitated reporter for the French newspaper, *Le Figaro*. He was confused by my use of the terms "Revelation" and "Apocalypse" interchangeably in my sermons. I tried to clarify that, while one is an English word and the other is Greek, both words mean the same thing. He couldn't grasp that fact but asked, "Do you think it is a useful and Christian thing to frighten the people with such things?" I replied, "Have you read the front page of *Le Figaro* lately? Every day your own headlines frighten the people with news of murder, disease, scandal, and corruption. Most of the world lives in a constant state of fear." The reporter interrupted me and said, "But those are daily things. Apocalypse is not a daily thing! I think you just want to frighten the people."

I understood what this man was saying, but it was obvious that to him the teachings of the Book of Revelation were only myths and fairy tales. He did not consider them the revelations of God concerning a very real and imminent end of civilization. So I said to him, "Sometimes it is my responsibility and my duty as a minister of the gospel to frighten people. I tell my children, 'Be careful when you cross the street, you could be hit by a car.' That is a legitimate fear. My wife and I live in the mountains of North Carolina, and we sometimes see poisonous snakes. I tell my children, 'Be careful where you walk; watch out for snakes!' That is also a legitimate fear. We have been told by God, 'If you sin against Me and break My commandments,

I will bring judgment upon the world.' That is also a legitimate fear, and if we don't listen to those warnings, we are living in great danger."

The Bible says that, "The fear of the LORD is the beginning of wisdom" (Psalm 111:10). We don't fear Him as a tyrant but as a loving and just Father who leads us in wisdom and truth to do what is good for us, what will prolong and preserve our lives. But since God is a just Father, we know He will discipline and punish us when we defy Him and break His rules. If we break those rules often enough and carelessly enough, He will take our privileges away completely. That is the risk this world faces even now. That is the message I must deliver.

As the Book of Exodus records, God sent plague after plague upon Pharaoh and the ancient Egyptians so His people would be freed from the slavery they had suffered for four hundred years. After a plague, Pharaoh would make promises that he did not keep. The Bible says, "Pharaoh's heart grew hard, and he did not heed them, just as the LORD had said" (Exodus 8:19 NKJV).

In Revelation we see a parallel situation from the end times, when God has warned His people and pleaded with them to obey and put away their idolatry, but they will not keep their promises. John writes, "But the rest of mankind, who were not killed by these plagues, did not repent of the works of their hands, that they should not worship demons, and idols of gold, silver, brass, stone, and wood, which can neither see nor hear nor walk; and they did not repent of their murders or their sorceries or their sexual immorality or their thefts" (Revelation 9:20-21 NKJV).

The grace, mercy, and goodness of God did not lead the people to repentance. They presumed upon His long-suffering, His negligence, or His powerlessness. But in both stories, the result is swift and ruthless judgment.

Today our promises of faithfulness to God's commandments have not led the nations to repentance. I have been preaching repentance for fifty years; there are thousands of ministers of the gospel all over this planet preaching repentance at this very hour; for two thousand years prophets, priests, preachers, and evangelists have been calling the world back to the righteousness of God, and most of the time the world has laughed in the face of the King of kings. Today men and women are still trying to ignore the very clear warnings of the approaching storm.

Recognizing Our Options

Apart from God, our hearts grow cold and unrepentant. What will it take to bring the world around to the Lord? If we do not succeed in helping the world to find repentance and renewal, the doom of this planet is ordained and irreversible. The second horseman of the Apocalypse will teach humanity its responsibility before our Creator God through the horror of a dreadful global war.

This brings us back to the question: Is there anything that we can do about war? Yes, as Christians we have a responsibility to seek peace and to make peace whenever and wherever we can. Jesus said, "Blessed are the peacemakers, for they shall be called sons of God" (Matthew 5:9 NKJV). We have been commanded by our Lord and Savior to work for a just peace on this earth. When the angels announced the birth of Jesus, they sang, "'Glory to God in the highest, And on earth peace, goodwill toward men!'" (Luke 2:14 NKJV). Just as the rider on the red horse comes into this world bringing war, Christ came bringing peace.

There are nonetheless disturbing passages in the New Testament regarding peace, such as these words of Jesus to His disciples recorded in Matthew:

> Do not think that I came to bring peace on earth. I did not come to bring peace but a sword. For I have come to "set a man against his father, a daughter against her mother, and a daughter-in-law against her mother-in-law"; and "a man's enemies will be those of his own household." He who loves father or mother more than Me is not worthy of Me. And he who loves son or daughter more than Me is not worthy of Me. And he who does not take his cross and follow after Me is not worthy of Me. He who finds his life will lose it, and he who loses his life for My sake will find it.
>
> Matthew 10:34-39 NKJV

While Jesus may not be talking specifically about armed conflict as I have described it, He is nevertheless talking about the spiritual warfare that follows both the hearing and the acceptance of the gospel. John Wesley interpreted this type of "sword" to be that of love, with the sense that Jesus came to spread love on the earth, and this love divides people. Some in the same home can be believers and some nonbelievers. This often generates friction, misunderstanding, and even division. But whether or not this is Christ's primary meaning in the passage, the gospel is always capable of unifying and dividing.

Peace with God, the peace of God, and peace between nations is possible if we repent of our sins, listen to Him, believe in Him, and follow Him. As servants, followers, brothers, and sisters of the Savior, we are commanded to be His allies in the cause of the true and lasting peace that He can bring. Nowhere does He promise that we will succeed apart from Him, but He calls us to try as best we can to confront the issues of war and peace and to work for peace in spite of seemingly insurmountable odds. Once again we are confronted by the mystery of God's sovereignty and our free will. We are to expect the coming of

Christ at any time, but we are to work as if He were not to come for a thousand years.

Understanding the consequence of sin and arrogance, I believe it should be the duty of every Christian to pray for repentance and revival in the land. We must do the work of believers, as Paul instructed, but we must also seek the face of God as never before. I believe it is time we led the world to pray.

In that regard, the National Day of Prayer organized in the spring of 1992 by Shirley Dobson and Vonette Bright was a remarkable event. Thanks to a lot of preparation and publicity, more than twenty-five hundred communities all across America held prayer vigils on the steps of their city and town hall buildings. Some five hundred diplomats and Christian leaders met in Washington, D.C. to pray for the youth of America and for a revival of Christian values. I believe this is the kind of commitment we must make in order to turn things around. As a people and a nation, we must come in honest and humble supplication before God before the storm carries us away.

According to a report in the *National and International Religion Report* (18 May 1992), more than 180 teenagers gathered in Spokane, Washington, to pray for solutions to the problems of drugs, violence, and promiscuity in the schools. In Atlanta, church members from all over Fulton County met on the steps of the state capitol to pray. In Houston, twenty-five hundred teens met for a concert of prayer at the city's coliseum. In Klamath Falls, Oregon, citizens prayed from dusk to dawn in a city park. This special day of prayer, decreed by President Bush, was a wonderful outpouring of God's Spirit, and this is precisely the kind of fervor and dedication that it will take, on a nationwide scale, to bring about change and revival in our land.

Unless we succeed in prevailing upon the mercies of God and gaining His clemency, I fear that the destiny of our civilization is already sealed. The second horseman of the Apocalypse sits high in the saddle, brandishing the sword of destruction in ever-widening arcs. Only God can intervene on our behalf. We must pray for peace because prayer is the most powerful weapon we have in our spiritual arsenal to bring an end to the threat of worldwide disaster and to bring about God's plans for His creation.

The Prince of Peace desires that we face the issue of disintegration and hostility in our world. Racism, hatred, economic imbalance, and a hundred other issues are raging out of control. The Scripture, however, commands us to wait with great anticipation upon the coming of the Lord; He alone will bring full and lasting peace. In the meantime, we are to work for peace and harmony among the nations of the earth and to love our neighbors even as we love ourselves.

God spared Nineveh for 150 years when the people of that ancient land repented under the preaching of Jonah; He may also give us peace if we turn to Him in true repentance! This is the only hope for today. We must repent of our wickedness and seek the mercy of God. We must now look into the prophecies concerning the next two seals: the black horse of famine and the pale horse of death.

12

Famine in the Land

I looked, and there before me was a black horse! Its
rider was holding a pair of scales in his hand. Then
I heard what sounded like a voice among the four
living creatures, saying, "A quart of wheat for a
day's wages, and three quarts of barley for a day's
wages, and do not damage the oil and the wine!"

Revelation 6:5-6

The image is stark but all too familiar: "Here they come:
the stick children with the flat, unseeing stares. Their
knee sockets are so large, and their calves are so thin that
you wonder how they manage to walk. They are too weak
to sweep away the flies that have settled on their mouths
and nostrils. They can only hold their bowls out toward
the television cameras." The scene being described is not
from Bangladesh in the 1970s or Ethiopia in the 1980s
but from East Africa today. Michael Ignatieff's article in
World Press Report, entitled "The Four Horsemen Are
Here to Stay," describes the dire tragedy of war, drought,
and starvation in East Africa: "Famine has come to Africa.
Again. Twenty-six million people are at risk in Sudan,
Ethiopia, Somalia, Malawi, Angola, and Mozambique. In all
those places where civil war conspires with drought in
wiping out the human race."

In this last phrase, Ignatieff echoes the portrait given
of the third horseman of John's revelation, riding the black

horse of famine, as he surges forth to unleash the fury of death by hunger upon the earth. This specter of starvation is perhaps the most ominous and recurrent fear known to humanity. It represents our helplessness and inability to cope with the forces of nature and the utter barrenness of life when the only alternative is hunger and death.

The black horse that appears before John in Revelation is ridden by a horseman holding a pair of scales in his hand. For an instant the rider stops the horse, restraining his mount in front of the prophet. While the animal stamps and snorts nervously, the rider holds the balance above his head, and a voice cries out from among the four apocalyptical beings, "A quart of wheat for a denarius, and three quarts of barley for a denarius; and do not harm the oil and the wine" (Revelation 6:6 NKJV).

In John's time a denarius was a day's wages. It amounted to perhaps twenty cents in our modern currency, and it would buy a quart of wheat or corn, from which a worker and his family could make a single meal. In those days barley was a cheaper grain, generally used for horses and cattle, but in times of famine it would be used for food. Three quarts of barley would be enough for a full day's meals. In the time of Christ, a denarius would purchase about twenty-four quarts of barley, but in John's vision the same amount buys only three quarts.

So when John hears the second cry, "three quarts of barley for a denarius," he realizes that the speaker is describing the hyperinflation that would naturally accompany a crippling famine. The value of money will be one-eighth, or just 12 percent, of its former value. In today's terms, that would be like a worker with an income of $20,000 suddenly earning just $2,400 a year. The loss will be shocking. Curiously, a recent news story from famine-ridden Mozambique included this comment: "The problem is that money has no value here anymore. How would you like to make half what you earned twelve years ago and you still can't supply the basic needs of your family?"

Holding up his scale to weigh the tiny amount of grain that will be available to the average worker, the rider on the black horse is a symbol of just such a desperate plight in the world. Through this rider, the Scripture indicates that deception, false religions, and apostasy lead to war, and that war in turn leads to famine and pestilence. Following the destruction wrought by the riders of the white and red horses, famine will engulf the earth. Millions will die of hunger and millions more will suffer malnutrition. With malnutrition comes disease, mental and emotional deterioration, despair, and death. The black horse and its rider are God's warning of the human suffering that lies ahead if we refuse to obey His commandments, humble ourselves before heaven, and pray for forgiveness and renewal.

Dissipation Amid Despair

The voice that had cried out with the appearance of the third horseman gave another command, "do not damage the oil and the wine!" (Revelation 6:6). Since ancient times oil and wine were associated with wealth and plenty, and perhaps this is a picture of famine coexisting with luxury. Jesus told Peter, Andrew, James, and John that prior to His return famine would stalk the earth and starve whole nations in various parts of the world (Matthew 24:7; Mark 13:8; Luke 21:11). But He also characterized those with power as eating and drinking, apparently to great excess. John later prophesied that there would be societies in the last times living in Babylonian splendor, living out the lifestyle of the rich and famous.

The reports of the famine in Africa and Asia contrast starkly with the image of overfed North Americans and

Europeans who are, almost without exception, living in luxury while the world starves. I saw an article characterize the self-indulgence around us by assessing that Americans weigh a billion pounds too much. We spend an annual $15 billion on diet formulas and $22 billion on cosmetics. Those expenditures alone would make the difference between life and death for the people of the world who are dying of starvation at this moment.

Many of the articles and television reports concerning the famine in Africa comment on the lack of public response. Some national news editors insist that the world is weary of hearing about starving Africans. They say, "Don't show us any more pictures of starving children. We don't want to know." But there is something terribly wrong when those who have so much are indifferent to those who have so little. This is a sign that Western society is hastening to its ruin, and this is the message of the rider on the black horse. The third horseman of the Apocalypse will herald the most exaggerated inequities in the long history of men and women on the earth. Millions live in splendor while millions more perish.

One of the great problems of this present age is that there is scarcity in the midst of plenty throughout the world. This is a crisis that will increase drastically as we approach the end of the age. It is a social maladjustment, a monstrous inequity on a worldwide scale. If the nations do not turn to God, the black horse and its rider will complete this work sooner. The storm of God's outrage will descend upon us, and the whole human race will suffer the consequences.

The world community is also wrestling at this moment with crop failures and food shortages. It is not simply a matter of the total quantity of food, but a problem of distribution in most places. Dishonesty among relief organizations, local government officials, and even the victims themselves complicates the problem of getting help to those who desperately need it.

Only a few countries in the world annually produce more wheat than they consume, including the United States, Australia, and Canada. Some of the members of the former Soviet Union (now known as the Commonwealth of Independent States, or CIS) have the potential to produce more than any other nation. But because of adverse weather, inefficiency, and the difficulties of reorganization after the events of 1991, farm regions such as the Ukraine and others may be lucky to get one good crop every four or five years.

Ironically, I remember a strident editorial in a Chicago newspaper just a few years ago that boasted, "By modern methods of agriculture we have solved the question of famine. We can produce any amount of grain we decide to produce. Science has triumphed over the constant dread of less enlightened communities." Not only was this newspaperman's assertion premature and contrary to fact, it also contradicted the predictions of the Bible. The Scriptures teach that famine and pestilence will continue and intensify until Christ returns as Prince of peace and Ruler of the world.

The Starvation Chronicles

No one really knows how many people die of starvation each year. Many underdeveloped countries keep irregular and often unreliable statistics, particularly concerning the deaths of infants and children. In addition, in regions where famine exists, people frequently die not from starvation directly but from indirect causes, such as illnesses and acute physical conditions that overcome people whose resistance has been lowered by malnutrition. Such deaths are sometimes not reported by family members; victims of disease may be reported to have died from unknown or natural causes.

Furthermore, there is a sociological and psychological component to famine and disease reporting. Bureaucrats and officials of many small governments simply do not report such disasters completely for fear that news of widespread deaths will damage business, trade, tourism, confidence, and other intangible factors. In reality, the death toll from such crises as famine, pestilence, disease, and epidemics of any kind is almost always much greater than the numbers reported.

Some years ago the Mennonite Central Committee reported that an estimated 12 million newborn infants die of the effects of malnutrition every year in the developing countries. The World Bank reports, "half of the people in absolute poverty live in South Asia, mainly in India and Bangladesh. A sixth live in East and Southeast Asia. Another sixth are in sub-Saharan Africa. The rest are divided among Latin America, North Africa and the Middle East." In these Southern Hemisphere and tropical regions that we now commonly refer to as the Third World, the United Nations estimates that at least 100 million children go to bed every night hungry.

The Effect of Population

During this decade, the population of the earth continues to grow at the staggering rate of about 100 million births per year. In an address on the campus of Indiana University at South Bend, Michael Marien, editor of *Future Survey*, reviewed the population dilemma facing the world. In 1930, he reported, there were approximately 2 billion people on this planet; by 1975 the number had doubled to 4 billion. By 1992 the total was 5.5 billion, and calculations suggest the number will exceed 6 billion in 1998. At that rate, we will pass the 8 billion mark by the year 2019. The bulk of this population growth will be in the Third World countries—the nations that are least able to meet the demand for food such growth would entail.

By 2020, Marien estimated, there will be 50 percent more people on this planet than there are today. In his remarks, the futurist ominously observed that these extrapolated numbers would only be lowered by war, famine, AIDS, or some kind of breakthrough in birth control technology. "Unfortunately," he added, "war, famine, and millions of deaths from AIDS are likely; major birth control advances are not."

Obviously in East Africa these potential problems have already become a dreadful reality. Drought, starvation, warfare, pestilence, and disaster are raging across the land, complicated by an uncontrollable and escalating AIDS epidemic. Most authorities believe that the current famine is the worst of the twentieth century. One front-page story in the *New York Times* called it "the worst drought in living memory." Subsequently a U.S. Agency for International Development communiqué reported that by January 1992 the drought in East Africa had "obliterated all hopes of successful yields this season." There is nothing left to eat.

From Somalia and Ethiopia in the horn of Africa to the Cape of Good Hope in the south, the entire east coast of the African continent has been devastated. The disaster has already surpassed the Ethiopian famine of the 1980s which left so many heartbreaking images in our minds. Relief workers estimate that, short of a miracle, 26 million people will starve to death.

Plague of Violence

Violence is a major secondary problem growing out of short supplies, hunger, and mounting anger. Lagos, Nigeria, on the west coast of Africa has been turned into an armed camp. Some reports say that rioting and looting there is largely uncontrolled. Mozambique, the worst hit in 1992 by the famine, is also suffering from more than a million violent deaths since 1976. Of its population of 15 million, 1.8 million people now depend on food supplied by overseas relief agencies . . . when they can get it.

Of the forty lesser-developed countries (LDCs) in the world, twenty-eight are in Africa. The complexity of the social and political problems in these countries has led to a situation that may be too big to solve under current conditions. International affairs specialist George Segal says, "with all the goodwill in the world, the root of the food problem lies beyond the reach of international agencies." Lagging food production, ineffective communications, plus the need for trade stimulation, revitalized market strategies, and land reform have made the mounting problems in the poor nations a pernicious and seemingly insoluble enigma.

Perhaps the classic example of effective foreign aid was the United States' Marshall Plan, which pumped $14 billion into Europe for four years at the end of World War II. By 1956, European productivity was 38 percent higher than in 1938 when the first signs of war appeared. Such an effort might indeed make a difference on the continent of Africa, but the $220 million appropriated by the U.S. Congress for disaster relief in East Africa will hardly make a dent in this crisis.

Compounding the disaster, many are reluctant to send money or food. The news reports call it a serious problem of "donor reluctance," or "donor fatigue," not only because of the uncontrolled violence, but also widespread corruption among the so-called Crocodile Rulers and bureaucrats. Money is consumed voraciously, especially in

Mozambique, where the government levies a surcharge of $150 per ton of food transported to its remote villages.

New York Times foreign affairs correspondent Leslie Gelb reported in May 1992 that poor countries annually spend twice as much on arms and soldiers as they receive in aid from all sources. The combined total surpasses $175 billion per year. War, famine, and unstable conditions have made most LDCs such bad credit risks, however, that the World Bank, the International Monetary Fund, and other traditional lenders will not extend loans to them. Gelb says that their only source of capital for arms and military budgets is increased taxation and withholding wages and benefits from their own citizens.

It is clear how such policies would intensify the health and welfare problems of these countries. The operating director of the World Food Program has said, "I'm afraid I foresee deaths in very large numbers." The numbers are already staggering. He added, "We can't reach large numbers of the population. If we can provide for half of these people, we will be doing very well." Many are already forced to subsist on roots and tubers. One elderly farmer told an interviewer, "When the donors come they don't understand why we are still alive."

These are all horrifying stories, but the problem of hunger and malnutrition is not limited to developing countries. Recently the Congressional Office of the Budget announced that many of America's children, too, suffer from malnutrition. Millions in North America live below the poverty line. Of course the poverty line here is very high compared to the developing nations, and what would be considered poor in America would be considered wealthy in many countries of the Third World. If you have a pair of shoes, or fresh water, or food, you would be considered rich in many places in the world today.

Suffer the Children

Remember that moment two thousand years ago when Jesus interrupted an important teaching seminar with His disciples? Perhaps the neighborhood children of Capernaum had interrupted Jesus' session with a loud game of tag. Perhaps they were playing nearby when a ball or a toy landed at Jesus' feet and the children burst in to retrieve it. Whatever happened, Jesus stopped His teaching, took the children in His arms, and said to the assembled throng, "But if anyone causes one of these little ones who believe in me to sin, it would be better for him to have a large millstone hung around his neck and to be drowned in the depths of the sea" (Matthew 18:6).

Just preceding that ancient biblical account is another deeply moving story which illustrates Jesus' compassion for children. A distressed father rushed into Jesus' presence begging Him to heal his mentally ill son. "I brought him to your disciples," he cried, "but they could not heal him" (Matthew 17:16). I imagine Jesus' eyes flashed as He turned to His disciples and said: "O unbelieving and perverse generation, . . . how long shall I stay with you? How long shall I put up with you? Bring the boy here to me" (Matthew 17:17). Jesus cast out the child's demon, and the child was cured.

The distressed parents of millions of children hold up the bodies of their dying infants to us who are Christians. We have the wherewithal to make a big dent in this problem, but we are not doing nearly enough. Jesus turns to us and says, "O unbelieving and perverse generation, how long shall I put up with you?" That is the message of the rider on the black horse who brings famine and pestilence. This is also the warning we must heed before we are judged guilty of neglecting so many hurting children.

We should repent of our neglect, ask God's forgiveness, and do what we can. We can't do it all, but we can do something! Both by His actions and by His command, Christ calls us to do all we can to heal the sick, feed the hungry, and help those who are suffering. Christ's great mission was to bring redemption to humanity through His death on the cross, and when He faced the cross He could say that He had finished the work His Father had given Him to do (John 17:4). But that did not mean He neglected the suffering and hunger of those around Him, quite the opposite. So you and I are called not only to proclaim the good news of Christ's salvation but to demonstrate His love for those who are yet in need.

An Ounce of Prevention

It is difficult to imagine the vast difference between health care in Western nations and in the least-developed countries. I have seen statistics which state that in Europe and North America there is one doctor for every 572 people. In East Asia there is one doctor for every 2,106 people. In Southeast Asia there is one for every 14,956 people. In East Africa, where such great suffering is found today, there is only one doctor for every 17,480 people! The shortage of nurses and midwives is similarly grim. In Europe and North America there is a nurse for every 194 people. In Central America there is one nurse for every 1,245 people, and in South Central Asia there is just one nurse for every 4,031 people.

Incomparably more vital than curing the sick is the prevention of illness. This is often primarily a nutrition concern. One child in three (of those who survive birth) in the poor countries is unhealthy because of inadequate nutrition. Every time we eat a balanced meal we should pause, not only to thank God for the food before us, but to pray for those starving children, and to ask God to show us how we can help feed even a few of the hundreds of millions of the starving children who have never once eaten a nutritious meal in their entire lifetime.

I was shocked by the findings of the Lausanne Committee for World Evangelization concerning children-at-risk (reported in the 1991-92 edition of the *Almanac of the Christian World*). According to Lausanne director Tom Houston, 250,000 children will go blind this year for lack of a ten-cent vitamin capsule or a handful of greens each day. Another 230,000 children will contract polio for want of immunization. More than 14 million children will die of common illnesses and malnutrition, and 100 million children living on the streets of cities will be drawn into crime, prostitution, and other forms of corruption. How much more urgent can anyone make the appeal to help?

I would counsel those who are young and looking for a purpose in life to consider the world's children. You who are older and looking for a way to serve out your retirement years, why not dream big dreams? I cannot tell you how you can best assist in helping to feed the hungry children of the world, but there is someone out there who can direct you. Pray for guidance. Call your church about the problem of hunger in your town or neighborhood. Call your denomination or a Christian service organization and volunteer.

If no one has a plan, create one. We have an Emergency Relief Fund in our organization. We never take one penny for administration. All of it, 100 percent, goes to the place of need. If you are interested in helping in any of these areas of need through us, why not write to me, **Billy Graham, Minneapolis, Minnesota,** and we will see that you get some literature on the Emergency Relief Fund.

My son Franklin, while on a visit to the central highlands of Guatemala a few years back, saw a family that had walked several days through thick jungles to government-controlled territory in order to escape from an area which was overrun by guerrillas. Their children were so malnourished that they could not even sit up by themselves. Franklin said that when he looked at those children, it was almost like looking at skeletons covered with a layer of skin. All the children could do was quietly sob—no expression or joy—just a constant low moan. The doctor who examined them was not even sure whether the children would live. As in the illness known as anorexia nervosa, there is a point in starvation where a person's vital organs begin to break down, and the damage that has been done cannot be repaired.

Clean Water and Health

There is serious concern over water and sanitation in the world's least-developed countries. Four children out of every five in the rural areas of the world do not have safe drinking water or sanitation. In Africa, ninety out of every hundred people have no piped water, and worse yet, the great rivers of Africa carry dangerous germs, liver flukes, amoebic dysentery, and other infections. One African authority calls the waterways of that continent "the waters of misfortune." If people in Africa are to survive, they must have pure water and delivery systems comparable to those we take for granted in this country.

I once saw a young girl in India with an empty five-gallon water drum on her head. She was walking from her home village to a dirty water hole several kilometers away. On many occasions I have seen the older women of these tribal villages return bent under the strain of unbelievably heavy loads. The water sources near their homes had dried up from a prolonged drought. As I stood watching, I knew that girl's spiritual thirst was more important than her physical thirst, but I couldn't force myself to separate the two. Like the woman at the well at Sychar in Samaria to whom Jesus ministered, she was a person who needed the water of life, both physically and spiritually.

I believe that to touch the hearts of a hurting world, we must also touch their need for food and shelter. Our loving witness for a lost soul must go hand in hand with loving concern for a dying body. We are called by God to bring the water of life for both soul and body. God created them both, and His purpose is to redeem them both. The death of Jesus Christ on the cross demonstrates God's concern for the eternal salvation of our souls. The resurrection of Jesus Christ from the dead—and the promise we have that our bodies will someday share in His glorious resurrection—demonstrates God's concern for our physical being.

Human beings are not just another animal whose life and death has little meaning. We are created in the image of God and even though that image is scarred and torn by sin, we are still God's creation. If we are believers, we will have not only a new heart as a result of the new birth, but someday we will have a new glorified body made very similar to the risen body of Jesus Christ.

The causes of trauma in our world—whether from starvation, famine, war, and intolerance, or from diseases as different as diphtheria, alcoholism, and AIDS—all cry out for compassion and care. God is concerned about those who suffer, no matter who they are, where they are found, or why they hurt. But He also cares about how we respond to their hurt. Christ told us to love those who are lost, to serve even "the least of these," to feed the hungry, and to clothe the naked. That is our Christian duty. Even in cases where famine or disease may possibly be seen as the judgment of God, Christians are to demonstrate the love of God and show compassion. We are not permitted to criticize and pass by on the other side: We *must* care and render aid.

Our Greatest Need

Several years ago Dr. Ernie Steury, a surgeon at Tenwek Hospital in Kenya, East Africa, told of a woman from the bush country who had been in labor for about two days. The family had sent for the witch doctors, but of course the witch doctors were not able to do anything to help her. Finally, in desperation, the family decided to take her to the mission hospital in Tenwek. They had to carry her several hours down a narrow jungle trail before they reached the road. Once they got to the road, they had to wait hours before a bus came. Then there was another delay of several hours before they reached the hospital. It was late in the evening when she arrived and was brought immediately to the emergency room. The nurse sent for Dr. Steury. He came and examined the woman only to find that she was already dead.

The husband was standing in the corridor waiting anxiously for the doctor's report. Dr. Steury went over to him and told him that it was too late. The man broke into tears, crying out, "Oh, but please sir, isn't there anything you can do? Isn't there anything at all you can do?" Dr. Steury explained that he could do nothing.

The doctor remembered later, "I turned, and what crushed me more than anything else was not the fact that she had died, but that she died never once having heard the gospel message. Thousands of people die every day, and they die never having heard about Jesus. This is what compels me to stay as a volunteer missionary doctor in Africa. This is what drives me to keep on. Last year we had more than eight thousand inpatients. Each one of those patients heard the gospel. More than five thousand made decisions to accept Jesus Christ as their Lord and Savior. We can't reach them all, but we can reach some. I have been told to go with this gospel message and go into all the world, and I am going to do my part."

I believe this is the sense of compassion that must inform our efforts to serve the afflicted. Dr. Steury knew that true servanthood does not allow us to separate the soul from the body: They are both vital parts of the total person. But when he saw the death of a patient, it wasn't so much the physical death that disturbed him—we all have to die—it was the spiritual death.

The Red and the Black

While famine and disease stalk much of the Third World, nearly all countries, even the smallest, are arming to the teeth. This is one of the most pathetic developments of our time. It is a problem that illustrates the precise contemporary relevance of ancient biblical truth. The red horse, the one who brings war, appropriately precedes and paves the way for the black horse, the one who brings famine, disease, and starvation.

Our world is obsessed with war, violence, and death. The trillion or more dollars spent annually on armaments would feed, clothe, and provide shelter for the billion or more people living below the subsistence level. Consider that the annual per-capita income of a family in Bangladesh today is just $176; in Mozambique, prior to the outbreak of famine and war, it was $220; in Somalia, now devastated by drought, famine, and anarchy, the average annual income was $300 prior to the troubles and only a fraction of that today.

In 1982, former Prime Minister Malcolm Fraser of Australia hosted the world leaders in a North-South Dialogue. In a part of the Melbourne Declaration, as it has come to be known, it was stated that "the protracted assault on human dignity and the deprivation from which many millions in developing countries suffer must inevitably lead to political turmoil." "Such turmoil," Fraser added, would be used "to extend the realm of dictatorship in the world."

Many at that conference felt that only a new political order or a new economic order could hope to solve such problems. I must say that they are right—only a world government can solve it. The only lasting "new world order," however, that will succeed in solving the problems of this world will be the dynamic spiritual leadership established by Jesus Christ when He comes to set up His kingdom on earth. Don't be fooled: Christ's new world order is not a myth; it is not a hyperbole or a metaphor for some mystical reality. It will be very real, very physical, and I believe it will come very soon.

The Widening Gap

The president of the United States was similarly warned in the *Global Outlook 2000* report, prepared by the United Nations in 1990, that the widening gap between rich and poor nations will inevitably "lead to economic disasters and open conflict." Former World Bank president Robert McNamara agrees: "Many of the poorest countries of the world are . . . doomed to economic and political chaos in the decade ahead." As the world rushes madly toward Armageddon, I cannot help but agree with former Soviet Premier Nikita Khrushchev, speaking of an anticipated World War III, "The survivors will envy the dead."

The world's situation may have reached a point of no return, and both Christians and secular analysts alike believe the dangers will continue to grow worse until we reach some sort of tragic climax. The Bible laid out the details of that climax in both the Old and New Testaments.

But it is not enough for Christians to stand glibly by and applaud the impending Apocalypse—in fact it would be wrong. It is up to us to pray and work. Even if we feel small and helpless before such unwieldy problems, we should remember the words of the man who said: "I only have one bucket of water to throw on the fire, but I am going to throw it with all my might, asking God to use it as He did the five loaves and two fishes."

The Coming Thunder

The storm clouds bringing the black horse and its rider thunder ever louder in our ears. Biblical prophecy is being fulfilled before our eyes. All around us we see the human tragedy of destitution and disease. Starving people rummage through garbage heaps and ditches for a few paltry crumbs to deaden their chronic hunger pangs. How should we respond? By my reading of Scripture I am convinced that we are called to action, not apathy, and to involvement, not detachment.

When Sargent Shriver was head of the poverty program in the United States several years ago, he asked me to help him, and I did. We made a motion picture together on poverty in Appalachia. I addressed about two hundred members of Congress and gave each of them a list of Scripture verses about our responsibility to the poor. Here are just a few of them:

> Do not go over your vineyard a second time or pick up the grapes that have fallen. Leave them for the poor.

> Leviticus 19:10

> There will always be poor people in the land. Therefore I command you to be openhanded toward your brothers and toward the poor and needy in your land.

> Deuteronomy 15:11

The poor you will always have with you.

Mark 14:7

Blessed is he who is kind to the needy.

Proverbs 14:21

He who is kind to the poor lends to the LORD,
and he will reward him for
what he has done.

Proverbs 19:17

The righteous care about justice for the poor,
but the wicked have no such
concern.

Proverbs 29:7

Learn to do right!
Seek justice,
encourage the oppressed.
Defend the cause of the fatherless,
plead the case of the widow.

Isaiah 1:16-17

One of the great judgments of Scripture was the judgment that God rained upon Sodom, and one of the great sins of Sodom was the neglect of the poor and the needy: "Now this was the sin of your sister Sodom: She and her daughters were arrogant, overfed and unconcerned; they did not help the poor and needy" (Ezekiel 16:49).

Jesus made our responsibilities very plain in Matthew 25:35, "For I was hungry and you gave me something to eat, I was thirsty and you gave me something to drink, I was a stranger and you invited me in, I needed clothes and you clothed me, I was sick and you looked after me, I was in prison and you came to visit me." Even though this passage may have a double meaning, its implications to us are very clear concerning our practical responsibility. He also warned of severe judgment if we fail in our duties.

The apostle Paul struck the same theme in Romans 12:20 and 1 Corinthians 13:3: "If your enemy is hungry, feed him; if he is thirsty, give him something to drink. In doing this, you will heap burning coals on his head." "If I give all I possess to the poor and surrender my body to the flames, but have not love, I gain nothing."

James approached it in a slightly different way, yet with the same meaning: "Has not God chosen those who are poor in the eyes of the world to be rich in faith and to inherit the kingdom he promised those who love him?" (James 2:5). "If you really keep the royal law found in Scripture, 'Love your neighbor as yourself,' you are doing right" (verse 8).

The Call of Suffering

As I have already pointed out, there are one or two passages that do not have easy explanations, for example where Jesus said, "The poor you will always have with you" (Matthew 26:11). In this verse Jesus was only pointing out the fact that poverty will never be eliminated until His kingdom is established; in the meantime, we should do all we can to help those who suffer. In fact, there is a very valid argument in the view that one reason God allows poverty and suffering is so that Christians may demonstrate the love of Christ to the hurting.

We have all seen the modern tendency to lay blame on the wrong party or circumstance. For example, the criminal (it is said) is only the victim of his environment. Yet the earth's first crime was committed in a perfect environment. Today, statistics prove that many of our crimes are committed in upper-middle-class or affluent environments. Poverty is no excuse for crime any more than the girl from a socially prominent family could be excused for murder because she had too much of everything. God created us with the power to choose. Each one of us will ultimately be held accountable for how we choose.

Another point that calls for clarification is the commandment, "Do not follow the crowd in doing wrong. When you give testimony in a lawsuit, do not pervert justice by siding with the crowd, and do not show favoritism to a poor man in his lawsuit" (Exodus 23:2-3), or as the Revised Standard Version puts it, "Nor shall you be partial to a poor man in his suit." Provision, yes; protection, yes; partiality, *No*. Leviticus 19:15 says, "Do not pervert justice; do not show partiality to the poor or favoritism to the great, but judge your neighbor fairly." Too often, I fear, some people compromise justice by overemphasizing the plight of the "disadvantaged." That is clearly wrong. But I am persuaded that the very threat of the four horsemen of the Apocalypse is not just to warn or judge, but to awaken. They come not merely to move us emotionally, but to motivate us to do something—to point men and women of the world in the direction that God Himself would have them go. I am convinced that we are to work against hunger and disease with all the power and energy at our command. I am equally convinced that we can make a big difference. Whether our efforts will feed all the hungry or heal all the sick is not the issue. It is always better to do something than to do nothing. To paraphrase James Kelley, "It is better to light one candle than to curse the darkness." God calls us to act; the rest is in His hands.

The Plague of Homelessness

Our country has never seen such a plague of homelessness as we have in today's world. A few years ago we had vagrants, tramps, and an occasional bag lady in our towns.

Today we have an epidemic of impoverished families and individuals who have lost their ability to make ends meet. Either through lost jobs, broken homes, desperate poverty, emotional problems, or through the effort of state mental health facilities to be rid of what some call "the walking wounded," tens of thousands of Americans live in night shelters, missions, or on the streets.

Nor is the problem limited to America. It is especially critical in poorer countries. There the trend toward urbanization of the past fifty years has been the largest contributor to the problem of homelessness. Since 1950 the urban population has doubled in most developed countries. In developing countries it has quadrupled. In the last sixty years urbanization has multiplied ten times. According to the *Almanac of the Christian World*, 1990 was the first year in world history when there were more people living in cities than in rural areas. To complicate matters, the United Nations projects that by the year 2000, seventeen of the twenty largest cities in the world will be in Third World nations.

All of these trends—urbanization, homelessness, growth in Third World populations—contribute to the plague of hunger in our time. But how can anyone deal with such stirring problems of such challenging dimensions? The 1982 General Convention of the Episcopal Church adopted a resolution on the church's response to the problem of hunger. I believe their advice still applies to the problems facing us today. It urged "all individuals and congregations . . . to deepen their commitment to the hungry." The resolution indicated five avenues such commitment could take. Allow me to cite them here.

The first of these is "*becoming familiar with local needs for food and assisting in establishing programs such as food pantries, food banks, cooperative programs on life style assessment.*" Many local churches have established donated or budget-purchased emergency food supplies in a storage area of the church or in a building or rental unit near the church. People in need of food can simply stop by the emergency food center, state their need and be supplied by the Christian volunteers manning the center. One church in Los Angeles established a store in the inner city where there are many suffering refugees. They sell food supplies and clothing to the needy at cost. I've noticed another commendable trend: Some local churches are examining their lifestyles to see where money can be saved from personal food bills so that they can share more with the poor and hungry in their neighborhoods.

Second, the resolution strongly urges "*each member of the Church to pledge at least one hour per week of volunteer time to direct service to those in need, and each congregation to provide facilities, food and money to meet those needs.*" I know a church that has a People Mover program, a system for keeping volunteers available, trained, and useful in Christian service organizations established either by the church or by other agencies in the community. This "talent bank" offers weekly opportunities for its members, young and old, to contribute to the needs of the community with their time and energy. One pastor asks for his people to volunteer one-tenth of their work time to the work of the kingdom in that town. Others limit volunteers to an easily manageable amount of volunteer time each week. It is important not to demand too much of any one individual, in time or in money. The struggle to help the destitute and oppressed should not lead to the destruction of a volunteer's vocational, spiritual, or family commitments.

I know of one family that has found a tremendous blessing in giving anonymously when they learn of those in need in their area. Together the family decides on projects. They work, pray, and sometimes struggle to fulfill their promises, but that is part of the lesson. The poor, hungry, or needy people helped—either directly or through the church—never know where their gifts come from. This family has learned the truth of the Scripture which says that it is more blessed to give than to receive. Perhaps your family would want to try to do something of this sort to help those in need where you live.

Third, the Episcopal resolution called for prayer *"for greater awareness and sensitivity among all citizens to the problems of hunger and malnutrition,"* and to work toward such awareness *"by distributing materials for educational programs."* Again, prayer is central to the problems of privation and human hunger, but prayer also goes hand in hand with action. Charles Schulz's cartoon series, "Peanuts," has an unforgettable strip in which Snoopy, the tragicomic beagle, is lying shivering on top of his doghouse in a terrible snowstorm. It is suppertime, and Linus and Lucy are enjoying the warmth of their fire. Lucy looks out the window at the cold and hungry dog and shouts: "Pray, be ye warmed and fed, Snoopy." So many times prayer without works is hypocrisy, and works without prayer is futile and short-lived. But together, praying and working for the hungry will make a tremendous difference and provide the community with an example of Christian love that leads to the most effective kind of Christian witness.

Fourth, the resolution counsels *"joining forces with other individuals and Christian organizations."* That is a practical and systematic approach to the problems. There are, of course, many denominational and parachurch organizations that could be recommended, from the Salvation Army to World Vision. One of the best of the small relief organizations in the world is Samaritan's Purse of Boone, North Carolina, headed by my son Franklin. Also, as mentioned above, we have our own emergency relief arm of the Billy Graham Evangelistic Association headquartered in Minneapolis.

After investigating these organizations and the work they do, decide on one or two groups you want to support. Once you have determined the denominational and/or parachurch organization that you feel is truly trustworthy and effective, work to support that group in its local, national, and international ministries.

Still, there is no way for any group or groups really to serve the entire world and its needs. There are plenty of needy areas, beginning in the houses around your home. Start in your own community. Serve your neighbors while reaching out to minister to the hungry and the needy around the globe. Remember charity always begins at home, and from there, around home.

Fifth, the resolution urges *"policymakers and the entire community to call for increased use of our national resources to meet basic human needs."* Our public officials appreciate a person's honest and informed concern. As we have seen, Christ called us to care for the widows and the orphans. In no uncertain terms, He commanded us to feed the hungry and to clothe the naked. Our taxes support national, state, and local service programs. It is our interest in those programs that keeps them effective. Our attention to their results will keep their executives honest and on target. Why should only nonbelievers work to influence the way our tax monies are spent? Why shouldn't we?

A Sense of Perspective

During the 1950s, it was my privilege to be a friend of Dwight D. Eisenhower both before and after he served as president of the United States. I hope I had some influence on him, and certainly he had a strong impact on my thinking. He made a statement to the American Society of Newspaper Editors in April 1953 and it has had a great influence on me. He said:

> Every gun that is made, every warship launched, every rocket fired signifies—in a final sense—a theft from those who hunger and are not fed, those who are cold and are not clothed. This world in arms is not spending money alone. It is spending the sweat of its laborers, the genius of its scientists, the hopes of its children. . . . This is not a way of life at all in any true sense. Under the threatening cloud of war, it is humanity hanging on a cross of iron.

Those words by our chief executive was part of what prompted me and some of my colleagues in 1956 to make our first tour of the developing countries. Before that time I had seen few people dying from starvation, and I had never experienced firsthand the horror of an almost entirely poverty-stricken nation gripped by hunger. Destitute people wearing tattered clothing or next to nothing at all were everywhere we went. In some places, beggars were so common, we could not make our way through the streets.

Such conditions would leave even the most insensitive sickened and horrified. When I returned to the United States it seemed that everyone looked as affluent as the rich man in Jesus' story in Luke 16:19. I went directly to the White House and shared my feelings with the president. He listened intently, and then he asked me to share my impressions with the secretary of state, John Foster Dulles. Dulles was a churchman. He had been president of the Federal Council of Churches before his appointment to the Eisenhower administration. Mr. Dulles was very cordial. He asked that I visit him at home rather than in his state department office. We talked at length about the hungry people I had seen. I was emphatic about the needs there and insisted that we should do something about them. "What about this nation's surplus wheat?" I asked. "Why can't it be used to help meet at least some of the basic needs of those around the globe who are dying because they have no grain to make bread?"

I feel even more strongly today about the social responsibility of the rich nations sharing their surpluses with the poor—even if it involves changing our thinking about how it should be done. There must be a way to shift grain and dairy products from the storerooms of the rich nations to the empty huts and hovels of those who are dying from hunger around the earth. It is time we put our best Judeo-Christian minds to work on this problem to solve it, for there is no reason why so many people, especially the children of the world, should suffer and die from hunger while we are so well fed. You can't read the epistles of either James or John and draw any other conclusion about where our responsibility lies.

For much of my life I spent little time thinking about the humanitarian responsibilities of the church. I was not really aware that millions of people throughout the world are living on the edge of starvation. The Bible was very specific about the obligations of believers to do something about such problems, but it was some time before I recognized the crisis. Today those problems are much easier to see. As I have traveled the world and studied the Bible on these issues—especially those New Testament verses that speak of our responsibility to the poor and hungry—my convictions regarding our responsibility as Christians has deepened.

I am fortunate enough to be a citizen of the United States, a nation that has been blessed in many ways beyond any other nation in the world. But I must not take these blessings for granted, and neither should you. We are stewards of what God has allowed us to possess. As long as we have more than our neighbors, Christ calls us to share with those in need around the world, especially those in the household of faith. If we fail Christ in that charge, we will be judged for our failure. The rider on the black horse carrying the scales rides to warn us that we can no longer escape our responsibility to the hungry in spite of all the barriers that stand in our way. There *are* formidable barriers.

Barriers to Progress

Sporadic shortages in grain harvests have been a large part of the famines in recent years. In some cases these problems are made even worse by both animal and insect pests. Unreliable and contaminated water supplies are another major factor. Some 600 million people live in marginal desert areas where both water and grain supplies are severely limited.

Traditionally Christians have seen missionaries as those who preach, teach, translate, or engage in ministries of healing. I believe that today we must also begin to train and equip our best brains, young and old, to serve Christ in the world through pest control, agricultural science, engineering, farm and soil management programs, and weather research. I congratulate the mission boards who are already working to train the new generation of missionary engineers and technicians, scientists, and managers who will join in using their vocational skills to save the lives as well as the souls of a world at risk.

World Vision's Information and Resource Center offers several suggestions for increasing our assistance to the peoples of the world. Their report suggests we need to volunteer our expertise to help nations design plans for storage of grain reserves, so that stored grain can be distributed whenever and wherever a food crisis may develop. This is precisely the mission that Joseph fulfilled in Egypt. As a result of his insight and leadership in building safe stores of grain, not only was Egypt saved, but Israel and the Middle East at large were also saved from famine and starvation.

Surely there are talented men and women who can find, create, and disseminate the technology to confront these agricultural challenges. North American engineers and agricultural specialists can also help impoverished nations to develop arable land by demonstrating how to conserve resources, fertilize, and irrigate what otherwise would remain unusable land.

In the Name of Christ

Over a period of years, my son Franklin and his associates in Samaritan's Purse have been building homes in Lebanon for Muslims who have been rendered homeless by the civil war in that country. This has been a mission designed to meet basic human needs, given freely in the hope that their acts of Christian charity will make a difference in the attitudes of Muslims toward Christians.

I know that those efforts are making a difference. As the men, women, and children of Lebanon have seen Christians sacrifice to help them rebuild their cities and their homes, they have also seen a kind of Christian witness that is different from what they have known before. They applauded Franklin and his friends as they passed by in the streets. They even embraced them with tears in their eyes, expressing their gratitude in every possible way. When they ask, "Why do you do this?" Franklin and his friends simply answer, "We do it because we love you and because God loves you. We do this in the name of Jesus Christ."

Many Christians working around the world are earning the right to be heard. They are backing their message with compassion. Of course it isn't a new idea. Missionaries, lay and clergy alike, have been in the field for generations, earning the right to be heard and backing up their message with compassion. They also stand before the rider of the black horse in the name of Christ.

We should never, despite our modern technology, criticize or despise the methods of those brave missionaries who paid a price during the last two hundred years to carry the gospel to the entire world. My father-in-law, Dr. Nelson Bell, was one of those great missionaries to China. He left a successful professional baseball career, studied medicine, and in 1916 went to China to help build a hospital. He combined medicine with the proclamation of the gospel.

Jesus said to His disciples, "I sent you to reap what you have not worked for. Others have done the hard work, and you have reaped the benefits of their labor" (John 4:38). The tremendous evangelical surge around the world today came because faithful men and women of God paid a price in blood, sweat, tears, and even death to lay the foundations upon which we are building today. When I read the reports of possibly as many as 50 million Christians surviving and even multiplying in China today, I realize how important our legacy of Christian love truly is to the world outside. As he has traveled back and forth to China with his East Gates ministry, my son, Ned, has been deeply moved to see firsthand some of the results of the labors of his grandfather and the other missionaries to China. These great planters of the faith paid a great price to leave home and venture to the other side of the world to minister in Christ's name and to sow the seed of the gospel.

My priorities are much the same as they've been since I was first ordained so many years ago. The salvation of the lost was, is, and always shall be my number-one assignment. But as I have said, Jesus didn't heal everybody. He didn't feed everybody. His primary mission was the salvation of the lost. When the paralytic was brought to Him, the first thing Jesus said was, "Your sins are forgiven" (Matthew 9:2). Jesus knew the man needed first to understand God's forgiveness, but then He reached out and met the physical needs of the man as well. It seems to me that is the right order of priorities.

Our Christian Duty

Jesus had compassion on all those He met who were in need. So must we. God has given each of us different gifts, talents, and abilities. We are different parts of the same body. Jesus was a carpenter before He was a minister, so He understood the importance of building things to make life endurable; that knowledge also informed His teaching. Today engineers, architects, weekend volunteers, pastors, and evangelists alike should all stand shoulder to shoulder to help slow the work of the black horse of famine and accomplish the work of the kingdom while there is still light.

Does that mean we are all called to give away everything we have? No, not necessarily. There is nothing wrong or immoral in having wealth. Some may be called of God to give away much and make great sacrifices, but God entrusts each of us to discover His will for us. Wealth may be a stewardship given by God. It can either be used selfishly and sinfully, or it can be used for the glory of God. Paul wrote to the Romans, "So then each of us shall give account of himself to God" (Romans 14:12 NKJV). We each have different talents and opportunities. The real question is, are we using what we have for the glory of God, and are we loving our neighbors as we love ourselves? Are you using your gifts for the physical and spiritual betterment of the world around you?

We are called by our Lord and Savior to proclaim the gospel and serve our fellow men and women in their psychological, physical, moral, and spiritual needs. It will require true spiritual muscle to put your life on the line for Christ. But before you rush to volunteer your life in the cause of need, or hunger, or health in the world, be sure you first rush to the cross of Christ for His forgiveness and strength.

The black horse of the Apocalypse makes it clear that we are engaged in a spiritual battle. Children are dying because evil rules the hearts and the minds of people. To feed and care for the world will require a spiritual revolution. As men and women turn to God in Christ they will be liberated to give up the false hope that weapons alone will save us from our enemies. They can reach out in love and share; for every possession we have is a gift from God. Let these words from the apostle Paul to Timothy be a guide:

> Command those who are rich in this present age not to be haughty, nor to trust in uncertain riches but in the living God, who gives us richly all things to enjoy. Let them do good, that they be rich in good works, ready to give, willing to share, storing up for themselves a good foundation for the time to come, that they may lay hold on eternal life.
>
> 1 Timothy 6:17-19 NKJV

We are only stewards of the world's resources. They are not ours; they are God's. When we find our security in Him, we can then give generously from what He has entrusted to us. That is our Christian duty.

13

The Shadow of Death

I looked, and there before me was a pale horse! Its rider was named Death, and Hades was following close behind him. They were given power over a fourth of the earth to kill by sword, famine and plague, and by the wild beasts of the earth.

Revelation 6:8

Death casts its shadow over the land. On every continent, in every nation, and through every city, town, village, and hut, death rides unfettered. It brings hardship, suffering, and sorrow wherever it goes. The specter of the Apocalypse is nowhere more visible than in the dreadful work of this grim reaper. Death is an accomplished master of destruction, and his credentials precede him: abortion, abuse, addiction, brutality, crime, disease, drugs, hatred, lust, murder, neglect, pestilence, racial conflict, rape, revenge, starvation, suicide, violence, and war. These are his calling cards.

Here is his record of achievement: 50 million deaths every year. Every year a million people die from man-made disasters; 80,000 die from earthquakes and 10,000 from floods. Each year there are a million new victims of desertification and 10 million environmental refugees; 625 million live in areas with unhealthy and potentially lethal air conditions. There are 250,000 new victims of environmental disasters every year, and a million are poisoned by pesticides. All these are targets of the dread stalker. Each day a shocking 25,000 die from pollution alone.

In the United States, 50,000 people die annually in traffic accidents; 11,000 die from falls; 5,000 from fires and burns; and 6,000 by drowning. Another 2,000 are killed each year by firearms; nearly 4,000 from ingestion of food objects; 1,000 are poisoned by gas; and 4,000 more die from other types of poison. This is complicated by the fact that there are currently 11 million alcoholics in this country, and 76 million families have at least one member who is struggling with alcoholism or alcohol-related problems.

Worldwide there are 5 million malaria deaths per year and 3 million from tuberculosis; 2.8 million children die annually from vaccine-preventable diseases, while infectious diseases kill 4 million unimmunized children. There are 5 million diarrhea deaths of children under age 5; 4 million die of pneumonia. We are told that by some estimates there are potentially 60 million AIDS/HIV carriers with an infection growth rate of 100 percent per year. There are an estimated 3 million AIDS victims worldwide with a mortality rate of 100 percent.

Add to these numbers the estimated 16.8 million who die from parasitic diseases, 13.3 million from circulatory disease, 5 million cardiovascular deaths, 4.3 million cancer deaths, 3.3 million perinatal deaths, 2.6 million tobacco-related deaths, and 401,000 suicides every year.

Accounting the Loss

How can anyone ever begin to comprehend the human toll of so much suffering, anguish, pain, and loss? This is only a tiny fraction of the evil at large in the world, raging and ravaging in our midst. Some 300 million suffer from chronic or acute arthritis; there are 85 million severely handicapped children; and 900 million people on this planet live in constant pain. On top of everything else, there are 51 million certified psychotics in the world, 10 million schizophrenics, and 950 million psychoneurotics.

These staggering statistics cause me to gasp at the toll death exacts from the world. But I have to wonder how such figures compare with the tragedy of combat casualties. I cannot imagine that the situation could be any worse in war time.

In August 1991 the *Journal of the American Medical Association* published a compelling study of the epidemiology of death in war which reported, among others things, the estimated average annual deaths from war over the past four centuries. The researchers found that the average annual death rate from war in the seventeenth century was 9,500. The yearly average was 15,000 in the eighteenth century, 13,000 in the nineteenth century, and an enormous 458,000 per year in the twentieth century . . . so far.

I was surprised to see that there was an average of just 6,000 military deaths per year during the Thirty Years War of the first half of the seventeenth century, for a total of about 180,000 killed. That is a large number, but less than I would have suspected for something called the Thirty Years War. By comparison, more than 620,000 died during just four years of the American Civil War some 250 years later. But more shocking was the estimated 5,561,000 combat deaths per year during World War II, for a total of more than 30 million soldiers killed, not including the more than 20 million civilian deaths.

Pale Horse, Pale Rider

In the Victoria and Albert Museum in London there is a painted reproduction of a series of seven tapestries woven in the fourteenth century. Some 472 feet long, it depicts

John's vision of the Apocalypse. Six hundred years ago the artists-weavers read the sixth chapter of Revelation and artistically interpreted the rider as a skull wrapped in graveclothes sitting upon a pale horse and carrying a Roman broadsword in preparation for the carnage he would inflict.

In the fifteenth century, Albrecht Dürer depicted John's vision in fifteen large, carefully cut woodblocks. These are perhaps the most famous illustrations of the horsemen. Death rides the pale horse in the more traditional form of Father Time, an emaciated, bearded harbinger of judgment carrying a three-pronged spear and riding at full gallop toward men whose faces are upturned in defenseless horror. For centuries artists have tried to portray this grisly scene, but nothing captures the horror of the reality.

Before we come to verse 6 of John's account, three horses have galloped into our presence. Each bears an instrument of God's wrath, and each has ridden off to bring terror and judgment on the earth. Now in verse 7, one of God's appointed emissaries steps forward at the command, "Come!" A new page is thrown open to reveal the fourth horse and its grim rider. In the verses that follow John writes, "I looked, and there before me was a pale horse!" (Revelation 6:8). The word in Greek is *chloros*. William Barclay, the late great Scottish professor at Glasgow University, calls it the color of a face "blanched with terror." Moffatt says the horse was the bloodless color of a corpse. We use the root of this ancient Greek word when we describe the color of chlorine gas, a pale, sickly green. At that moment John's eyes were confronted with a terrifying sight. Seated on the pale horse was a rider "named Death, and Hades was following close behind him" (Revelation 6:8).

The little phrase, "and Hades was following close behind him," has puzzled scholars over the centuries. Was there a second rider on the pale horse riding in tandem with Death? Or was there a fifth horseman of the Apocalypse? Hades is the transitional abode of the dead. This is the place that for a time swallows up the spirits of those who die outside of Christ. In the vision, John sees Death and Hades in all too ordinary terms of a man cleaning up refuse along a public road, spearing a bit of trash and dumping it into the trash bag he lugs along.

The Vision of Hell

When he sees this image of Death and Hades, John uses the mysterious phrase, "They were given power . . ." (Revelation 6:8). In that awful instant when horse and rider paused, something transpired between God and Death giving him the power to kill one of every four people living on earth.

It is important to realize that the horrors unleashed by the four horsemen have a compounding effect. The first horse is not replaced by the second and so on; rather, the first is joined by the second, then by the third, and then the fourth. The rider who brings pestilence and death is accompanied by each of the others we have already observed. The combined effect of the four horsemen is devastating.

One of the objectives of Satan is to deceive. We have seen this portrayed so vividly in the image of the white horse. The deceiver came to conquer and mislead the nations. In John 8:44, Jesus said, "he is a liar and the father of lies"; and his desire to bring death is also seen in the same verse: "He was a murderer from the beginning, not holding to the truth, for there is no truth in him." Here in Revelation 6:8, he is given permission to go forth to kill hordes of humans, a holocaustic one-quarter of the population of the earth.

By the end of this decade it is estimated that the population of the world will surpass 6 billion. That means, if this harbinger of judgment were given divine permission to kill one-fourth of the world's population at that time, 1.5 billion people would be slain. That is more people than currently live in Europe, South America, and North America combined.

Why would God allow such suffering to take place? John's vision is consistent with ancient biblical pictures describing what happens when God sends His wrath upon those who disobey Him. William Barclay warned, "at the back of it all there is the permanent truth that no man and no nation can escape the consequences of their sin" (*The Revelation of John*, 2:12). Lynn Howard Hough explains that Death, here, does not bring meaningless destruction, "but destruction which serves the purposes of the justice of God. [Death] is a part of the divine administration. A fourth of the earth feels his power that the rest may see and have the opportunity to repent" (*The Interpreter's Bible*, 12:414).

The whole world was horrified by the Holocaust in which Hitler cold-bloodedly sent some 6 million Jews (as well as millions of Poles and other non-Jews) to the gas chambers. But no one was more grieved than God. It breaks His heart when His own children die. It is not God's intent that any should perish, but when people defiantly refuse God's plan, the consequence of this disobedience is death. The rider on the pale horse is only taking his due.

The Love of God

Still, in this vision, God reaches out in love. He illustrated His great love by giving His Son to die on the cross—the most horrible death a person can die. God hopes that through this evidence of love and this warning of the fourth horseman given to John nearly two thousand years ago, the rest of the world may yet see the wages of sin, turn from its sinfulness, seek God's forgiveness, and be saved from the jaws of hell.

We should not be horrified at what God is doing. We should be grateful. In some cases physical death is actually a blessing. What if Adolf Hitler or Joseph Stalin were still alive? This world would be a living hell had they lived forever. But people not only die physically; they are spiritually dead while they are physically alive until they find new life in Christ. The Bible also speaks of the second death, or eternal death. This refers to hell. God, through this rider, hopes to cheat hell of the billions who have by their own sinfulness chosen death over life. If the love He offers is accepted and the warning He gives is heeded, then billions will be spared.

But the order is even more specific. The weapons of death are clearly described: sword, famine, plague and wild beasts are named. These New Testament instruments of the apocalypse are taken directly from Old Testament texts. The vision of John has roots in a vision of Moses almost thirteen hundred years before John's island vision. Barclay reminds us that in Leviticus (26:21–26) Moses described the judgment God would send upon His people because of their disobedience. Barclay says, "Wild beasts will rob them of their children, and destroy their cattle, and make them few in number. The sword will avenge their breaches of the covenant. When they are gathered in their cities the pestilence will be among them. He will break the staff of bread and they will eat and not be satisfied" (*The Revelation of John*, 2:11-12).

The Sword of the Lord

Later, the prophet Ezekiel heard the sovereign Lord say, "How much worse will it be when I send against Jerusalem my four dreadful judgments—sword and famine and wild beasts and plague—to kill its men and their animals!" (Ezekiel 14:21). But even these promises of horror bring hope. God assures Ezekiel that "there will be some survivors," and those survivors will console the prophet when he sees "their conduct and their actions, for you will know that I [God] have done nothing in it without cause" (Ezekiel 14:22-23).

But the Bible teaches that God, too, has swords. "The sword of the LORD, and of Gideon" (Judges 7:20 KJV) was the war cry of the ancient Israelites when they went forth to destroy the invading Midianites. In the New Testament we read of the Lord's "sword of the Spirit, which is the word of God" (Ephesians 6:17).

The weapon of Satan is, of course, counterfeit. It would represent "the spiritual lie" as opposed to the truth of God. In 2 Thessalonians 2:7-12 (NKJV), Paul says:

> For the mystery of lawlessness is already at work; only He who now restrains will do so until He is taken out of the way. And then the lawless one will be revealed, whom the Lord will consume with the breath of His mouth and destroy with the brightness of His coming. The coming of the lawless one is according to the working of Satan, with all power, signs, and lying wonders, and with all unrighteous deception among those who perish, because they did not receive the love of the truth, that they might be saved. And for this reason God will send them strong delusion, that they should believe the lie, that they all may be condemned who did not believe the truth but had pleasure in unrighteousness.

The passage in Revelation 6 concerning the pale horse probably has a double interpretation. One is literal; the other is spiritual. The Bible teaches that there will be a famine of the Word of God in the last days (Amos 8:11). Spiritual death follows spiritual starvation.

But there is also physical starvation in the world. For example, forty thousand children died from hunger and disease last night while you were sleeping. Add those to the total numbers of victims of plague and pestilence sweeping East Africa, Asia, and Latin America. The Amplified Bible translates Deuteronomy 28:15, 21-22, 27-28:

> If you will not obey the voice of the Lord your God. . . . The Lord will make the pestilence cling to you until He has consumed you from off the land, which you go to possess.
>
> The Lord will smite you with consumption [wasting, degenerative diseases?], with fever, and inflammation [communicable diseases?] . . . and the tumors [cancer?], the scurvy [deficiency diseases?] and the itch, of which you cannot be healed [such as genital herpes, syphilis, and AIDS?]. The Lord will smite you with madness [mental illness?] and blindness [birth defects?] and dismay of [mind and] heart [emotional traumas?].

The bracketed questions in the above quotation are inserted to stimulate your own thoughts on this descriptive passage. This is only a short list of what pestilence will inflict the population when the rider on the pale horse traverses the earth.

Also to be considered are those slain by wild beasts. Moses, Ezekiel, and John lived in a world where wild beasts frequently stalked wayfarers as they trudged the primitive roads between villages. Predators invaded the unwalled settlements, terrorizing and dismembering their inhabitants. In most civilized cultures today wild beasts are locked away in zoos or traveling circuses. But like the evolution from sword to nuclear missile, so wild beasts have evolved into modern killers that stalk us everywhere we are or go. Oh, there is still the very real threat of actual wild beasts sweeping down into modern cities in search of food and water, like the coyotes of Southern California, or the herds of wild boar that occasionally invade a Third World village. But there are other wild beasts among us, and this may also be what the Scripture suggests. Consider, for example, abortion.

The Abortion Holocaust

Few issues have polarized our society as much as the debate over abortion. It is not my purpose to get involved in the complex legal and political issues that swirl around this difficult question. There admittedly are isolated cases where abortion is the lesser of two evils, such as when the mother's life is clearly at risk. However, for many people today abortion has become little more than another means of birth control, practiced for mere personal convenience with no regard for the fate of the infant growing in the womb—and from the Bible's standpoint, that self-centered approach is wrong. All too often the right to life of the unborn child has been tragically lost in a tidal wave of cries for the "right" to choose.

The Bible makes it clear that God sees the unborn infant not as a piece of superfluous biological tissue, but as a person created by Him for life. The psalmist said, "For you created my inmost being; you knit me together in my mother's womb. . . . My frame was not hidden from you when I was made in the secret place. When I was woven together in the depths of the earth, your eyes saw my unformed body. All the days ordained for me were written in your book before one of them came to be" (Psalm 139:13,

15-16). God expressed a similar truth to the prophet Jeremiah: "Before I formed you in the womb I knew you, before you were born I set you apart; I appointed you as a prophet to the nations" (Jeremiah 1:5). When Mary, the virgin mother of Jesus, visited her cousin Elizabeth who was pregnant with John the Baptist, we are told that Elizabeth declared to Mary, "As soon as the sound of your greeting reached my ears, the baby in my womb leaped for joy" (Luke 1:44). This is a clear indication that that unborn infant was a person, not just a piece of tissue.

From these and other passages I cannot escape the conclusion that the unborn child is worthy of our concern and protection just as much as a newborn infant or an adult. The unfettered practice of abortion on demand is yet another grim sign of the thundering hoofbeats of the rider on the pale horse in our time.

According to a May 1992 article in a popular women's magazine, American teens have one of the world's highest rates of pregnancy. The U.S. rate is twice as high as England, France, or Canada; three times as high as Sweden; and seven times as high as the Netherlands. A million teens get pregnant every year. Half of those give birth; 36 percent choose abortion; 14 percent miscarry. Also 623 teens get syphilis or gonorrhea every day. Since the beginning of the nationally funded Planned Parenthood program to "educate" teens on sexuality, there has been a 230 percent increase in teen pregnancy in this country.

In 1960, there were fewer than a hundred thousand abortions in this country annually; in 1972 there were nearly six times that number, but in 1978, with the legalization of *Roe* plus the backing of pro-abortion and feminist groups, more than 1.4 million abortions were carried out. Today the annual average is about 1.6 million abortions per year in the United States. The death toll is staggering.

Since 1973 there have been approximately 30 million babies cut off from life while still in their mother's womb.

Sexual promiscuity is obviously another of the major pandemics of our age, along with famine, violence, and disease. In 1988, one of every four births in this country was to an unwed mother. This has been a particular tragedy in our inner cities where, in 1990, 61 percent of all births and 52 percent of all abortions were among unwed, poor, black women.

Almost without exception, the media have staunchly defended a woman's "right" to abortion. One of the few meaningful expressions of disapproval I have found in any newspaper is this prophetic cry against this specter of immorality and suffering raised after the *Roe v. Wade* decision by an editorial writer in the Orlando, Florida, *Sentinel:*

> The devaluation of morality induced by abortion could, and in all likelihood will, have far-reaching effects. Among them are the promotion of promiscuity, depersonalization of the concept of life and activating the destruct button on the family unit as we know it. . . . And what of the woman herself? Abortion by whim could have grave future consequences to her. There is enough unavoidable pain in living without inflicting on oneself, in a period of extremity, the haunting memory of a child that might have been.

This really comes to the heart of the matter. Easy morals and promiscuity lead inevitably to disappointment, despair, and death. Even history declares the tragic legacy of promiscuous societies—from Carthage and Rome to Renaissance France. And the Bible declares repeatedly the wrath of God on those who persist in such sin.

As we approach the end of this millennium, millions of men and women all over the world have turned away from

God and indulged in hedonism and the idolatry of self. In their search for absolute freedom from moral restraint or personal responsibility, many believe they can pay for their sins with cash. When pregnancy is the problem, or when the love and nurture of a child is not in their plans, they simply pay a specialist to cut out the problem, even when the problem is a human life. This libertine mentality of playing now and avoiding the consequences has blinded many young mothers; only later do they discover that they must deal with the physical and emotional scars forever.

I have heard some people say, "Well, I'm against abortion, but with the population crisis and all the unwanted childbirth in the world, especially among the poor, abortion is probably for the best." Let me be quick to say that this kind of reasoning is false and dangerous. The way to solve the population crisis is first to tell men and women that God loves them and has a personalized plan already designed for each one of them. They need to understand that human life is a sacred gift from God. Lead them to a new life in Christ through repentance and a change of heart. Then teach them about self-control and moral responsibility, as God has defined it, and help them with food and shelter if they need it. We can demonstrate God's love, but we must never think that we can solve one moral crisis by condoning another, especially the crime of murder, for unrestrained abortion is nothing less than that.

In this issue alone we can see all the evidence of the four horsemen: the first horseman who deceives, the second who brings violence and strife, the third who brings pestilence, and the fourth who brings death. All life is sacred, created in the image of God; yet the horsemen have no greater intent than to destroy God's creation.

The AIDS Epidemic

The mysterious disease known as acquired immune deficiency syndrome (AIDS) is another crisis of our time that has become a major component of the disasters now afflicting the world. This fatal disease appeared suddenly just a decade ago and has already left a staggering trail of death and destruction in its wake. The *Journal of the American Medical Association* reported in June 1991 on the incidence of AIDS since the first cases appeared in 1981. In that year, a total of 189 cases were reported to the Centers for Disease Control (CDC) from fifteen states and the District of Columbia. The large majority—more than 76 percent—were from New York and California. Of all known cases, 97 percent were among men, 79 percent of whom were homosexual/bisexual men. There were no known cases in that early period among children.

By 1990, however, the picture had changed dramatically. In that year 43,000 cases were reported from all states, the District of Columbia, and the U.S. territories. Two-thirds of the cases were from outside New York and California; 11 percent of all cases reported among adolescents and adults were among women; and nearly 800 cases were reported in children under the age of thirteen.

By any standard, such a rapid spread of a disease would be seen as epidemic in nature. Since the first reports of the disease in 1981, the public health departments in Washington received reports of more than 179,000 AIDS-infected persons. Of these, 63 percent (113,000) have since died. At the same time, AIDS has become a leading cause of death in both men and women under the age of forty-five and in children between the ages of one and five in the United States.

The World Health Organization (WHO) has predicted that the number of AIDS cases will multiply ten times by the end of the century. From the total estimated number of 1.5 million cases in 1992, the toll by the turn of the century will likely exceed 15 to 18 million. Since many of the cases take place in impoverished countries where statistics are at best imprecise, the real toll may be much greater.

In its Resolution 46/203 enacted in December 1991, the WHO urged all member-states to make the AIDS epidemic a top national priority. It also encouraged health providers to protect the human dignity of those affected with the disease. In one of his last addresses to the United Nations before his departure in late 1991, Secretary-General Javier Pérez de Cuéllar said, "If not controlled, AIDS may ultimately prove to be the single greatest assault, beyond the deprivations of poverty, on the health and development of human beings."

A Worldwide Disaster

The magazine *World Press Review* has chronicled the AIDS epidemic from the start. The cover story of its January 1992 issue spotlighted the impact of this new disease around the world and provided research which shows that the spread of AIDS is much greater than anyone has yet documented.

AIDS is the most dreadful epidemic of our generation and may yet be the most fearful killer of all time. According to the World Health Organization, by the year 2000, 90 percent of AIDS cases are expected to be in Third World countries.

AIDS reporting is a serious problem, however, since the WHO suspects that less than 10 percent of the actual occurrences of the disease are ever reported. While the total number of cases being treated worldwide is approximately 420,000, the WHO fears that figure may double, with as many as 8 to 10 million yet undetected infections.

One of the most frightening aspects of HIV is its ability to mutate rapidly. It literally hides from antibiotics and virus medications. So far the only approved anti-viral drugs, AZT and DDI, have at best only slowed the progress of the disease.

In Africa today AIDS is no longer considered an epidemic: rather, as the French magazine *Le Nouvel Afrique Asie* reports, it is a pandemic; that is, an out-of-control, raging global epidemic. Dr. Dorothy Blake of Jamaica, deputy director of the Global AIDS Program, concurs with previous estimates that there are as many as 8 to 10 million AIDS cases worldwide, with 70 percent of those in the Third World. She projects that by the year 2010 the total number of cases may surpass 40 million affected men, women, and children.

Prostitutes are the largest source of contagion in some areas. In countries like Thailand, it is estimated that 75 percent of the male population has visited prostitutes, many of whom, it is now clear, are infected with the AIDS virus. Dr. Jim McDermott, co-chairman of the International AIDS Task Force of the U.S. Congress, in an interview with the Asia News Agency of Manila, reported that the average prostitute in Bombay, India, has six customers per night. Then he offered this frightening estimate: "If one assumes then that 600,000 contacts with prostitutes take place nightly in Bombay, and that a third of these prostitutes are infected, then each night there are 200,000 contacts that might result in AIDS infection."

The Toronto *Globe and Mail* reported that every week in Rio de Janeiro more than 3,000 young women, mostly from rural Brazil, come to join the legion of prostitutes there. Already Brazil has the highest number of AIDS cases in Latin America and the fourth largest in the world. An estimated 700,000 Brazilians have been infected.

Mexico, with just over 7,000 known AIDS cases, seems mild in comparison, but authorities believe the number of reported cases may be a fraction of the actual number. For comparison, nearly 1,200 cases have been reported in Poland and 1,000 in South Africa. In France, both AIDS and hepatitis are on the rampage due to distribution of AIDS-infected blood supplies by the public health service. Beyond the known cases of AIDS and HIV, the French ministry of health estimates that 400,000 people may have been infected with the virus through contaminated blood transfusions.

The Epidemic Explosion

AIDS activist Larry Kramer stated in a May 1992 article in *USA Today* that we have already lost the war against AIDS. Despite the expenditure of more than a billion dollars on research into AIDS and HIV, no cure or even promising therapies have been discovered, and the disease continues to escalate at an alarming rate. Kramer reported that there is one new HIV infection every 54 seconds, and 267 new cases of AIDS every day, or about 8,000 a month. There is one AIDS death every nine minutes; at least 4 in every 1,000 college students are now infected with the disease.

"When I first started hearing about and fighting against what was to be called AIDS," writes Kramer, "there were only 41 cases. When I first started getting really scared and vocal, there were 1,000. America rapidly is approaching 200,000 cases of full-blown AIDS, with up to 10 million people infected with the HIV virus worldwide. No one knows how many there really are. No one knows how to count them."

"The worst thing about these numbers," the writer says, "is that they're terribly low." He adds one further note: "If the U.S. health care system nearly collapsed under the burden of the first 100,000 cases, imagine what another 100,000 will do." But the AIDS pandemic will not be the only drain on public health services. In addition to the statistics above, sexually transmitted diseases (STDs) are reaching epidemic proportions both in the United States and around the world. Research suggests that 63 percent of all STD infections affect people under the age of twenty-five. Among these are a million new cases of pelvic inflammatory disease, 1.3 million new cases of gonorrhea (some strains resistant to treatment), 134,000 new cases of syphilis (a forty-year high), and 500,000 new cases of herpes. There are currently 24 million cases of human papilloma virus (HPV) in the United States, and 4 million new cases of chlamydia each year. Each year 3 million teenagers in this country are affected by STDs.

Christian Compassion

Is there anything to be done about this crisis situation? Are there things that you can do to express your concern and be of some help while continuing to stand for traditional Christian values? Yes, I believe there is, and I believe it is our Christian duty to do something.

To begin with, it would help to be informed on these issues. In addition to recent magazine features, such as *Newsweek*'s special issue on "Teens and AIDS" (August 3, 1992), many excellent books have been published in the past four years describing each of these problems in detail and offering suggestions for ways to get involved. In this regard, I would especially recommend those from the major Christian publishing houses; that is, those affiliated with the Christian Booksellers Association. However, there are others from secular publishing houses that offer informative and objective insights into the scope of the problems, the statistics, the remedies being attempted, and the underlying problems.

The second thing you can do is to learn more about the organizations that educate, inform, and assist men and women on these issues. Your pastor may be able to point you to responsible national or local organizations that focus on these concerns.

Third, you can volunteer to help in your church, civic organization, or local special-interest group. Many of these organizations have a nonmoral, nontheological policy, demanding either that ethical and religious issues not be discussed or that no such discussion may invoke Christian beliefs. Others, however, have a strong religious base and seek to minister to the needs of others with love and Christian compassion. They also seek to tell others how they can find peace with God through faith in Jesus Christ.

The Rise of Racial Conflict

At the same time the world is being ravaged by sexual promiscuity and disease, the horror of ethnic and racial violence has surfaced with new potency. This ancient beast refuses to die. Fifty years after Auschwitz, Bergen Belsen, Buchenwald, and Dachau, armed bands are once again persecuting minorities in Germany. In the first ten months of 1991 there were more than fifteen hundred reported attacks on immigrants in both the eastern and western sectors of this once-divided nation. Neo-Nazi skinheads are the main offenders, but not only have law-abiding citizens not protested their acts, in many cases crowds stand by and applaud the beatings, verbal abuse, and other forms of brutality.

The situation is particularly volatile in the recently liberated cities of East Germany where more than a million factory workers lost their jobs when their inefficient and nonproductive factories were shut down. Many East Germans believe that African, Middle Eastern, and Turkish workers—who generally receive lower wages and, for that reason, are more readily hired for labor positions—are responsible for their plight. Attacks in the factory towns surrounding Dresden and Leipzig have been bitter. Homes have been vandalized or destroyed, and in some places non-Germans have been killed.

But the shadow of rage, hatred, and death all over the world is never far from sight today. Racism has become an issue in France, Britain, Italy, and Scandinavia as well. Recent assault cases in the U.S.—for example, in Brooklyn and in Los Angeles—are only the most visible incidents. Shootings, muggings, beatings, and other forms of racial assault are on the rise in every American city. The fourth horsemen is taking the world by storm.

The evidence of brutality is everywhere. Simply scan the morning headlines, listen to the radio news as you drive along the freeway, or catch the network news on television tonight for a report on the death and tragedy in our midst. Add up the tally of his victims. It no longer takes a science fiction writer to imagine the horrible faces this ancient villain now wears in his mission to ravage, conquer, and destroy.

Since mid-1991, violence has terrorized Yugoslavia and escalated ancient ethnic hatreds in that divided country. Since the conflict began, more than 2 million people were forced from their homes, creating the largest refugee crisis in recent history. The war has been another stark example of racial violence, with more than a million Arab and Muslim families expelled from Serbia and Bosnia-Herzegovina.

Local officials called the atrocities carried out by the Belgrade-based Serbian Army a "cleansing" of ethnically undesirable peoples. In its most sinister forms, the violence, extending from Slovenia to Macedonia, has given that ancient land where the first shots of World War I were fired the atmosphere of Nazi Germany. The fact that inflation has soared, approaching 12,000 percent since the Communist breakup, simply fuels further violence and disorder. Grim scenes portrayed night after night on the network news merely confirm the atrocities and prove, once again, man's inhumanity to man.

Count the bodies slain by the sword in just the past dozen years: terrorist attacks in London, bombings in Beirut, pipe bombs and machine-gun fire in Belfast, another massacre in Africa, a riot in California, a hurricane in Florida. Before World War II the images of death described in Revelation and elsewhere in the prophetic Scriptures would have been unimaginable. Such images must have seemed like fantasy in those times, something totally out of reason. Today, however, we have seen what was once called fantasy become the very shadow of death.

To Save the Earth

For at least the past twenty-five years, the depletion of natural resources and the destruction of the environment have loomed as ever larger issues on the political agenda. The first widespread public visibility of such issues at times focused on blocking economic development and returning the earth to some sort of pre-industrial paradise. In more recent years, the focus has been on finding appropriate ways to dispose of society's waste products, of stopping manufacturing industries from releasing hazardous chloroflourocarbons which damage the ozone layer and increase global warming, of stopping the spread of deforestation and desertification in Third World countries, and of legislating a global program for "biodiversity"—the movement to preserve endangered species, etc.

As with any movement of this kind, many special interests and many kinds of activists (including some extremists) have attached themselves. Some readily grant higher status to insects and mollusks than to human life. They are a small, fringe element, but academic credentials and scientific research give them a stronger influence than their numbers would warrant on issues of concern to voters. Some are entrepreneurs or bureaucrats who hope to profit from the issue. Still others are public-spirited citizens sensitized by the media who want to see a healthy and productive balance between the various components of the ecosystem.

There is no doubt the earth is in trouble. Garbage dumps are bulging, sewage treatment is unmanageable, consumerism has created mountains of virtually indestructible waste, rivers are drying up or being polluted, the seas are being endangered by illegal dumping, nuclear contaminants and other hazardous materials are being stored in unsafe places and, in some cases, seeping into the water table to become the carcinogens and sources of contagion for the next generation. Compounding the tragedy, the earth's tropical rain forests are disappearing, being leveled at a pace of up to twenty thousand acres a day by timber or agricultural operations. These are genuine problems, but there must be some sense of priority in addressing them.

One troubling aspect of the environmental debate is the pseudo-religious tone it has sometimes taken on. The language of ecology is apocalyptic and evangelical at the same time. *Newsweek* magazine began its coverage of the 1992 Earth Summit in Rio de Janeiro with an allusion to the fall of Adam in the Garden of Eden and featured a global survey of nations to determine if "apocalypse soon" was a reasonable threat. Supporters of the movement calling for "environmental stewardship" often appear to worship, not the God of heaven, but the God of nature. This is a dangerous form of idolatry in itself. Furthermore, any time animal life becomes more sacred in our view than human life, we have lost sight of our proper priorities.

Nevertheless, the possible death of our planet by some type of ecological suicide is not God's will. The Bible says, "The earth is the LORD's, and the fulness thereof; the world, and they that dwell therein" (Psalm 24:1 KJV). We must take into consideration God's authentic purpose for this planet. We must be responsible stewards of the resources we have been given by God, and I believe we have gone too far too fast and put elements of the environment in jeopardy. I also believe we can accomplish much by discipline, resourcefulness, and prayer. The earth will not be saved by legislation or by compulsion alone, but by the responsible concern of men, women, and children who care for God's creation. If we do not, the pale horseman of death will march across our world.

A Return to Righteousness

The plagues, diseases, famines, and wars of our day should arouse the world not only to righteous action but to repent of their sins and turn to God while there is still time. John's words make it clear that they exist to awaken humanity to obedience. The Bible teaches that peoples and nations are bringing this pain upon themselves by their secular outlook, hatred, and violence. God has chosen to allow men and women to reap what they sow, to help them learn the lesson that sin brings pain. God does not condone abortion; He deplores it, but He allows it to happen.

God does not infect people with herpes, AIDS, or other diseases. They do it to themselves; God only allows it.

That is the lesson of the four horsemen. They ride in part to warn us. They ride to point the world back to God and His way of righteousness. God's love is forever! There is nothing that can separate us from it, except our own continuing disobedience. Even then, God loves and pursues us despite our self-inflicted ailments. Furthermore, God observes how we respond to moral crises. Do we take His side, or do we simply go along with the crowd? Do we participate in the sin, or do we cry out and speak the truth in love? God gives us fair warning, first to help us, then to examine our hearts.

We cannot simply mourn the crises all around us. We cannot go on pretending that someone else will do the work God expects us to do. We cannot act as though we are helpless to work for repentance and renewal. We must do what we can, with energy and compassion, even though we know that God's ultimate plan is the making of a new earth and a new heaven. Signs indicate that the end of this age is near, yet there is no certainty. It could be centuries from now.

In Matthew 24:7 (KJV), after Jesus had warned about counterfeit religion, the maddening escalation in wars, and the raging famines, He pointed to rampaging pestilences. This word "pestilence" can be translated as "death," a word meaning any infectious malady that is fatal. There have been virulent wars, famines, and plagues during the long period of human history, but nothing comparable to the storm that is yet to come. Its fury is depicted in its devastation of everything before it, killing a large part of the earth's population.

Jesus said, "those will be days of distress unequaled from the beginning, when God created the world." Yes, "and never to be equaled again. If the Lord had not cut short those days, no one would survive" (Mark 13:19-20). Thus, under the fourth seal we see Death and Hades given authority over a fourth of the earth to kill with God's four judgments listed in Ezekiel 14:21: sword, famine, pestilence, and wild beasts.

Suddenly all of our programs for bringing peace, plenty, and longevity through science and technology will be eclipsed by a cataclysmic apocalypse and overturned in appalling brevity—unless in the meantime the world turns to God. This is one of the reasons I feel compelled to continue my preaching all over the world. Medical science has made such quantum leaps to bring to the brink of paradise whole peoples who a short century ago were living at primitive subsistence levels in the jungle. Science continues to make incredible breakthroughs by which we are all benefited.

But pestilence is coming! Many are saying, "Peace, peace," where, despite our best efforts, there will be no permanent peace because we have ignored the Prince of Peace. We have rejected God's commandments that would have helped us live in peace. Thus the sword is coming. There are those who are promising prosperity and plenty if we adopt their particular programs, regime, or ideology. But ultimately the worst disaster ever to strike our world is coming, bringing terrible suffering and death in its wake. What we see today is but a foreshadowing of those days.

14

Hope for the World

Almost every headline, every television news report, and every radio bulletin these days proclaims one essential truth: The modern world is in chaos and no one has a realistic solution. Wherever you look today there are storm clouds of anger and outrage. There is violence, abuse, and unhappiness swirling about us. We see crime and unrest in the inner city, and the economy is dangerously out of control. The whole world is crying out for some word of hope, but all we hear is the babble of wishful thinkers and charlatans. Psychologists, educators, social scientists, physicians, and media wizards of every stripe offer pronouncements and preachments, but even the best ideas generally collapse under closer scrutiny. So far, our modern secular society has produced no positive answers; yet we continue to reach out in hope.

Actually, there is still good reason to hope; there is still time. For with society's failure comes the chance to repent and seek renewal. If we recognize the failures of living without God and turn from our foolishness and disobedience, we may yet be able to receive God's mercy and forgiveness.

Today's headlines are God's warning to a sinful world. The television news flashes are a shadow of His loving hand at work, pushing for the world's redemption. The radio bulletins are a reminder that in spite of our compulsive determination to ruin the earth and destroy God's program of salvation, He has not given up on us completely. Until that day when God's final judgment affixes each of us into place for eternity, there is a chance to begin again. Jesus said, "You must be born again" (John 3:7). That is the last best hope for this world. Ultimately it is our only hope.

At the risk of eternal peril, men and women must not fail to recognize the primary purpose of the riders in John's prophecy, for they come to bring a warning of future judgment. We can still hear the rolling thunder, flee the rising storm, and humble ourselves before Almighty God while there is yet time. Jesus repeatedly warned us of this reality, saying, "do not fear those who kill the body but cannot kill the soul. But rather fear Him who is able to destroy both soul and body in hell" (Matthew 10:28 NKJV). If we truly fear the ultimate Judge of all mankind, we must turn from our sin and be renewed through faith in Christ.

Sobering Realities

If anything, the events of the past three years should cause many people to realize just how real Bible prophecies are for us today. Consider, for example, how the Persian Gulf War focused our view of the biblical references to Babylon and the Middle East, making them as contemporary as today's headlines.

God has not revealed how His work is accomplished, and often God's ways are hidden from us. The writer of Ecclesiastes says, "He has put eternity in their hearts, except that no one can find out the work that God does from beginning to end" (Ecclesiastes 3:11 NKJV). But He has put a longing for truth in our hearts, and He has given us His own truth in the revelations of Scripture. Can that instinctive longing for truth and hope persuade us to respond in time and turn to the source of our salvation? Can we yet be saved?

When the time is complete, the fourth horseman will come forth to kill men and women with the sword, famine, pestilence, and wild beasts. Jesus made it clear that we should not fear the empires and ideologies of the world, no matter how evil they may be, but we must fear the one who controls the activities of this ruthless horseman. Over against the grossest political injustice is put the justice of a God of love. As we examine the fourth horseman we must not forget that he comes not only at the permissive will of God, but also at the command of the One who opens the seven seals; namely, Jesus Christ.

The Bible teaches that the devil is the one who has the power of death (Hebrews 2:14), but he can only act by God's permission, for as Jesus Christ had said to John five chapters earlier, "I am the Living One; I was dead, and behold I am alive for ever and ever! And I hold the keys of death and Hades" (Revelation 1:18).

In the Old Testament we see Satan's using this permission to kill the family of Job. There's a mystery here that none of us can really comprehend. This is "the mystery of iniquity" (2 Thessalonians 2:7 KJV) that we do not yet fully understand. It involves all the great attributes of God including His righteousness, holiness, and justice. It also includes the cleverness, the subtlety, and the power of Satan, and also includes our yielding to Satan's temptations and defying God and the passing down of this sin from generation to generation.

Separation from God

Death is tragic but inevitable. The Bible tells us that what we must fear is the second death, which is eternal judgment and separation from God. That is the ultimate tragedy. If we were two-dimensional beings who had total mortality but no immortality, death would simply end our earthly existence. But the everlasting separation from God is a penalty far worse than the most tortured physical death and something no man, woman, or child should ever have to experience.

Four months before being discovered and deported to a concentration camp by the Nazis, Anne Frank wrote in her now famous diary: "I want to go on living even after my death" (*The Diary of Anne Frank*, 6). After learning that he had serious heart trouble, Simon Wiesenthal, the famous Nazi hunter who brought approximately eleven thousand war criminals to justice during his extraordinary thirty-six-year campaign, said, "I cannot fight against the calendar. . . . As for the Nazis, we are rapidly reaching a biological solution. As I die, so will they" (*The Mail*, 26 June 1983).

This is the reality of death: It is universal and total in every generation. The generation in which we are now living, that is struggling with the problems of the world, will soon be dead and another generation will follow to wrestle and try to cope with similar problems. For many intellectual unbelievers, life is meaningless and hopeless. They do not know where they came from, why they are here, or where they are going. They stumble on in the cosmic darkness. Those of us who have put our trust and faith in Christ know where we have come from, the purpose of our existence, and the glorious future toward which we are headed. This makes life more than worth living. It gives us a hope for the future.

I cannot help but be reminded of the statement that Paul made as a great comfort to all those who believe in Jesus Christ. He said, "Christ Jesus . . . brought life and immortality to light through the gospel" (2 Timothy 1:10).

That is a wonderful comfort to those of us who believe. But it's one of the most terrifying verses in all the Bible for the unbeliever because it means that if you have never repented of your sins and received Christ by faith you are doomed and you live under a curse. You may be able to commit suicide physically, but you cannot self-destruct your soul. You are going to live forever whether you like it or not. But you have a will: You can choose whether you live with God or without him.

The fourth horseman rides to warn us. He warns us first of all of *physical death*—the death of both us and our planet—and what we must do if it is to be delayed. The fourth horseman warns us also of the *spiritual death* of humanity (eternal separation from God) and what Christ has done to save us from this second death, which is far more serious.

If Nothing Else Matters

The great Methodist preacher, author, and missionary of the past generation, Dr. E. Stanley Jones, described how he was once addressing an Indian university on the verities of eternity. When he sat down, the thoughtful Hindu president stood up and sonorously solemnized, "If what this man says is not true, then it doesn't matter. But if what he says is true, then nothing else matters." I feel strongly that my love for Christ and love for people demands of me, as it did of the ancient John the Baptist, to warn people to "flee from the coming wrath" (Matthew 3:7) by putting their faith in Jesus Christ. "Since, then, we know what it is to fear the Lord, we try to persuade men. . . . For Christ's love compels us" (2 Corinthians 5:11, 14).

Therefore the sword in the hand of the rider on the pale horse should arouse us to call people to repentance and faith in Christ and thereby be saved from the second death. It also points us to all jobs yet undone to uplift our fellow humans. The famine and plagues point to the responsibilities God has given us to help Him preserve life on earth and witness the Judgment Day further in the distance. It also points us to the millions who have never heard of Christ.

According to Matthew 24:14, God has tied the second coming of Christ with the success of world evangelization: "And this gospel of the kingdom will be preached in the whole world as a testimony to all nations, and then the end will come." For the first time in history we now have the technology and the capability of reaching the entire human race with the gospel of Christ in this century. While the Bible teaches only a minority will accept and the vast majority of humanity will reject God's offer of mercy, yet God has spared many nations and cities because of a dedicated minority. The wild beasts in their modern forms are red lights to stop our perilous journey away from God and His design and turn us back toward His loving, everlasting arms.

The Weapons of Our Warfare

The fourth horseman of the Apocalypse is the rider who brings death. To achieve his goals, the horseman on the pale horse is armed, as we have seen, with four deadly weapons: the sword, famine, plagues, and wild beasts. Let us take a closer look at these four weapons and their designated role in the physical death of one-quarter of the world's population.

First, the rider carries the sword—the symbol of warfare. In chapter 3 I referred to the interesting story of Damocles. He was a young man who used flattery to endear himself to Dionysius, tyrant ruler of ancient Syracuse. To instruct and warn the ambitious youth, Dionysius invited the flatterer to a banquet and seated him under a sword suspended over his head by a single hair. This graphic lesson was designed to illustrate the perilous nature of one's happiness. We are one hair away from death. The sword of Damocles is a graphic figure of speech and an apt analogy for the state of the world now that the fourth rider closes in on us, sword in hand.

North Americans and Europeans, in contrast to much of the world's population, appear to sit at that banquet of pleasure. By the world's standards we are still feasting in relative luxury, while we forget that just above our heads hangs the Damoclean sword of our own design. At any moment the hair could break, the sword could fall, and the luxuries and pleasures of this world could evaporate for millions.

In John's time the sword of the fourth rider was actually a sword. In those ancient cultures when a weapon could be broken across the knee of a conqueror, there was hope of containing warfare. Now the sword of the fourth rider is no longer easily sheathed. There are monstrous machines of war that may or may not be controllable. No ancient swordsman could kill millions of the world's people. But currently one rider is capable of pushing a button that could set off a chain reaction of death.

Without reference to the Bible, or certainly these passages in the Book of Revelation, the world's scientists are saying many of the same things. Today the fourth horseman rides on his potent pale steed in our very direction waving his sword overhead. How will you respond?

To me, one of the most amazing passages on this theme in the whole Bible is 2 Peter 3:9-10. Verse 10 says: "The day of the Lord will come like a thief. The heavens will disappear with a roar; the elements will be destroyed by fire, and the earth and everything in it." But despite this inevitability,

Peter says we are to reflect Christ who is "not wanting anyone to perish, but everyone to come to repentance" (verse 9). Christians are always—and with every passion and persuasion at their command—to work for the eternal salvation of the souls of men and women. We are also to work in every way for the salvation of society from mass holocaust, even though it seems hopeless.

In the Gospel of Matthew, Jesus says:

> If anyone desires to come after Me, let him deny himself, and take up his cross, and follow Me. For whoever desires to save his life will lose it, but whoever loses his life for My sake will find it. For what profit is it to a man if he gains the whole world, and loses his own soul? Or what will a man give in exchange for his soul?

Matthew 16:24-26 NKJV

That is a thrilling concept for believers, for in giving everything for the Master, we receive even more in return. It should, however, be a sobering thought for the unbeliever who sells his eternal soul so cheaply for the trinkets of today. You don't need to be a certified financial planner to see the inequity of that transaction.

Getting Involved

As we see the storms of famine, starvation, violence, pestilence, and death, we must also see the importance of being concerned and involved. I have suggested that every follower of Christ must be responsible to do something for the hungry, the hurting, and the sick in the world. I also suggest that every one who believes in Jesus Christ must stand up for moral integrity, faithfulness to Scripture, and obedience to His call to resist the oppressors and destroyers of this age. Doing something, even if it feels hopeless or seems insignificant, is better than doing nothing. We must never forget that Jesus made Himself one with the poor saying, "I tell you the truth, whatever you did for one of the least of these brothers of mine, you did for me" (Matthew 25:40).

Jesus Christ has the power right now to feed every hungry person in the world. He had that power in His own day. This was one of the temptations of Satan: If Jesus would turn stones into bread and feed the hungry then He would not have to go to the cross to redeem the world. But Jesus refused Satan's temptation. He overcame the appearance of evil by resisting. Today Christ calls us to resist sin and temptation and to do what we can to change the world. In the past, God spared those who cried out against sin; He challenges us today to be His messengers of truth and hope in the world.

We must never get away from the central truth of the world's need of eternal salvation. We must first gather at the foot of the cross, for the cross and its eternal redemptive power is the only way to know God. Then through Christ, we are empowered to follow Him in obedience in helping the hungry and the hurting wherever they may be.

In John's revelation we are warned of death through plagues and pestilences. Jesus also warned of pestilences. Our Lord prophesied the period of Apocalypse in Luke 21. He warned us there would be plagues. In *The Living Bible* it is translated "epidemics." We are being warned by scientists today about bacteria, viruses, and insects that are highly resistant to radiation, antibiotics, or insecticides. Some feel the tilt of nature has already been affected by modern chemicals. One scientist said: "If the meek don't inherit the earth, the cockroaches will."

As we read on in the Book of Revelation, many things that we find are highly symbolic, but some are literal. One of the judgments referred to in Revelation 9:3 indicates "locusts came down upon the earth." Some years ago in Florida millions of toads overran whole counties. We have been warned in many articles of the possibility that insects could take over the earth in the coming decades. They have become resistant to many insecticides. I read the cover story in one of our most reputable national news-magazines called, "The Insects Are Coming." It was a frightening article to read, especially for those who do not know the Bible. It reminds us of what happened in Egypt when Pharaoh refused to let the ancient Israelites leave.

Examples of Mercy

One of the people most identified with Christian com-passion in our day is Mother Teresa of Calcutta. There are thousands of unknown servants of Christ who quietly and without fanfare invest their lives in feeding, clothing, and caring for the poor. But Mother Teresa has become a kind of representative of them all. I remember the first time I met this tiny, wrinkled, radiant lady. An American consul in Calcutta offered to drive me to Mother Teresa's com-pound in the heart of that sprawling city. When I was introduced to her, she was ministering to a dying person, holding him in her arms. I waited while she helped him face death. When he died, she prayed quietly, gently low-ered him to his bed, and turned to greet me.

We talked till dusk that day. I was surprised to learn how much she knew about me and about our crusades. In her lilting, broken English she asked if I would like to hear some of her experiences with the hungry and the dying. Very simply, she explained her calling to me. Mother Teresa looks past the physical features of every needy man, woman, or child, and she says that she sees the face of Jesus staring up at her through them. In every starving child she feeds, she sees Jesus. Around every sick and frightened woman she cares for, she sees Jesus. Surrounding every lonely, dying man she cradles in her arms is Jesus. When she ministers to anyone, she is ministering to her Savior and Lord.

I also recall the story from my son's book, *Bob Pierce: This One Thing I Do*, about a missionary who ministered to the lepers in China. Through sheer hard work and her own ingenuity, Beth Albert supported the lepers outside the city of Kunming. She was "a merry heart [that] doeth good like a medicine" (Proverbs 17:22 KJV). She loved these people and they loved her. This was the first time these lepers ever had anybody do anything for them, and they all became Christians because of Beth's love. When they asked Beth, "Why are you doing this?" she replied, "Because I love Jesus and He loves you. He loves you so much He sent me to help you. You are precious to God and He sent His Son to earth to die for you so that you might be saved and be in heaven with Him and have a wonderful body. He sent me to show you that He loves you, and I love you" (pp. 68-71).

Until the day the new government gave the edict that every missionary had until sundown to get out of the area, Beth helped her patients in every way she could. She gave sulphatone injections to treat their leprosy. She showed them how to grow some of their own food. She helped them beautify their surroundings with flowers.

Uniting Body and Soul

The debate that existed in the church between the liberals who supposedly minister to the body, and the evangelicals, who supposedly minister to the soul, can only be resolved if both sides learn from each other—and from the Bible. If the conservative church will come to see that the Bible also teaches that we must be concerned about both the soul and the body, and if the social church, on the other hand, will begin to realize that social action without the faithful proclamation of the truth of God's Word is futile, we can serve the kingdom of God together. We are called to minister to human bodies and human spirits simultaneously. As many have said, a starving man will not heed the Word unless he can see Jesus in your life; the two are inseparable.

We are commissioned to follow our Lord onto the streets, trails, and byways of the world and minister to the whole person, whoever he or she may be. As a Christian I am called to minister to the soul and body. But the Lausanne Covenant makes it clear that the priority must always be spiritual. For example, when Jesus was in Capernaum a great crowd came to hear Him preach, and four men brought a man sick of the palsy. But they couldn't get into the house the normal way, so they went up on the roof and broke it up and let down the bed in front of Jesus.

The Scripture says, "When Jesus saw their faith, he said to the paralytic, 'Son, your sins are forgiven'" (Mark 2:5). Jesus' first concern was with the man's sins, then later He healed him of the palsy. I have visited places in the world where I felt I must help meet these physical needs before I could preach the gospel to them. Yet I have always known that their deepest need was spiritual, and that they needed the Water of Life and the Bread of Life more than anything else in the world. But I must follow the example of Jesus and have compassion on suffering humanity.

In one Third World city I have seen dilapidated old vans rumbling up and down the streets at sunrise picking up the corpses of those who had died in the night. When I reflect on those heartrending scenes, I think of Death riding up and down those same streets with Hades close behind. Men and women in the Salvation Army, Mother Teresa, and thousands like them have thrown their lives into the path of the fourth horseman. They are reluctant to let anyone within their reach starve to death or die unattended. They stand in Christ's name squarely in the path of the pale horse of death as he thunders in their direction.

The odds on beating him are ultimately hopeless, because we all die eventually. Still they stand, solitary and strong, doing all they can to prevent premature death. People call them naive, do-gooders, and fanatics. Yet they stand. Still the storm clouds gather, and the sky grows ever darker. This very day, you and I, like the Good Samaritan, must do what we can to help in a torn, bleeding world. Evangelical Christians have built hospitals, nursing homes, clinics, and sent doctors and nurses by the thousands wherever there was need. But still it is only a drop in the bucket. Much more is needed.

The Rich Young Man

Do you remember that moment in Jesus' life when a rich young man came up to Him and asked, "What must I do to inherit eternal life?" Jesus answered, "You know the commandments." The young man answered, "All these I have kept since I was a boy." It was quite a claim. Jesus must have looked carefully at the young man. He must have seen that this seeker was telling the truth. The rich man was sincere, a struggler, a lover of truth. So Jesus answered him, "Sell everything you have and give to the poor. . . . Then come, follow me." The young man couldn't do it. It would have cost him too much. So "he became very sad" (Luke 18:18-23) and turned away. He missed the chance of a lifetime. He asked for life and missed it. He clung to the standards of living to which he had become accustomed, to his security, and he lost everything. We must not let this happen to us.

As I have said earlier, that does not mean Jesus necessarily calls all of us to renounce all wealth. God may entrust wealth to some individuals who are to use it for His glory. But the rich young ruler's problem was not that he was wealthy, but that his wealth came before his commitment to Christ. Is there anything in your life that is keeping you from Him? If so, there is no shortcut. You must loosen your grip on it before you can reach out to Christ.

In a baccalaureate address at a theological seminary, a visiting minister looked down on a large graduating class. He knew firsthand the struggle every student would have at making enough money to live in the vocation of the Christian ministry. So, instead of a formal sermon he used an offering plate and passed out a newly minted dollar bill to each member of the class. Then, to this startled crowd who had never taken from an offering plate before, he told the story of the rich young man. Because of this power of the dollar in his life, he missed the priceless opportunity. "Frame this dollar," the baccalaureate speaker suggested. "Hang it up in your office or home, and write across the face of it, 'Remember the rich young man.'"

That speaker knew the power for good or evil that money could be in our lives. Once we really discover that all our resources are His, then we are free to spend them on others. They are God's gift to us. They are simply tools God has given us to aid Him in proclaiming His love and mercy.

The rich young man clung to God's resources believing they were his, and in clinging to them he lost his way to life eternal. If only he had shared his possessions; if only he had trusted God for his future, he would have found life everlasting.

The Meaning of Life

As the fourth horseman rides we must not forget the rich young man, for if ever a nation could be compared to him, it is the Western world at this time. By continuing on in waste and self-indulgence and rejecting God's plan of salvation, we risk losing not just our homes and the earth, but the life everlasting in heaven, which Christ has gone to make ready for those who have been born again. Meanwhile, Jesus taught those who are His: "Give, and it will be given to you. A good measure, pressed down, shaken together and running over, will be poured into your lap. For with the measure you use, it will be measured to you" (Luke 6:38).

An elderly Isaac told his children, "I am now an old man and don't know the day of my death" (Genesis 27:2). None of us knows the day of our death. We do not know exactly how we will die. But we do know one thing: We are all sentenced to death, and we are all going to have to face the judgment. The writer of Ecclesiastes said, "There is . . . a time to be born and a time to die" (Ecclesiastes 3:1-2).

The Scripture emphatically teaches that all humans carry in themselves a death sentence, but that's not the end. "Man is destined to die once, and after that to face judgment" (Hebrews 9:27). Here is the pale horse with Hades riding just behind him. Because of Adam and Eve's sin, death has come upon the human race. But Christ has conquered sin and death and hell by His cross and resurrection. When we know Christ, we know that we too need not fear the grave. In 1 Corinthians 15:21-22, 26, 55-57, we read:

> For since death came through a man, the resurrection of the dead comes also through a man. For as in Adam all die, so in Christ all will be made alive. . . . The last enemy to be destroyed is death. . . .

273

"Where, O death, is your victory? Where, O death, is your sting?" The sting of death is sin, and the power of sin is the law. But thanks be to God! He gives us the victory through our Lord Jesus Christ.

Jesus Christ came for the purpose of abolishing death, suffering, social injustice, and oppression from this earth—all of which are the result of sin. He came to forgive us our sins and to give us the assurance of eternal life. At this very moment He is preparing a place for us who know Him (John 14:3). Meanwhile He bequeaths the gift of everlasting life which "has now been revealed through the appearing of our Savior, Christ Jesus, who has destroyed death and has brought life and immortality to light through the gospel" (2 Timothy 1:10). In Hebrews 2:14-15, we are assured "that by his death he might destroy him who holds the power of death—that is, the devil—and free those who all their lives were held in slavery by their fear of death." Not only is He going to eliminate death, He is going to remove forever the devil who is the cause of suffering and death.

Defeating the Destroyer

Thank God, the power of this great enemy of mankind, death, has been broken. The last enemy to be destroyed or nullified is death (1 Corinthians 15:26). That is what Jesus Christ did on the cross. God raised Him from the dead. Paul exclaimed: "Where, O death, is your victory? Where, O death, is your sting?" (1 Corinthians 15:55). By the death and resurrection of Christ we can read with joy and certainty, "I am the Living One; I was dead, and behold I am alive for ever and ever! And I hold the keys of death and Hades" (Revelation 1:18).

For the unbeliever, however, death is solemn and terrible. The unbeliever goes immediately to await the Great

White Throne Judgment. One cannot read the Bible and miss the references to hell. They are unmistakable in the teachings of Christ Himself. For every time He spoke of heaven, He spoke of hell several times. To be in hell is to be out of the presence of God forever.

Three words are used by Jesus to describe hell. First, fire. "For our God is a consuming fire" (Hebrews 12:29). Jesus used this symbol over and over. I believe that it means a thirst for God that is never quenched. The second word that is used is darkness. The Scripture teaches that God is light (1 John 1:5). Hell will be the opposite for those who are outside of Christ, for they "will be thrown outside, into the darkness" (Matthew 8:12). Those who have rejected Christ will be separated from this light and subsist in eternal darkness. The third word is death. God is life. Therefore hell is separation from the life of God: "Then death and Hades were thrown into the lake of fire. The lake of fire is the second death" (Revelation 20:14). God takes no delight in people going to hell. He never meant that anyone would ever go to hell. He created hell for the devil and his angels.

But if we persist in going the devil's way and serving the devil instead of God, we are going to end up there. The Scripture says that God's desire is that all men should be saved. The death of Christ was a judgment. God laid on Him the iniquity of us all (Isaiah 53:6). He bore our judgment. He bore our hell. In that brief span of time, He endured hell for every person who ever lived. We cannot be saved by our good works. Only Christ can save us, because on the cross He took our place and bore the punishment we deserve for our sins. All we have to do is put our trust and confidence in Him.

But we have a responsibility to accept His free gift of salvation. We are not automatically saved just because

Christ died for us; the Bible does not support universalism (the idea that all people will be saved). You personally must make your decision for Christ, and if you refuse to do so you are, in a sense, already making a decision—the decision to reject Him and turn your back on His salvation.

The Gift of Life

For the true believer in Christ, one who has repented of sin and has been born from above, the judgment is past. There will be no hell. There will be no eternal death. Christ died for our sins and by His death He destroyed death. In Christ, we no longer regard death as the king of terrors. Paul wrote, "I desire to depart and be with Christ, which is better by far" (Philippians 1:23). Why? Was it because he worked so hard for Christ and had suffered so much? No. He was ready because half a lifetime earlier he had met Christ on the Damascus road. In 1 John 3:14 we read that we have already "passed from death to life." You can have eternal life now. The conquest of death is the ultimate goal of Christianity. Physical death is a mere transition from life on earth with Christ to eternal life in heaven with Christ. For Christians there is such a thing as the shadow of death. Death casts a shadow over those who are left behind.

An unbeliever only sees a hopeless end to life. But the Christian sees an endless hope. In a network television program Malcolm Muggeridge reflected that a true Christian "is longing for the termination of life in time as one longs for the end of a long and arduous three-week sea voyage when one is in the last three days. I look forward to the time when my life will partake of eternity with near irrepressible eagerness."

Perhaps these words of Muggeridge do not describe your feelings about death. Perhaps you are afraid of death and don't relate to the quiet confidence this famous British journalist and television personality felt. The torturing, tormenting fear of death is a condition that is perfectly normal for any who have never come to Christ.

Death is an experience from which people instinctively shrink. Yet for Christians the fear is removed. They have the assurance that the sins for which they would be judged at death have been dealt with, whereas the non-Christian has no such assurance. I do not look forward to the prospect of dying, but I do look forward to death itself. It will be a glorious release. It will be the fulfillment of everything I have ever longed for. The Scripture says, "In thy presence is fulness of joy; at thy right hand there are pleasures for evermore" (Psalm 16:11 KJV).

The Lesson of Justice

Many non-Christians try to convince themselves that they believe neither in the supernatural nor in the hereafter. Try as they will, however, there lingers the nagging, irrepressible realization that we have not been created just for time. We instinctively know that justice alone demands some judgment day. Unless we have knowingly settled the question of our sinful guilt, we are chronically beset by this fear. Until you acknowledge this fact, your fears will worsen. If you admit the possibility of the supernatural and acknowledge the facts of the gospel as they apply to your own life, you would find the fear of death removed and the glorious peace of believing present as a part of your life.

You can have peace in your heart and the personal and perennial assurance of salvation if you will humbly acknowledge yourself as a sinner in God's sight, ask for His forgiveness and cleansing by the blood of Christ shed on the cross, and trust in Jesus, God's Son, as your Savior and

Lord. Christ died to do all this. Let me urge you to get a Bible and read, or ask someone to help you read the following verses: Romans 3:12, 23; 2 Timothy 3:5; Romans 3:19; Ephesians 2:8; Luke 19:10; Romans 5:8; Hebrews 7:25; and Romans 10:13, 9-10.

These are not magical verses. They simply tell us about our need and how to find that need met in Jesus Christ. You do not have to do some wonderful thing to be saved. All you have to do is to accept the wonderful thing Christ has done for you. After you have this assurance in your heart, tell other people about it. Also, show by your daily life that Christ has changed you for His own glory. I invite you to bow your head right now and ask Christ to forgive you and come into your heart and make you part of His family forever. God has promised in His Word, "Yet to all who received him, to those who believed in his name, he gave the right to become the children of God" (John 1:12). This can be your experience today as you turn in faith to Christ and give your life to Him. Don't let another day go by without committing your life to Christ.

The fourth horseman, Death and Hades, rides across our horizons even as you read this page. Can't you hear the thunder? Can't you see the darkening clouds banking in the east? How will you respond?

Part 5

Toward the Coming Sunrise

15

A Voice in the Storm

W hat is this world coming to? Every morning people pick up their morning newspapers, read the headlines, and ask that question. But no one has an answer. No one knows what tomorrow will hold because the changes of our time have been so sudden, so unpredictable, and so wide ranging. Since the fall of 1989, we have seen changes in our world that no sociologist, no scientist, and no scholar could have anticipated. Some of the happenings I have written about in this book will be almost forgotten by the time you read this, crowded off the news by still other crises.

Looking back, we can easily see where we have come from. The 1960s have been called the decade of rebellion, the 1970s the liberation years, the 1980s the decade of indulgence, and the 1990s may be known someday as the decade the whole world changed. It seems as if the world changes radically from day to day. No one knows what will happen next.

In the midst of these rapid changes, people all over the world are desperate to know what the future holds. False prophets of every variety are doing a booming business. Television commentators and authorities in every field are consulted for their wisdom. Some tell us how to thrive amidst the chaos; others tell us how to adapt to the reality of "fractured families"; and still others teach us how to liberate the primal-male or the earth-mother spirit within.

One popular PBS series, "Millennium," proclaims the death of God and the old world order and heralds the birth of a new order in which men and women merge with their environment in a metaphysical search for "the god within."

There is a brisk trade in crystal balls, tarot cards, and Ouija boards. New Age religions are booming everywhere, with such arcane expressions as goddess worship, earth worship, fertility cults, astral projection, and many others mentioned earlier. People everywhere are planning their lives by the signs of the zodiac. Spiritual mediums are prospering. Even computers are being used to predict the future. But there is only one authoritative source that accurately predicts what will happen in the future, and that is God's revealed Word, the Bible.

John's short vision of the martyrs beneath the altar summarizes the Bible's promise of the future and how we are to prepare for it. John must have gasped at the sight. We see his description in the second half of Revelation 6. In a place the writer calls "under the altar," he saw "the souls of those who had been slain because of the word of God and the testimony they had maintained" (Revelation 6:9). They were crying out their loud complaint in one voice: "How long, Sovereign Lord, holy and true, until you judge the inhabitants of the earth and avenge our blood?" (Revelation 6:10).

Westminster Abbey in London and St. Peter's Basilica in Rome have great altars with marble crypts beneath them. Imagine such a church at midnight when it is dark and silent. The tombs of the saints and martyrs lie sealed as they have been for centuries. Then suddenly, seals break, coffins spring open, stones roll away, and hundreds, maybe thousands, of spirits pour into the cathedral, all crying out with one voice, "How long, Sovereign Lord?

How long until we are avenged?" John was witness to just such a vision. Now the scene was packed with the souls of men and women who had died because they were faithful. They were asking the obvious question. When would justice be done? When would they be relieved? When would their faith be rewarded?

This is the question Christians ask even now; yet no one but God Himself can answer it. What we do know for certain is this: when the commotion was subdued, each martyr was given a white robe, and, the prophet says, "they were told to wait a little longer, until the number of their fellow servants and brothers who were to be killed as they had been was completed" (Revelation 6:11).

We learn two important facts from this mysterious moment. First, there will be a point at the end of time when God will judge the inhabitants of the earth. Second, before that moment can come, other men and women equally dedicated to God and His kingdom will be martyred for the Word of God and for the testimony they will maintain. Are you prepared for the risk such words describe?

The Financial Threat

Risk is inevitable, but overshadowing everything we do in the 1990s is the evidence of greed, self-indulgence, and financial irresponsibility; not just on the part of individual consumers, but in government and industry as well. Today, we read, the world is $25 trillion in debt; the United States has become the largest debtor nation with a huge foreign trade imbalance. As a result of these and other problems, thousands of banks folded, the savings-and-loan industry collapsed almost completely, the insurance industry stood for a time on the very threshold of collapse, and the stock market grows more volatile and unpredictable every day.

The great flaw in the American economic system for the past four decades has been an unrealistic faith in the power of prosperity rather than in the ultimate power and benevolence of God. The American Dream became America's god, and wealth and abundance became the symbols of America's devotion. Writing in the March 2, 1992, issue of *Newsweek* magazine, Robert J. Samuelson addressed the practical expression of this faulty thinking. He said:

> Every age has its illusions. Ours has been this fervent belief in the power of prosperity. Our pillars of faith are now crashing about us. We are discovering that we cannot, as we had once supposed, create prosperity at will. . . . Worse, we are learning that even great amounts of prosperity won't solve all our social problems. Our Good Society is disfigured by huge blemishes: entrenched poverty, persistent racial tension, the breakdown of the family, and staggering budget deficits. We are being rudely disabused of our vision of the future. The result is a deep crisis of spirit that fuels Americans' growing self-doubts, cynicism with politics, and confusion about our global role.

The payback for this misplaced investment is all too visible now in the trading columns of the local newspaper.

The Troubled Economy

In 1992 American workers had to work four and a half months to pay their taxes. But there is no end in sight for the government's debt. Today the United States has a direct debt of $3 trillion and contingent liabilities of $6.5 trillion. America's foreign debt alone is in excess of $650 billion. We have gone from being the world's largest creditor to being the largest debtor nation. Such statistics add to the storm warnings we are seeing.

As the world watched the utter collapse of the savings-and-loan industry, the collapse of the $200 billion junk-bond market, the "October Massacre" of the U.S. stock market in 1987, the consolidation of Wall Street financial institutions, the ongoing litany of bank and insider trading scandals, and the near default status of the Social Security Administration, we have to realize that America is in deep financial trouble. Americans of this generation are already spending their great-grandchildren's inheritance. No wonder the economy refuses to rise out of the current recession.

Financial adviser Larry Burkett, author of *The Coming Economic Earthquake*, warns Christians to prepare for a day of reckoning. His evidence is compelling, and his calculations of the financial and moral failures in America and the world show just how far the ravages of the Apocalypse have already taken us. I have no doubt that a financial judgment day is coming for the United States before the end of this century unless our financial problems are addressed.

At the moment this does not seem likely. Items that were luxuries when I was a boy have come to be necessities to many people today. We are living far beyond our means, and eventually it will catch up to us.

Many commentators on the world situation have been comforted by the recent breakup of the Soviet Union and the democratization of the former Communist states of Eastern Europe. Dissolution of the Warsaw Pact, the KGB, and other supporting totalitarian bodies would seem to open the horizons for unlimited peace and accord among nations.

But no reasonable person believes that the transition from a defunct, morally and economically bankrupt system to an enlightened democracy will happen overnight.

It is clear that many in Russia and the other republics are in desperate straits today, and the euphoria over freedom and democratic rights has not so far made hunger, cold, and disappointment any easier to bear. During my recent travels in Russia, I could see the fear and weariness etched in the faces of the people. What I saw in those faces was a very unusual phenomenon; I could only describe it as an expectant euphoria mixed with a somber sense of helplessness and a fear of the unknown future.

In Russia, the new government of the republic had to create a Ministry of Social Protection to ensure that foreign aid actually makes it to those who need it and not to the more profitable black market. In cooperation with its Commission on Humanitarian Aid, the Russian social welfare system is trying to care for more than 65 million needy and disadvantaged persons in thirty-one regions. Clearly the task is formidable. There has been an outpouring of aid and concern from the West, but the depths of the nation's hunger and uncertainty have not really been touched. The European Community voted in 1991 to send 240 million European Currency Units (ECU) of humanitarian aid to Moscow and St. Petersburg. An officer of the Humanitarian Aid Commission, Gennadi Zhukov, commented sardonically, "Of course, that way it is more convenient for them, and easier to show on television."

By the first quarter of 1992 more than 352,000 tons of foreign aid had been shipped to the CIS. In January 1992, representatives of forty-seven nations met in Washington, D.C. to orchestrate aid and assistance plans, including $450 million in loans to Russia to buy Korean rice.

The delegates to the July 1992 Helsinki Conference have had perhaps the most difficult task, discussing and debating ways to provide both economic and military security for the recovering Eastern European nations. As the first post-Communist world summit, there would be little reason to expect the delegates from thirty-five nations to agree on such complex matters since they are so widely separated politically and ideologically on virtually every issue. Whether or not any of their resolutions will actually bring security and stability to the CIS remains to be seen.

Nations like Romania, where I had the great honor and joy of preaching in 1985 prior to the fall of the hated Ceausescu regime, are seeking desperately for their own forms of order and balance. They want to make it on their own, but millions in Romania, Bulgaria, Albania, Latvia, Estonia, and other parts of the former Soviet Union are suffering, starving, and dying from the years of neglect and abuse that they have endured.

Terrible Realities

The vicious war in Yugoslavia underlines the tensions that may emerge in many regions now that self-determination is a possibility. Despite the good intentions on both sides, nuclear weapons remain a threat to the entire world. The very real and imminent danger we face at this moment is the nuclear menace itself and the dangers of a runaway technology we apparently lack the sophistication or knowledge to control. In March 1992, *World Press Review* relayed an article from Poland on the continuing fallout and devastation from the 1986 Chernobyl accident. Despite millions of dollars spent on containment, Chernobyl continues to burn with the ongoing meltdown of its nuclear material. The cement "sarcophagus" built over the reactor is cracked and broken in many places, infiltrated by wind, water, and wild life, and continually pouring out radioactive death and destruction.

The writer says,

> The real danger is posed by radioactive dust.
> High temperature and strong radiation are causing
> the concrete to crumble into dust and mix with the
> fuel, which also turned to dust at the time of the ex-
> plosion. Supposedly, there are now 35 tons of this
> material. If the sieve-like sarcophagus collapses, a
> geyser of deadly dust will erupt through the cracks.
> Even now, little dust storms break out all the time.
> Staying in such a cloud for more than three minutes
> can be deadly.

Chernobyl indeed remains a live time bomb, still killing, still threatening, still polluting the underground rivers
that flow beneath the site, still demonstrating the monstrous evil of nuclear energy gone awry. I can only wonder
what new element this or similar situations may add to the
perilous storm approaching our world today.

The Promise of the Future

Whenever you look closely at the prophecies of the end
times, you will inevitably raise dark specters and enigmas
that trouble the soul. That is as it should be, and that is
why God has given us such pronounced warnings of this
coming storm. But let me also remind you of God's promise. For in the midst of the pessimism, gloom, and frustration,
there is a marvelous hope, and in this present hour of concern there is still the overarching hope, the promise made
by Christ: "If I go and prepare a place for you, I will come back"
(John 14:3). He died on the cross for our sins. He was
raised again. He ascended to heaven. The Bible says that
He's going to return in triumph.

One day after His resurrection, He was talking to His
disciples. "They asked him, 'Lord, are you at this time going to restore the kingdom to Israel?' He said to them: 'It

is not for you to know the times or dates the Father has set by his own authority. But you will receive power when the Holy Spirit comes on you; and you will be my witnesses in Jerusalem, and in all Judea and Samaria, and to the ends of the earth'" (Acts 1:6-8). After He had said that, He was taken up from them. They watched His ascent and a cloud enveloped Him beyond their sight.

The faith of the disciples was still small, and some of them probably had nagging doubts that they would ever see Him again in spite of His promises. They must have been looking intently into the sky, with a sense of loss and sadness as He was ascending. Then there appeared beside them two men dressed in white. "'Men of Galilee,' they said, 'why do you stand here looking into the sky? This same Jesus, who has been taken from you into heaven, will come back in the same way you have seen him go into heaven'" (Acts 1:11).

The time of His return, Jesus had assured them, was a secret known only to His Father. However, indications as to when it will happen are foretold in various books of the Bible. In the ninth chapter of Daniel we are told that an angel brought the word to the prophet that God had appointed seventy weeks to His people and their holy city. There have been scores of books written about these seventy weeks, and I do not intend to spend time here discussing what they mean. I can only meditate, think, and interpret as best I can. There are some things I believe we can know for certain about this and other prophetic passages; there are other passages where we must be more cautious, and sincere Bible scholars may disagree on some details where God has chosen not to speak as clearly concerning the future. But virtually everything has been fulfilled that was prophesied in the Scriptures leading up to the coming of Christ. We know His coming is near!

What needs to be noted here is that the angel did say
something to Daniel that relates to the four horsemen:
"War will continue until the end, and desolations have
been decreed" (Daniel 9:26). This gives us a clear clue to
the whole history not only of the Middle East, but of the
past several thousand years of the human race. It has been
a great battleground and a scene of unfulfilled dreams,
dashed hopes, broken hearts, mutilated bodies across
thousands of battlefields on which hundreds of millions
have died.

The Hope of His Coming

The promised coming of the Lord has been the great
hope of believers down through the centuries. Emil Brunner
said, "What oxygen is to the lungs, such is hope to the
meaning of life." Some years ago in a Telstar discussion,
Lord Montgomery asked General Eisenhower, "Can you
give any hope?" Mr. Eisenhower prescribed a way out,
"which if man misses," he said, "would lead to Armageddon." Winston Churchill's favorite American song was,
"The Battle Hymn of the Republic," which begins with the
stirring phrase, "Mine eyes have seen the glory of the coming of the Lord."

The great creeds of the church teach that Christ is coming back. The Nicene Creed states, "He shall come again
with glory to judge both the living and the dead." Charles
Wesley wrote seven thousand hymns, and in five thousand
he mentioned the Second Coming of Christ. When Queen
Elizabeth II was crowned by the archbishop of Canter-
bury, he laid the crown on her head with the sure pro-
nouncement, "I give thee, O sovereign lady, this crown to
wear until He who reserves the right to wear it shall return."

But till that time, one of America's best-known columnists summed it up when he said, "For us all, the world is disorderly and dangerous; ungoverned, and apparently ungovernable." The question arises: Who will restore order? Who can counter the danger of the nuclear holocaust? Who can bring an end to AIDS and the other epidemics of our time? Who alone can govern the world? The answer is Jesus Christ!

The psalmist asked centuries earlier: "Why do the nations conspire and the peoples plot in vain? The kings of the earth take their stand and the rulers gather together against the LORD and against his Anointed One. 'Let us break their chains,' they say, 'and throw off their fetters.' The One enthroned in heaven laughs; the Lord scoffs at them. Then he rebukes them in his anger and terrifies them in his wrath, saying, 'I have installed my King'" (Psalm 2:1-6). He promises the Anointed One, "I will make the nations your inheritance, the ends of the earth your possession. You will rule them with an iron scepter. . . . Therefore, you kings, be wise; be warned, you rulers of the earth. Serve the LORD with fear and rejoice with trembling" (Psalm 2:8-11). Then He advises the whole earth, "Blessed are all who take refuge in him" (verse 12).

Yes, God has promised this planet to His Son, Jesus Christ, and someday it will be His. He will bring an end to all the injustice, the oppression, the wars, the crime, the terrorism that dominate our newspapers and television screens today. But before that time comes, the four horsemen are going to vent their storm of fury across the pages of history.

For the Christian believer, the return of Christ is comforting, for at last men and women of faith will be exonerated. They will be avenged. The nonbeliever will see and understand why true Christians marched to the sound of another drum. But for the sinful unbeliever, the triumphant return of Christ will prove disastrous, because Christ's return ensures final judgment.

The Final Judgment

Consider what happened in John's next vision. It is a picture of the absolute horror of the final judgment. Carefully, the Lamb opened the sixth seal (Revelation 6:12-17). Suddenly, chaos gripped the universe. An earthquake that no Richter scale could measure shakes the entire world. The sun is eclipsed completely. In fact, reports John, "the sun turned black . . . the whole moon turned blood red, and the stars in the sky fell to earth, as late figs drop from a fig tree when shaken by a strong wind" (Revelation 6:12-13).

Here is a storm of apocalyptic proportions. The world trembles with terror. The great cities collapse. John sees kings, princes, generals, the rich, the mighty, slaves, free, every human being left on the earth running to escape the horror of God's final judgment. They flee to mountain caves. They cower behind rocks and boulders. But there is no escape. Desperately they cry out, "Hide us from the face of him who sits on the throne and from the wrath of the Lamb! For the great day of their wrath has come, and who can stand?" (Revelation 6:16-17).

There will be a day of reckoning when God closes His books on time and judges every creature, living and dead. This vision of the judgments leading to the final judgment permeates the sixty-six books of the Holy Scripture. Before John's vision it was called the "day of wrath" (Zephaniah 1:15; Romans 2:5). Amos called it "the day of the Lord" (Amos 5:18), as did Jesus' own disciple, Peter (2 Peter 3:10). Paul, again and again, called it "the day of our Lord Jesus Christ" (1 Corinthians 1:8; Philippians 1:6). It is often referred to as the Great Tribulation.

All through history there have been days of judgment. The first judgment of God fell on Adam and Eve at the beginning of time (Genesis 3:16-19). Their original sin brought God's day of wrath and a permanent curse on all who followed. God judged Cain. God judged the descendants of Cain with the flood that Noah escaped. Other judgments include the confusing of tongues at Babel, the fiery destruction of Sodom and Gomorrah, the captivity and dispersion of the Israelites.

The Wheat and the Tares

Throughout this book, I have pictured the coming judgment of the human race as a combination of the biblical prophecy of the four horsemen and the image of a coming storm in Matthew 24. The New Testament record makes this picture perfectly clear: the final judgment will be a tempest of unimaginable proportions and the four horsemen will ride forth on the winds of God's wrath.

Jesus pointedly charged the Pharisees who doubted His teachings about the coming storm, saying, "When it is evening you say, 'It will be fair weather, for the sky is red'; and in the morning, 'It will be foul weather today, for the sky is red and threatening.' Hypocrites! You know how to discern the face of the sky, but you cannot discern the signs of the times" (Matthew 16:2-3 NKJV). He warned that the storm He would one day unleash upon the earth would surpass anything they had ever known. Later he said, "As the lightning comes from the east and flashes to the west, so also will the coming of the Son of Man be" (Matthew 24:27 NKJV). The time of judgment will come swiftly and at a time known only to God, but it will certainly come.

In the wilderness outside Jerusalem, John the Baptist warned of the coming judgment. He instructed those who would hear him that true repentance is the only way to escape that judgment day. Then came Jesus Himself. He, too, spoke of the final judgment, often in the language of fields and harvest. "At that time," our Lord warned, "I will tell the harvesters: First collect the weeds and tie them in bundles to be burned; then gather the wheat and bring it into my barn" (Matthew 13:30).

At another place, Jesus met a Jewish teacher and explained the judgment to him. "For God did not send his Son into the world to condemn the world," Jesus informed the man, "but to save the world through him" (John 3:17). Then He made perfectly clear how one can be saved from the wrath of God's judgment. "Whoever believes in him is not condemned, but whoever does not believe stands condemned already because he has not believed in the name of God's one and only Son" (John 3:18). The man who does not believe dooms himself to the judgment.

My wife and I are parents. When our children disobeyed our family rules, it was necessary to correct them. Where there is no judgment, there is no justice. We didn't like reprimanding the children. To the contrary, we hated it. We loved them, and it hurt us to see them suffer. But simply to allow them to get by with those acts that were destructive to them in the long run would not have been good parenting. It would have been soft, uncaring parenting. We threatened judgment for their own good. We carried out the judgment for the same cause.

I know a wealthy family whose oldest son was exposed to the drug culture during his senior year of high school. At a party the boy snorted cocaine with his rich friends. The father found out and confronted his son. Carefully he explained the risks of drug use, especially cocaine. He took the boy to the library and they read together the stories of lives ruined by drug habits begun at similar high-school parties. But the teenager laughed at his father's old-fashioned ideas. So, hoping to prevent his son from further experiments with cocaine, the father threatened the boy with a day of judgment. "If you try it again," he warned, "you will be grounded, and your car will be parked in the garage."

Still the boy disobeyed. The father discovered his son's disobedience and evoked the judgment. The son was grounded. His car keys were taken from him. All this was motivated by a desire to help the son, to save him from the horror of drug addiction. But nothing worked; the son continued using cocaine in college. Knowing of their son's growing addiction, his parents refused to supply him with any funds to maintain the habit. Instead, they worked and prayed and telephoned. They poured out their love to their son. They begged him to come home for treatment and offered to pay for a drug rehabilitation program in a local hospital. The son ridiculed their fears and ignored their warnings. He began to steal to pay for his drugs. Then, one Saturday night, he was killed in an attempted robbery of an all-night liquor store.

That young man brought judgment on himself. Like God, the parents threatened judgment not to condemn him but to save him. Still, the son's disobedience frustrated the purposes of the father and brought even worse judgment on himself. Death came, not because of the father, but through the son's disobedience.

Learning Obedience to God

As God, our loving Father, looks on, we, His disobedient children, continue to disobey. It would not be just for Him to let our sins go unpunished. Justice requires judgment. But God loves us and works to save us from the results of our own disobedience. In His Word, God has repeatedly warned us of the coming judgment. He has offered us a way of escape through repentance of sin and faith in Christ His Son. He has sent harbingers like the four horsemen to sound the alarm, to awaken us from our deadly sleep, to point us in the right direction, to get us on the trail again. There is a final judgment coming, but God hates that day and continues to postpone it so that the world might be saved.

But we fool ourselves if we think our God will hold back the storms of judgment forever. He will not. God *is* a God of love. We sing, "Jesus loves me; this I know, for the Bible tells me so," when we are children. We sing, "Love lifted me," as adults. We must never forget that God loves us more than we can ever begin to realize because God is a God of mercy. But we must remember as well that He is also a God of justice. He is a consuming fire.

Nothing we have ever seen or heard compares to the holiness of God. He is absolutely pure. Our purest thoughts are ugly in the sight of God compared to His purity. Like the woman in clean, white clothing who looks gray and faded while standing in the new-fallen snow, our attempts at holiness are as filthy rags compared to God's purity. He can never change. He cannot look upon evil. Evil is the enemy, and those who ignore God's warning and continue to be allied with evil will be judged.

Still He has done and continues to do everything He can to save us from that judgment day. We have already referred to Jonah, who preached to the people of Nineveh, a very idolatrous and wicked people. Like the four horsemen, this reluctant prophet warned the people of God's day of judgment. The king and all the people obeyed; they repented in sackcloth and ashes. Estimates of the number of those who confessed their sins through Jonah's preaching range from three hundred thousand to 2.5 million souls. It was probably the largest spiritual awakening in history.

The Harvest of Repentance

Because Nineveh repented, God changed His mind. He spared them and withheld His hand of judgment. In fact, as we mentioned earlier, judgment did not fall on Nineveh for 150 years. Then Nineveh was destroyed by invading armies on God's day of judgment.

Huldah, the prophetess, was told by the Lord to send a message to the people of Judah that judgment was going to fall, "This is what the Lord says: I am going to bring disaster on this place and its people" (2 Kings 22:16). However, the message to the king himself was different:

> Because your heart was responsive and you humbled yourself before the LORD when you heard what I have spoken against this place and its people, that they would become accursed and laid waste, and because you tore your robes and wept in my presence, I have heard you, declares the LORD. Therefore I will gather you to your fathers, and you will be buried in peace. Your eyes will not see all the disaster I am going to bring on this place.
>
> 2 Kings 22:19-20

I believe the judgment of God can be withheld for a period of time. It doesn't take the repentance of a whole city to delay God's judgment plans. Abraham was granted a delay if he could find a mere ten righteous men in Sodom. Still, the judgment day is coming. The thunder and lighting grow louder every day. How long will God postpone the storm of His wrath? We do not know. But we do know from this wonderful vision of John what we believers must do in the meantime: We must continue working as God's allies in the salvation of the lost and in social justice.

Again, remember John's vision. The saints under the altar were instructed to wait longer until their brothers and sisters in the faith "who were to be killed" would join them. The martyrs and the saints had been killed because of the Word of God and the testimony they had faithfully maintained. When we hold up the Word of God, when we maintain our testimony faithfully, we too will suffer. Some of us will die.

We must not be content with easy answers. The call to follow Christ is not easy. It is easy to receive salvation, but there can never be cheap grace. Our redemption by the cross of Jesus was costly to God. So also we must be willing to deny self and take up a cross and follow Christ. It is not easy to follow Him. It is not easy to decide what tasks you can do and what tasks you must leave for others. It is not easy to take a stand when issues are complex and two-sided. It is not always easy to witness for Him. It is not easy to work against evil that judgment might be postponed, but it is the task to which we all are called.

This is why the Bible's prophecies are in such stark contrast with the synthetic predictions of computers. The Bible takes human nature into account. The Bible prophesies a swift descent into lawlessness and world chaos so shocking that only God Himself can intervene and save the human race. With his mind illuminated by the Holy Spirit, the apostle Paul predicted that "the final age of this world is to be a time of troubles. Men will love nothing but money and self; they will be arrogant, boastful, and abusive; with no respect for parents, no gratitude, no piety, no natural affection; they will be implacable in their hatreds, scandal-mongers, intemperate and fierce, strangers to all goodness, traitors, adventurers, swollen with self-importance" (2 Timothy 3:1-4 NEB).

Such people, he said, will not long enjoy the fruits of their scientific attainments, however marvelous. He predicted, "Destroyed they shall be, because they did not open their minds to love of the truth, so as to find salvation" (2 Thessalonians 2:10 NEB).

When Christ was asked by His disciples, "What will be the sign of your coming and of the end of the age?" He replied along the same line. Instead of picturing a future filled with scientific achievements amid an era of perpetual peace, He foretold an endless sequence of disorder and tragedy until He Himself would return to bring it to an end. He said, "Nation will rise against nation, and kingdom against kingdom. There will be great earthquakes, famines and pestilences in various places" (Luke 21:10-11). The Bible teaches that there will be no break in the chain of sorrows and disasters that will afflict the human race until they see "the Son of Man coming in a cloud with power and great glory" (Luke 21:27).

A Compassionate Warning

Before the storm of judgment comes, however, God always warns the people. He warned the people of Noah's day before destruction came. He warned the people of Sodom before destruction came. He warned the people of Nineveh before judgment came. He warned the people of Jerusalem before destruction came.

What happened in Noah's day will be repeated at the end of history. We have the word of Jesus who said, "As it was in the days of Noah, so it will be at the coming of the Son of Man" (Matthew 24:37). The two experiences will run parallel in many important aspects, not only in the vast extent of lawlessness and the universality of catastrophe, but also in the earnestness of warning and the provision of a way of escape. At God's bidding, Noah preached for 120 years. During that time he warned the people to repent of their sins and turn to God, but the people laughed and sneered. Then, as time ran out, astonishing things began to happen. Clouds appeared in the sky for the first time. Animals began to gather. The rain came. Jesus said, "The flood came and destroyed them all" (Luke 17:27).

Something just as devastating and just as global in its effects is going to happen again, unless man repents. The massive devastation we mentioned in chapter 1 wrought by Hurricanes Andrew and Camille is a mere snapshot of the wrath to come. The tragedy and the irony of the portrait with which I began this book is really just a tiny taste of the inconceivable reality that is yet to come upon this earth. Now, as then, people try to deny the fury of the coming storm. They want to continue in their self-gratification and intoxication with the world's pleasures. But denial will not stop the hand of God.

The apostle Peter wrote, "In the last days mockers will undoubtedly come—men whose only guide in life is what they want for themselves—and they will say: 'What has happened to his promised coming? Since the first Christians fell asleep, everything remains exactly as it was since the beginning of creation!'" (2 Peter 3:3-4 PHILLIPS).

But Peter warned, "The day of the Lord will come as suddenly and unexpectedly as a thief. In that day the heavens will disappear in a terrific tearing blast; the very elements will disintegrate in heat and the earth and all that is in it will be burned up to nothing" (verse 10).

Before all of these terrifying things take place, the Bible indicates there will be a turning away from the true faith on the part of many who profess Christ, and much social and political unrest all over the world.

A Word for the World

Jesus, however, also said another interesting thing that I have already elaborated on: "This gospel of the kingdom will be preached in the whole world as a testimony to all nations, and then the end will come" (Matthew 24:14). Today, for the first time in history, we are witnessing the preaching of the gospel on a global scale such as the world has never known, using radio, the printed page, and television. It's one of the signs that we are to look for as we approach the end of history. The Bible teaches that there is deliverance from the things that are about to come upon the world for those who put their faith and trust in Jesus Christ. Not by chemicals, but by Christ. Not by smoking crack cocaine or injecting heroin, but by bringing their minds and hearts into harmony with God through submission to His will and accepting His forgiveness as offered from the cross. In Christ alone there is deliverance from the world's tortured thoughts, healing for weakened minds and bodies, and freedom from the sordid, destructive, and immoral habits that are destroying so many today.

But more important, there is hope for the future. The Bible teaches that God has planned utopia. There *is* a glorious new social order coming, but it is going to be brought by Jesus Christ Himself when He returns. I believe the time is short; we must each tell that good news however we can. Listen for the voice of Jesus above the storm, saying, "So you also must be ready, because the Son of Man will come at an hour when you do not expect him" (Matthew 24:44). Are you ready?

16

The Promise of Peace

The world we live in is like a hurricane—ever-changing, ever-changeable, always unpredictable, and frequently destructive—but there are some things that never change: The love of God. His matchless grace and mercy. His boundless forgiveness. Until that day when Christ shall come "with shout of acclamation," there is still hope for the human race. While there is yet time, we must earnestly seek Him.

The more I learn of the realities of the Book of Revelation, the more I realize there are still many mysteries, ambiguities, and complex uncertainties which cannot yet be fully understood. But we are not without understanding. From the truth we have already learned of God, we have proof of His love and provision for humanity. From the unfailing accuracy of biblical prophecy, we have evidence of the faithfulness of Scripture and its often stunning relevance to the circumstances and events of our lives. Thus we know His Word is true.

Paul wrote to Timothy, "All Scripture is given by inspiration of God, and is profitable for doctrine, for reproof, for correction, for instruction in righteousness, that the man of God may be complete, thoroughly equipped for every good work" (2 Timothy 3:16-17 NKJV). With that assurance, we study this Word and discover how its truth can be applied to our individual lives and needs.

Paul also understood the implications of his message.

He writes: "I charge you therefore before God and the Lord Jesus Christ, who will judge the living and the dead at His appearing and His kingdom: Preach the word! Be ready in season and out of season. Convince, rebuke, exhort, with all longsuffering and teaching" (2 Timothy 4:1-2 NKJV).

I do not fully understand everything that will happen when the events I have described in this book come to pass, but I also realize we do not have the complete picture yet. God reveals to each age what His children are able to understand. I am prepared to rest in that knowledge until God opens up the next chapter in this incredible adventure.

His Name Is Faithful and True

For now, let us look ahead to a yet future time in which another horse and rider appear before the prophet—One who rides to bring the kingdom of God in all its fullness to earth. Like the first horse in chapter 6, the horse we see later in chapter 19 is also white. But there the resemblance ends. The rider of this horse is Jesus Christ Himself, coming in glory and power to the earth.

As I draw this narrative to a close, I would like to look ahead to those verses to see what the Spirit of Christ will reveal to us in the account in Revelation 19. Chapters 7 through 18 deal with that catastrophic saga of history, perhaps just ahead, when "there will be great distress, unequaled from the beginning of the world until now—and never to be equaled again." Jesus says, "If those days had not been cut short, no one would survive, but for the sake of the elect those days will be shortened" (Matthew 24:21-22).

I believe it will be a time of nuclear conflagrations, biological holocausts, and chemical catastrophes spilling over the earth, bringing humanity to the edge of the precipice. History will bottom out on the battlefield of Armageddon. We already see its storm clouds creeping over the earth.

Will the human race exterminate itself? It *almost* will, as Jesus stated. But just before it does so, Christ will come back! The demonized leaders "of the whole world" will have mobilized both as antagonists and protagonists of that coming world's anti-God system, probably headed by the antichrist. They'll be gathered, we're told, "together to the place that in Hebrew is called Armageddon" (Revelation 16:16).

Woodrow Wilson spoke of "the war to end all wars," and Ellen Goodman, the columnist, wrote of the possibility of an ominous war ahead "to end all life." But rest assured, *it won't happen.* God has other plans for the human race. Life is not going to be brought to a catastrophic end. God's intervention will see to that.

Everywhere I go, people ask, "Are you an optimist or a pessimist?" My reply is that I'm an unswerving optimist. In the words of Robert Browning, "The best is yet to be." I believe that, too, and in the final pages of this book I want to explain why.

With forty or more wars raging in the world at this moment, we have to wonder about our hopes for peace on earth. Any one of those wars could lead to the beginning of the end. So I ask: Can paradise be restored? Is there light at the end of the tunnel? Or as the late Winston Churchill asked a young American clergyman thirty years ago, "Young man, can you give me any hope?"

Back to the Bible

For the answer to Churchill's question, I take you back to the future. In Revelation 19:11-13, the ancient apostle writes, "I saw heaven standing open and there before me was a white horse, whose rider is called Faithful and True. With justice he judges and makes war. His eyes are like blazing fire, and on his head are many crowns. He has a name written on him that no one knows but he himself. He is dressed in a robe dipped in blood, and his name is the Word of God."

The four horses of the Apocalypse of chapter 6 have gone on before. Other judgments have fallen. Now God is about to make His final move. The identity of the rider on the white horse in chapter 19 is the Lord Jesus Christ, Israel's Messiah, head of the church, the King of kings and Lord of lords.

The white horse of deception in Revelation 6 darkens to a dirty gray in comparison to the impeccable, immaculate white horse here in Revelation 19. Whereas the red horse in Revelation 6 inflicts war to kill and defoliate, this white horse, with the mounted King of kings draped in a robe dipped in blood, declares war on the killers to establish His kingdom of salvation and peace. Whereas the black horse of Revelation 6 carries famine and disease, the white horse of Revelation 19 brings healing and the Bread of Life. Whereas the pale horse of Revelation 6 brings death and hell, the white horse of chapter 19 brings life and heaven to all who place their faith in Him.

When will the Man on the white horse, as outlined in Revelation 19, appear? The clear teaching of the Word of God is that He will come when the human race has sunk to its lowest and most perilous point in all history—the time when the four horses riding on the storms of Apocalypse have run their course and driven mankind to the very edge of the precipice.

There is an eerie feeling throughout society today. Albert Schweitzer described it when he lamented, "Man has lost the capacity to foresee and to forestall. He will end by destroying the earth." Left to ourselves, that is precisely what we will do. Barbra Streisand put her finger on the problem when she said, "I do believe the world is coming to an end. I just feel that science, technology and the mind have surpassed the soul—the heart. There is no balance in terms of feeling and love for fellowman."

Who better than the late behaviorist, B. F. Skinner of Harvard could respond to such a question? At the age of seventy-eight, Skinner shocked the American Psychological Association Convention by asking in understandable anger and anguish, "Why are we not acting to save the world? Is there to be much more history at all?" When Skinner was asked afterward, "Has the observer of social conditioning lost his optimism?" his reply was, "I have. . . . When I wrote *Beyond Freedom and Dignity*, I was optimistic about the future. A decade ago there was hope, but today the world is fatally ill. . . . It is a very depressing way to end one's life. . . . The argument that we have always solved our problems in the past and shall, therefore, solve this one is like reassuring a dying man by pointing out that he has always recovered from his illness" (*Philadelphia Inquirer*, 25 September 1982).

Of Peace and War

In an article entitled "Psychology and Armageddon" in *Psychology Today*, Harvard Professor of Psychiatry Dr. Robert Coles described a prevailing feeling worldwide that humanity is heading for Armageddon. The gamble ahead will be the worst in all history. The antichrist (or his system) will be a monstrous impostor, the incarnation of iniquity. All people the world over will think and say, "We've been had!"

There is coming a time in the future—whether near or far I do not know (especially since Jesus warned us not to speculate on dates)—when a counterfeit world system or ruler will establish a false utopia for an extremely short time. The economic and political problems of the world will seem to be solved. But after a brief rule the whole thing will come apart. During this demonic reign tensions will mount, and once again the world will begin to explode with a ferocity involving conflict on an unparalleled scale. Even the grip of the world leaders will be unable to prevent it. This massive upheaval will be the world's last war, the battle of Armageddon. According to secular and scientific writers, there is an inevitability to humanity's date with Armageddon.

Arming for Apocalypse

If I were not a believer in Christ, I might at this point succumb to total pessimism. A while back I read a column by Ellen Goodman in which she asked, with "Armageddon perhaps around the corner, what are intelligent people to do? Wrap ourselves in mourning sheets and wait for the end?" Are we to stare up at that intimidating nuclear sword of Damocles that "has hung over us like some apocalypse without the promise of redemption?"

Definitely not! Jesus urged that when universal holocaust begins "to take place, stand up and lift up your heads, because your redemption is drawing near" (Luke 21:28). Rather than pulling sheets around us, we are to look for redemption in Christ. We are also to work as if these events are far in the future. Jesus promised a blessing on those who would be found working when their Lord returns.

I do not want to linger here on the who, what, why, how, or when of Armageddon. I will simply state my own belief that it is near. Without a sudden and massive worldwide revival of God's people and a return to the morality and the values set down in the Word of God, earth is already under the condemnation of God, and its judgment will be swift, unavoidable, and total. In the face of this coming storm, we have only one sure hope: Armageddon will be interrupted by the return of Jesus Christ on the white horse leading the armies of heaven, as clearly prophesied in many Bible passages.

In no place is this more definitively or dramatically described than in Revelation 19. When John foresaw "heaven standing open and there before me was a white horse, whose rider is called Faithful and True," he went on to describe the rider as "the Word of God" followed by the armies of heaven "riding on white horses and dressed in fine linen, white and clean." Turning his focus back on the coming Messiah, John saw that "out of his mouth comes a sharp sword with which to strike down the nations. 'He will rule them with an iron scepter'" (Revelation 19:11-15).

In case anyone gets confused as to His identity or authority, John makes it unmistakably plain, "On his robe and on his thigh he has this name written: KING OF KINGS AND LORD OF LORDS" (Revelation 19:16).

The Man on the White Horse

What does the Man on the white horse do? John makes clear that He and His army from heaven are faced with the antichrist and the military forces gathered together to make war not only against each other but against the armies of heaven. But the antichrist is "captured, and with him the false prophet who had performed the miraculous signs on his behalf. With these signs he had deluded those who had received the mark of the beast and worshiped his image. The two of them were thrown alive into the fiery lake of burning sulfur" (Revelation 19:20). The antichrist's collaborators and colleagues are all conquered by Jesus Christ.

Adolf Hitler's grandiose notion of Nazism was that he would establish an imperialist empire over the entire earth, and that it would "last a thousand years." It didn't happen. A *Time* magazine writer pointed back to Mao Tse Tung's global "export of revolution" as an obsessive vision "to hasten the Communist millennium." But today Mao's empire has vanished, his vision already radically altered with even greater changes on the horizon.

People may ask: Is John the only one who made Christ's Second Coming to this earth so plain? No, the oldest quotation from all literature is Jude 14-15. Jude cited "Enoch, the seventh from Adam, who prophesied that the Lord is coming with thousands upon thousands of his holy ones to judge everyone" alive, including "all the ungodly." The ungodliest man or system ever will be the antichrist. Paul wrote to the Thessalonians, "The Lord Jesus will overthrow [that lawless one] with the breath of his mouth and destroy [him] by the splendor of his coming" (2 Thessalonians 2:8).

The return of Jesus Christ is the great assurance for the Christian. Seymour Siegel has commented, "The central problem of Christianity is: If the Messiah has come, why is the world so evil? For Judaism, the problem is: If the world is so evil, why does the Messiah not come?" The Messiah is coming to solve both dilemmas, and soon. Every devout orthodox Jewish worshiper prays every day, "I believe with complete faith in the coming of the Messiah. Even though He tarry, yet I will wait for Him every coming day."

The Scripture says, "The government will be on his shoulders. And he will be called Wonderful Counselor, Mighty God, Everlasting Father, Prince of Peace. Of the increase of his government and peace there will be no end. He will reign on David's throne and over his kingdom, establishing and upholding it with justice and righteousness from that time on and forever" (Isaiah 9:6-7).

Arnold Toynbee of Cambridge foresaw that "only a world government could save mankind from annihilation by nuclear weapons." That's right. Jesus Christ will be the King over all the earth in His theocratic world government.

Jonathan Schell's book *The Fate of the Earth* envisages a day when "existing institutions must give way to some sort of transcendent sovereignty and security, presumably by a government that embraces all mankind," in fact world government. That may happen in some secular fashion on the road to Armageddon, but it will not happen as part of a complete, harmonious, and productive system until Jesus Christ returns to rule this world.

The Nuclear Monster

We know that the world has entered a somewhat less volatile and less confrontational period. There is no East-West standoff as there once was; supposedly there is no United States-Soviet nuclear balance of terror. President Bush proclaimed this a kinder, gentler world. Yet, as we have seen, the risks of nuclear warfare and even peaceful uses of nuclear energy turning ugly are very much with us.

There is a statue across from the United Nations building in New York bearing the inscription, "They will beat their swords into plowshares." Where does that quotation come from? From the Bible! In Micah 4:2, only one of many scriptural prophecies which deal with this catastrophic question, we read that the world's "nations will come and say, 'Come, let us go up to the mountain of the LORD, to the house [of the true God who] . . . will teach us his ways.'"

That passage goes on to tell us that, as King of the world, "He will judge between many peoples and will settle disputes for strong nations far and wide. They will beat

their swords into plowshares and their spears into prun-
ing hooks. Nation will not take up sword against nation,
nor will they train for war anymore. Every man will sit
under his own vine and under his own fig tree, and no one
will make them afraid, for the LORD Almighty has spoken"
(verses 3-4). That is a marvelous prophecy of a coming
time of peace, but it will not come from the United Nations. The president of the United States will not bring this
miracle. In the long run, the beating of our swords into
plowshares is something Jesus Christ Himself, as King
over all the earth, will bring to pass.

The New Catholic Encyclopedia points out that the
result of Christ's triumph over antichrist and the forces of
evil will be a reign of Jesus Christ and His saints of all the
ages over an earth that will know unprecedented prosperity and peace. From time immemorial, mankind has longed
for a combination of true law and order, of peace and
prosperity, of freedom and fulfillment, of health and happiness, of godliness and longevity on this earth. It will happen
when Christ comes again to set up His kingdom.

A New World Order

There can be no new world of lasting peace under the
present conditions. Something dramatic has to happen to
alter human nature. That leaves us with only one absolute
certainty about the future: Christ as the Prince of Peace,
with the government upon His shoulders. The utopian
dreams and schemes of the Platos, the Bellamys, the Owens,
and similar philosophers and idealists throughout history
will all be fulfilled through His rule. That's the message of
the God-Man on the white horse coming down out of heaven,
which the apostle John foresaw and recorded in Revelation 19.

John Milton yearned for "Paradise Restored." I'm sure
that for nearly a thousand years Adam longed to get back

into the Garden of Eden from which he was driven because of his sin. But he couldn't! Professor John Walvoord puts it concisely, "The longing for perfect government, righteousness, equity, economic prosperity, and deliverance from insecurity and fears which plague the modern world finds its answer in the Return of Christ and the establishment of His kingdom."

The Scriptures have a great deal to teach us about the world of the coming Christ. The Messiah will take complete charge of the peoples of the entire earth. He "will stand as a banner for the peoples; the nations will rally to him, and his place of rest will be glorious," assures Isaiah (11:10). "The Spirit of the LORD will rest on him—the Spirit of wisdom and of understanding, the Spirit of counsel and of power, the Spirit of knowledge and of the fear of the Lord" (11:2). Throughout the world today people crave a society of peace and provision, but also one of goodness and justice. The Messiah Christ will implement all these, as "with righteousness he will judge the needy, with justice he will give decisions for the poor of the earth," as "righteousness will be his belt and faithfulness the sash around his waist" (11:4-5). Will it work? Yes: "they will neither harm nor destroy . . . for the earth will be full of the knowledge of the LORD as the waters cover the sea" (11:9).

So transformed will the prevailing order be that even the animal world will be completely tamed: "The wolf will live with the lamb, the leopard will lie down with the goat, the calf and the lion and the yearling together; and a little child will lead them. The cow will feed with the bear, their young will lie down together, and the lion will eat straw like the ox. The infant will play near the hole of the cobra, and the young child put his hand into the viper's nest. They will neither harm nor destroy" is the promise of the coming King (Isaiah 11:6-8). This will be in complete contrast to the savage beasts, scavenger birds, devouring insects, and raging diseases that have been among the most ferocious foes of primitive and civilized man from the Adamic to the atomic ages.

A Message from Messiah

This leads me to consider what the Scriptures have said about that future era under the reign of the Messiah. The storms will all have passed. The sky will be clear. The horsemen will ride no more. Sickness will be remedied by Christ, the great healer of nations. He will remove all deformities and handicaps. At that time there'll be no designated spots on parking lots, or graduated ramps on buildings for the handicapped. There will be no blindness, deafness, muteness, paralysis—no need for eyeglasses, hearing aids, speech therapy, wheelchairs, crutches, or white canes. "No one living," assures Isaiah (33:24), "will say, 'I am ill.'" "I will restore you to health and heal your wounds, declares the LORD" (Jeremiah 30:17). "I will bind up the injured" (Ezekiel 34:16).

Isaiah prophesies:

> Be strong, do not fear;
> your God will come, . . .
> Then will the eyes of the blind be opened
> and the ears of the deaf unstopped.
> Then will the lame leap like a deer,
> and the mute tongue shout for joy.
> Water will gush forth in the wilderness
> and streams in the desert.
> The burning sand will become a pool,
> the thirsty ground bubbling springs.
> In the haunts where jackals once lay,
> grass and reed and papyrus will grow.
> And a highway will be there;
> it will be called the Way of Holiness.
>
> Isaiah 35:4-8

"Surely the day is coming" prophesied Malachi (4:1-2) in the last chapter of the Old Testament, when the peoples of the world will finally "revere my name, the sun of righteousness will rise with healing in its wings." In the last chapter of the New Testament, we read that there will stand in that era "the tree of life, bearing twelve crops of fruit, yielding its fruit every month. And the leaves of the tree are for the healing of the nations. No longer will there be any curse." (Revelation 22:2-3). "He will wipe every tear from their eyes. There will be no more death or mourning or crying or pain, for the old order of things has passed away" (Revelation 21:4).

Currently, as Paul wrote to the Romans (8:22, 18-21), "the whole creation has been groaning as in the pains of childbirth right up to the present time." But "our present sufferings are not worth comparing with the glory that will be revealed," for the whole "creation waits in eager expectation for the sons of God to be revealed. For the creation was subjected to frustration, not by its own choice, but by the will of the one who subjected it, in hope that the creation itself will be liberated from its bondage to decay and brought into the glorious freedom of the children of God."

An End to Dissent

We've had enormous controversies in recent years over birth control, abortion, and euthanasia. Today these crises are escalating in every community with increasing violence and dissent. Within a very short time, I believe they will evolve into full-fledged Supreme Court debate and state-by-state legal dogfights, touching the very core of what we believe. But Revelation tells us these problems will all vanish as the curse of evil on the earth is removed. In place of thorns and thistles, drought and deserts, we will discover fruits and vegetables, fountains and fertility. This is the promise of God.

Rabbi Dr. Harvey Fields was so right when he exclaimed, "Without the Messiah, the human enterprise would crash into darkness forever." But thank God, the Messiah is coming. He saves individuals today. In the great tomorrow, He will remake all creation.

One day it *will* happen. The prophet Isaiah predicted, "The desert and the parched land will be glad; the wilderness will rejoice and blossom. Like the crocus, it will burst into bloom; it will rejoice greatly and shout for joy." Yes, the world will be like the "splendor of Carmel and Sharon; they will see the glory of the LORD, the splendor of our God" (Isaiah 35:1-2).

With that kind of future ahead for believers, and beyond that in eternity with Christ and the believers of all the ages in a new heaven as well as a new earth, I could not finish a book like this without another pointed invitation to you as a reader to be absolutely sure that you are Christ's. In feeling this way so strongly, I am only reflecting exactly the way the ancient apostle John felt. He simply could not conclude the Revelation of Jesus Christ without making the last six verses of his book one of the most compelling invitations to repent of sin and receive Jesus Christ as Savior and Lord to be found anywhere in the entire Bible.

"I, Jesus, have sent my angel to give you this testimony for the churches," is what we read in Revelation 22:16. Jesus Christ Himself wants John to make no mistake about it. After envisaging a panorama of scenes covering the past, the present, and the future; after peering deep into the heavens, the earth, and hell; after being introduced to God, to man all the way from his best to his worst, and to Satan himself—Jesus wants the last word!

Why? Because, as we read in Revelation 1:5, He is the One above all others "who loves us and has freed us from our sins by his blood" shed on the cross for our sins to purchase our pardon and peace. He is, therefore, the One to whom we are ultimately as well as immediately answerable. Later in that first chapter (verses 17-18), He assured, "I am the First and the Last. I am the Living One; I was dead, and behold I am alive forever and ever! And I hold the keys of death and Hades"—of hell itself!

In Revelation 3:20, Jesus comes a step closer and declares, "Here I am! I stand at the door and knock. If anyone hears my voice and opens the door, I will come in and eat with him, and he with me." Jesus is saying to you, right now, that if you have never admitted Him as Savior and Lord into your life, you not only vitally *need* to do so now, you *can* do so now! Many say, "There is no need." But the goodness of God should lead to repentance.

When, however, difficulties and heartaches come into your life, God can use those hard knocks to show you your need of Christ in every circumstance. It may be a business disappointment, a reversal in your love life, a broken marriage, a tragic bereavement, a hopelessly severed or even strained relationship between you and a parent or child. It could be the gradual or rapid deterioration of your own health. Whatever your disappointment, it's His appointment!

God Working in Our Midst

God's plan is not abstract or unclear. It is not secret. He says very clearly, "I love you!" He has called tens of thousands all over the world to proclaim His love to the world and to call every man, woman, and child to His loving arms. To exemplify the army of God that is going forth at this moment into the world I can think of no better example than the thousands of "barefoot preachers" and other itinerant evangelists we helped train in Amsterdam during the past decade.

The Amsterdam International Conference for Itinerant Evangelists in July 1983 was a ten-day ministry and training session. Approximately 70 percent of the participants in that first event were from Third World countries. The original goal had been to invite twenty-five hundred young evangelists for a series of hands-on seminars. But more than eleven thousand applied, and ultimately about four thousand were actually invited.

When we went back to Amsterdam three years later, we had the same enthusiastic response—even greater perhaps. Preachers, teachers, students, and mission helpers came from all over the world. Thousands came from Africa—people who, in many cases, had never traveled more than a few miles from their villages—they were stunned, not only by the fellowship with believers from more than 170 countries and territories, but by their first glimpse of European culture. They came from all over Asia, Latin America, and Eastern Europe, and they went out into the streets of Amsterdam to see and learn and share the love of Jesus Christ with others.

I have never known such a passionate outpouring of the Spirit of God. On Pentecost, described in the second chapter of Acts, the Spirit of God descended with the sound of a mighty wind and with visible tongues of flame. There was electricity in the air in that first visitation of God's Spirit on the Christian church, but in Amsterdam we felt something just as electric and just as inspiring. There were moments when there was not a dry eye in the house.

Today that mighty army of traveling preachers from every corner of the world is traveling from village to village and house to house preaching the good news of God's love. Why do they do it? For the money? No, they receive almost no support for what they do. Many are lucky if they have a bicycle, a Bible, and a change of clothes. Do they do it for fame and fortune? There is none. In most cases only God knows what good works these humble, sincere pastors have done.

They do it because Jesus Christ is alive! He is living in their hearts, and that good news is something worthy to share with the world. They are compelled by the life that is in them to tell everyone that Jesus is Lord. If Jesus Christ is *not* the son of God, nothing matters. But if He is, *nothing else matters!*

Is He knocking at your heart's door today? If someone comes to your house and knocks on the door, you can either open the door and invite him in, or you can ignore the knock and he will go away. That's the way it is with Jesus knocking at your heart's door. You can bow your head on an airplane, in a jail cell, in an office building, in a hotel room, in your hospital bed, or in the privacy of your home, and you can open your heart to Christ by a simple prayer of faith. Jesus Christ is the ultimate good news. He is bigger than the "Man of the Year." He is the biggest news story of all time!

I love these words of that dear Christian saint, who is now with the Lord, Corrie ten Boom. Corrie was from Holland, and she was imprisoned by the Nazis during World War II for hiding Jews in her home. All the members of her family died in German concentration camps. In her book, *Amazing Love*, she asked this question:

> If I straighten the pictures on the walls of your home, I am committing no sin, am I? But suppose that your house were afire, and I still went calmly about straightening pictures, what would you say? Would you think me merely stupid or very

> wicked? . . . The world today is on fire. What are
> you doing to extinguish the fire?

I would like to ask that question in this way: If Jesus is Lord, and He is, and I do not tell you, what would you say? Would you think me merely stupid or very wicked?

So we have this good news made possible in the past by Christ's everlasting love and His death on the cross for us. We have His knocking at our heart's door in the present, seeking possession of our lives, not only for our eternal benefit, but—incredibly—for His also. Jesus wants to show us off to the rest of the universe as an example of what His grace can do.

In Revelation 4:1 we are shown the future, invited through John's eyes to look ahead: "And there before me was a door standing open in heaven. And the voice I had first heard speaking to me like a trumpet said, 'Come up here, and I will show you what must take place after this.'" Jesus gives us a preview of the heaven He has gone to prepare for us.

Freedom of Choice

You may ask: What if I reject Jesus Christ and choose instead the way of sin? He is also loving and caring enough to warn you of the peril of that route. In Revelation 21, He makes unmistakably clear that "the cowardly, the unbelieving, the vile, the murderers, the sexually immoral, those who practice magic arts, the idolaters, and all liars—their place will be in the fiery lake of burning sulfur." Then He assures, "This is the second death" (Revelation 21:8), so "I, Jesus," initiate this final biblical invitation. "I, Jesus . . . give you this testimony" (Revelation 22:16).

The same powerful voice of the Holy Spirit who moved among us in Amsterdam speaks to you, saying, "Come!" (Revelation 22:17). It would be completely futile for me to preach the gospel, as I have done to many people every year for the past generation, if the Holy Spirit were not convincing the hearers of their sin and prompting them to open their hearts to Christ. Your reading of this book is entirely in vain if through doing so the Holy Spirit has not inspired you to new spiritual growth or, if you are not a believer, to give your life to Him. Right now, the Holy Spirit is saying one thing to you, "Come!" Come to Christ! Open your life to His salvation and to His control.

In verse 17 we read, "The Spirit and the bride say, 'Come!'" The bride of Christ is His church. It is made up of those who have received Him as Lord and Savior. Doing so, we take His name and are thereafter known as Christians. We love Him and we live with Him as our Lord, to the exclusion of all others. He has promised to provide for all of our needs. So, we're the bride! He is the bridegroom!

Then again, Jesus invites, "Let him who hears say, 'Come!'" (verse 17). We're told that "faith comes from hearing the message, and the message is heard through the word of Christ" (Romans 10:17). One of the verses I have used most frequently to lead people into a saving experience with Jesus Christ is John 5:24. It is Jesus speaking, "I tell you the truth, whoever hears my word and believes him who sent me has eternal life and will not be condemned; he has crossed over from death to life." That's one of the clearest promises in all of the Bible as to how to come to Christ. Then, when we come to Christ, we'll urge others to come to Christ. When we confess Jesus as Lord of our lives, we'll want to confess Him before others.

"Whoever is thirsty, let him come" (Revelation 22:17), testifies Jesus! So many are chronically thirsty but can't put a finger on what that thirst is or a handle on how to quench it. Blaise Pascal, the great French physicist and philosopher of the seventeenth century, noted that all humans have in their hearts a God-shaped void that only Jesus Christ can fill. Years before John had written in his Gospel what Jesus said to a morally mixed-up woman at the Samaritan well: "Everyone who drinks this water will be thirsty again, but whoever drinks the water I give him will never thirst. Indeed, the water I give him will become in him a spring of water welling up to eternal life" (John 4:13-14).

Do you have that thirst deep down in your soul that has characterized all people who have ever lived, but especially many of the great men and women of history? Riches cannot quench that thirst. Knowledge cannot quench that thirst. Alcohol cannot quench that thirst. Drugs cannot quench that thirst. Sex or romance cannot quench that thirst. But Christ can! He asks you right now, wherever you are, to come to Him. Believe in Him. Tell Him that you do. Call upon Him to satisfy your thirst with the water of eternal life.

Again, in Revelation 22:17, Jesus repeats the invitation one final time with the strongest and most inclusive call of all: "And whoever wishes, let him take the free gift of the water of life." By this, Jesus is saying that—from our human viewpoint—a decision for Christ is entirely a matter of the will.

God has done everything possible to bring you salvation; you can add nothing to what He has done. He has shown us the vision of the coming storm to give advance warning of the judgment so that we can flee from His wrath and come to Him. If you wish to be saved and go to heaven, you can, by believing in the Lord Jesus Christ as your Savior. If you wish not to be saved and therefore to be lost forever, that also is your privilege. Like those men and women in the Richelieu Apartments, standing defiantly before the wrath of Killer Camille, ultimately you must choose if you wish to be saved from the hurricane. Insofar as Jesus is concerned, He "wants all men to be saved and to come to a knowledge of the truth" (1 Timothy 2:4).

He Will Never Leave You

Peter, writing the closing chapter of his two letters, pleads that Christ is certainly "not wanting anyone to perish, but everyone to come to repentance" (2 Peter 3:9). I cannot think of how God could open the door wider for you to enter into the household of faith. To be sure that no one thinks salvation is something we buy, contribute to, or earn, He clarifies, "Take the free gift."

Jesus Christ rose from the dead to be alive forever. Because He is alive and because He can be everywhere at once, He is right there where you're reading. All you have to do is take Him, receive Him, accept Him personally into your heart as your Lord and Savior.

You might reply, "But I've received people into my life before, in relationships that didn't last and I'm wondering, will Jesus Christ love me and leave me? Will He take me and then forsake me, even perhaps forget that I exist?" No. In the next to the last verse in the Bible, Jesus testifies to you, "Yes, I am coming soon." The old apostle is so happy about that reassurance that he replies, "Come, Lord Jesus." When you really mean your commitment to Christ not just as a momentary, but as an ongoing relationship, you will have Jesus Christ as your Lord and Savior forever. You can choose to "be with the Lord forever" (1 Thessalonians 4:17).

You may have one final hesitation. You may ask, "But could I live the Christian life on my own?" No, you can't. But you will not be on your own. Christ gives you His unmerited favor day by day and moment by moment. He strengthens, energizes, and directs your life. The last verse in the Bible, Revelation 22:21, promises, "The grace of the Lord Jesus be with God's people. Amen." What more could you desire, ask, or ever hope for than that the grace of our Lord Jesus Christ be with you forever?

> You asked me how I gave my heart to Christ,
> I do not know;
> There came a yearning for Him in my soul so
>   long ago;
> I found earth's flowers would fade and die,
> I wept for something that would satisfy
> And then, and then, somehow I seemed to dare
> To lift my broken heart to God in prayer.
> I do not know, I cannot tell you how;
> I only know He is my Saviour now.
>
> Anonymous

Let me offer you a final suggestion. I have led tens of thousands who have come forward to make decisions for Christ in every part of the world in this simple prayer: "O God, I am a sinner. I'm sorry for my sins. I'm willing to turn from my sins. I receive Christ as Savior. I confess Him as Lord. From this moment on I want to follow Him and serve Him in the fellowship of His church. In Christ's name. Amen."

If you want the assurance of His eternal presence in your life, won't you pray that prayer right now? If you prayed this prayer, write to me and tell me about it. Write to Billy Graham, Minneapolis, Minnesota 55403, USA. We will reply with a letter and some literature that will help you to renew, or to begin, your walk with Jesus Christ.

God bless you.

Postscript: A New Dawn

As the debates during the 1992 elections pointed out so clearly, big changes are taking place in the world today: Changes in government, changes in public attitudes, changes in our hopes and dreams, and changes in the opportunities for the average man and woman to do something about the world's problems. People once reluctant to participate in the political process are coming forward in record numbers, and there is a new surge of vitality all across the land. The massive outpouring of private help given recently to the victims of Hurricane Andrew recently is an example of this.

Out of the storm clouds of disappointment and despair we see new signs of hope and a new unity of spirit. For the past three decades, we have been going through a time of turbulence. Many forces have conspired to divide this nation and to separate us from each other. Social trends have separated men, women, and especially children from the traditional values that have always represented truth and security and stability.

But today we are seeing a new movement to restore family values and tested moral foundations in this nation and to bring back a new sense of worth and dignity through faith and worship. This is a very positive sign; for I believe that only a return to decency and morality on a broad scale, combined with a new attitude of openness and caring, can hold back the coming storm of Apocalypse. We can have that kind of love as we open our hearts to Christ and allow His Holy Spirit to fill us and control us.

If America and the world are to be spared and to avoid the holocaust of John's Revelation, we must rediscover what it means to love one another. The apostle Paul said that "the fruit of the Spirit is love, joy, peace, patience, kindness, goodness, faithfulness, gentleness and self-control" (Galatians 5:22-23). In the thirteenth chapter of 1 Corinthians Paul went on to say: "Love suffers long and is kind; love does not envy; love does not parade itself, is not puffed up; does not behave rudely, does not seek its own, is not provoked, thinks no evil; does not rejoice in iniquity, but rejoices in the truth; bears all things, believes all things, hopes all things, endures all things. Love never fails" (1 Corinthians 13:4-8 NKJV).

Clearly Paul is not describing some weak, ineffective, or empty emotion. He identified love as a force of power and authority. It is the ultimate power, since it is the power of God Himself. John tells us: "God is love, and he who abides in love abides in God, and God in him" (1 John 4:16 NKJV). Paul described the virtue of love as the first characteristic and obligation of the believer in Jesus Christ and the way to transform the world around us.

The apostle said that prophecies and gifts would cease when Christ's kingdom is established. He writes: "where there are prophecies, they will cease; where there are tongues, they will be stilled; where there is knowledge, it will pass away" (1 Corinthians 13:8). But regardless of what else may happen on this planet and regardless of what other changes may come in the years ahead, Paul assures us that "love never fails."

I know that the enemy, Satan, is at work trying to divide or discourage us. We are often divided on peripheral issues. Our ability to practice our faith openly, to pray, to evangelize, to speak honestly and openly are sometimes threatened by the world and even by those who have accommodated themselves to the secular standard of our age. But over the past decade I have begun to witness an awakening among evangelical Christians. God is at work in the world; thousands are coming to Jesus Christ as their Lord and Savior and are finding peace with God.

God has been reaching out to all people, and today they are reaching back to Him in record numbers. This has been a thrilling and busy time for all of us in the Billy Graham Evangelistic Association (BGEA), but there is no time to lose. I have seen the same kind of growth and excitement in Eastern Europe and the former Soviet Union that we are seeing in America, Western Europe, Africa, and Asia today. We have clear evidence of the awakening that is taking place.

As just one example, on the final day of our five-day crusade in Hong Kong in 1990, I preached to an audience of 49,000 people while another 30,000 watched on a mammoth, large-screen television at a nearby athletic field. More than 5,000 came forward that night to receive Christ. But even more astonishing was the fact that as many as 100 million viewers were able to watch that broadcast in 30 Asian nations, translated into their own languages. We had the support of some 125,000 churches all over Asia and 400,000 counselors. We distributed 10 million pieces of follow-up literature to go along with the 70,000 satellite and videotape presentations our people helped organize. Only eternity will reveal the results of these efforts and the efforts of countless other organizations and individuals who are faithfully proclaiming the gospel in the far corners of the world.

The Bible says, "where the Spirit of the Lord is, there is liberty" (2 Corinthians 3:17 NKJV). When people come to

Christ, there is always a spiritual awakening that leads to liberty—liberty from sin and liberty to serve Christ. I believe that this is what took place in the former Soviet Union over the past decade. The return to faith is reshaping the world and bringing liberty where there has been oppression.

As I have reconsidered each of the issues in this book and reexamined both the teachings of Jesus and the writings of the apostle John concerning the end times, I have been forcefully reminded of the urgency of these issues. From the vantage point of the 1990s, we can now see the genuine dangers behind us, and we can imagine those still ahead. The worst thing any man or woman can do is to ignore these writings and assume that either they are fantasy or hyperbole.

Like the reporter from *Le Figaro* I mentioned earlier who thought I was simply trying to scare the people, some people may assume that nothing so horrible as the Apocalypse can ever happen. But I must assure you, it can, it must, and someday it will. The Apocalypse will come when God, in His wisdom and mercy, decides that this world cannot go any further in its rebellion against Him. But until that time, I believe we have the future, as it were, in our own hands. If we turn to Christ and, with His help, change our lives to conform to the will of God, we can prolong the days of planet Earth.

The purpose of this storm warning has not been to frighten or alarm people without reason. I have not written these things to cause panic or to create uncertainty, but to offer the bright hope of Jesus Christ as the one who will indeed bring a new and glorious dawn to all humanity. If you have been led to a better understanding of the promise of new life in Christ and a deeper commitment to Him by reading this book, then I have accomplished my purpose.

There is no greater joy than the peace and assurance of knowing that, whatever the future may hold, you are secure in the loving arms of the Savior. If the world should fall into perilous times; if the antichrist should arise to mislead and destroy; or if we should witness the full unveiling of Apocalypse in our midst, we can rest completely in Christ, for those who come to Him in faith and humility belong to Him and nothing can remove us from His eternal kingdom. We are secure in His love. If you turn to Him now and seek in His name to bring renewal and restoration to this broken world—through the power of God's love—we may yet drive away the dark clouds of warning.

But whatever happens, there is hope on the horizon. Jesus Christ is our hope. He is our hope for the future, and He is our hope right now. Even in the midst of the storms of our daily lives, Christ can give us inner peace and joy. He has promised—and He cannot lie—that we are secure in God's hands when we know Christ. Our peace comes not from our circumstances, for they change and at times they may be hard and painful. Our peace instead comes from Christ and from the firm knowledge that "I give them eternal life, and they shall never perish; no one can snatch them out of my hand" (John 10:28). Jesus' promise to you is certain: "Peace I leave with you; my peace I give you. . . . I have told you these things so that in me you may have peace. In this world you will have trouble. But take heart! I have overcome the world" (John 14:27; 16:33).

Christ is the light of the world. There is a new dawn coming even now. With that promise, I urge you now to put your hope in the One who holds tomorrow and to hold firmly to His promises, whatever storms may lie ahead.

Works Cited

Adams, Ruth, and Sue Cullen. *The Final Epidemic: Physicians and Scientists on Nuclear War.* Chicago: Educational Foundation for Nuclear Science, 1981.

Aldridge, Robert C. *The Counterforce Syndrome: A Guide to U.S. Nuclear Weapons and Strategic Doctrine.* Revised edition. Washington, D.C.: Institute for Policy Studies, 1979.

Augsburger, Myron S. *The Christ-Shaped Conscience.* Wheaton, Ill.: Victor, 1990.

Augustine. *Confessions.* Translated by Edward B. Pusey. New York: Macmillan Co., 1961.

Barash, David P., and Judith E. Lipton. *Stop Nuclear War! A Handbook.* New York: Grove Press, 1982.

Barclay, William. *The Revelation of John.* 2 vols. Philadelphia: Westminster Press, 1959.

Brown, Lester R. *Building a Sustainable Society.* New York: W. W. Norton, 1981.

Busséll, Harold. *Unholy Devotion: Why Cults Lure Christians.* Grand Rapids, Mich.: Zondervan, 1983.

Buttrick, George A., et al., eds. *The Interpreter's Bible.* 12 vols. New York: Abingdon Press, 1957.

Chandler, Russell. *Understanding the New Age.* Dallas: Word, 1988.

Dobson, James C., and Gary L. Bauer. *Children at Risk: The Battle for the Hearts and Minds of Our Kids.* Dallas: Word, 1990.

Draper, Edythe, et al., eds. *Almanac of the Christian World.* Wheaton, Ill.: Tyndale, 1990.

Eckholm, Erik P. *The Picture of Health: Environmental Sources of Disease.* New York: W. W. Norton, 1977.

Editors of *The Ecologist. Blueprint for Survival.* Boston: Houghton Mifflin Co., 1972.

Falk, Richard A. *This Endangered Planet: Prospects and Proposals for Human Society.* New York: Random House, 1972.

Frank, Anne. *The Diary of Anne Frank.* New York: Modern Library, 1958.

Frankl, Viktor. *Man's Search for Meaning.* Boston: Beacon Press, 1963.

Freeman, Leslie J. *Nuclear Witnesses: Insiders Speak Out.* New York: William Morrow & Co., 1981.

Graham, Billy. *Approaching Hoofbeats: The Four Horsemen of the Apocalypse.* Waco, Tex.: Word, 1983.

———. *The Holy Spirit.* Waco, Tex.: Word, 1978.

———. *Hope for the Troubled Heart.* Dallas: Word, 1991.

———. *Till Armageddon: A Perspective on Suffering.* Waco, Tex.: Word, 1981.

———. *World Aflame.* New York: Doubleday, 1965.

Graham, Franklin, and Jeannette Lockerbie. *Bob Pierce: This One Thing I Do.* Waco, Tex.: Word, 1983.

Gribbin, John. *Future Worlds.* New York: Plenum Press, 1981.

Gwertzman, Bernard, and Michael T. Kaufman. *The Collapse of Communism.* New York: Random House, 1991.

Hersey, John. *Hiroshima.* New York: Alfred A. Knopf, 1946.

Johnston, Jerry. *The Edge of Evil: The Rise of Satanism in North America.* Dallas: Word, 1989.

Ladd, George Eldon. *A Commentary on the Book of Revelation of John.* Grand Rapids, Mich.: Eerdmans, 1971.

Mackarness, Richard. *Living Safely in a Polluted World: How to Protect Yourself and Your Children from Chemicals in Your Food and Environment.* New York: Stein and Day, 1981.

McClung, Floyd. *Holiness and the Spirit of the Age.* Eugene, Oreg.: Harvest House, 1990.

McMinn, Mark, and James Foster. *Christians in the Crossfire: Guarding Your Mind Against Manipulation and Self-Deception.* Newburg, Oreg.: Barclay Press, 1990.

Marine, Gene, and Judith Van Allen. *Food Pollution.* New York: Holt, Rinehart & Winston, 1972.

Montagu, Ashley. *The Endangered Environment.* New York: Mason/Charter, 1974.

Naisbitt, John, and Patricia Aburdene. *Megatrends 2000: Ten New Directions for the 1990s.* New York: Morrow, 1990.

Office of Technology Assessment, Congress, U.S. *The Effects of Nuclear War.* Totowa, N.J.: Allanheld, Osmun & Co., 1979.

Osborn, Frederick. *The Human Condition.* New York: Hugh Lauter Levin Associates, 1973.

Petersen, William J. *Those Curious New Cults*. New Canaan, Conn.: Keats Publishing, 1973.

Rankin, William W. *The Nuclear Arms Race—Countdown to Disaster: A Study in Christian Ethics*. Cincinnati: Forward Movement Publications, 1981.

Renneker, Mark, and Steven Leib. *Understanding Cancer*. Palo Alto, Calif.: Bull Publishing Co., 1979.

Robinson, J. A. T. *In the End God*. New York: Harper & Row, 1968.

Schell, Jonathan. *The Fate of the Earth*. New York: Knopf, 1982.

Segal, George. *The World Affairs Companion*. New York: Simon & Schuster, 1991.

Sine, Tom. *The Mustard Seed Conspiracy*. Waco, Tex.: Word, 1981.

Strong, Maurice, ed. *Who Speaks for Earth?* New York: W. W. Norton, 1973.

Terry, Randall. *Accessory to Murder: The Enemies, Allies, and Accomplices to the Death of Our Culture*. Nashville: Wolgemuth & Hyatt, 1990.

Walvoord, John F. *The Blessed Hope and the Tribulation*. Contemporary Evangelical Perspectives. Grand Rapids, Mich.: Zondervan, 1976.

———. *The Nations, Israel, and the Church in Prophecy*. Grand Rapids, Mich.: Academie Books, 1968.

———. *Return of the Lord*. Grand Rapids, Mich.: Zondervan, n.d.